HOLT McDOUGAL LITERATURE

Resource Manager

Unit 1

GRADE 6

HOLT McDOUGAL

a division of Houghton Mifflin Harcourt

Printed in the U.S.A.

ISBN 13: 978-0-547-61850-0

5 6 7 8 9 10   1409   18 17 16 15 14 13 12

4500352189

^ B C D E F G

Resource Manager

What Is It?

The Resource Manager brings together in one place the rich body of resources provided by *Holt McDougal Literature*. These are some of the tools you'll find here:

Beginning the year

- an overview of program components
- planning for differentiated instruction
- resources for creating a classroom profile
- options for instructional paths
- thematic opportunities for teaching the selections

Teaching a unit

- tools for grammar instruction
- academic vocabulary for English learners

Teaching a selection

For you, the teacher
- lesson plan and resource guide
- leveled selection questions
- ideas for extension
- answer keys

For your students
- copy masters customized to teach and reinforce the focus standards in each selection and workshop
- copy masters to preteach and reinforce vocabulary
- reading fluency copy masters

Resource Manager Pages

The selections and workshops in the anthology are supported by the following types of Resource Manager pages.

SELECTION AND WORKSHOP RESOURCES

Teacher Planning Pages	**Student Copy Masters with Workshops**
Lesson at a Glance	Unit Introduction
Lesson Plan and Resource Guide	Academic Vocabulary
Additional Selection Questions	**Text Analysis Workshop**
Ideas for Extension	Note Taking
Teacher Notes	**Media Study**
Student Copy Masters with Selections	Summary
Summary (translations in Spanish, Haitian Creole, Vietnamese)	Viewing Guide
	Close Viewing
Text Analysis	Media Activity
Reading Skill	Production Template
Vocabulary Study	**Writing Workshop**
Vocabulary Practice	Planning/Prewriting
Vocabulary Strategy	Drafting
Reading Check	Revising and Editing
Question Support	Ask a Peer Reader
Grammar In Context	Scoring Rubric
Reading Fluency	Speaking and Listening Workshop
	Technology Workshop
	Writing Support (for English language learners)

A Sampler of Resource Manager Pages

The **Lesson at a Glance**, a teacher planning page, outlines the lesson. It includes a summary and readability scores for each selection.

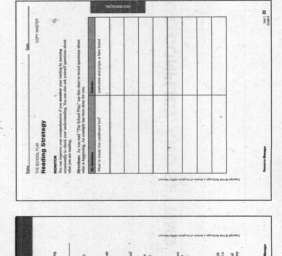

The **Lesson Plan and Resource Guide** suggests a step-by-step plan for teaching a lesson, along with the program resources to use at each step.

The **Ideas for Extension** feature offers a variety of ways to enrich and extend the lesson concepts through activities, research, and writing.

A **Reading Strategy** copy master contains the graphic organizer introduced in the Student's Edition. Students use the organizer to track the focus skill while reading a selection.

Table of Contents

STARTING THE YEAR

INTRODUCTORY UNIT
THE POWER OF IDEAS: INTRODUCING THE ESSENTIALS

Unit Planning

Workshop Resources

UNIT 1
WHAT'S HAPPENING: PLOT, CONFLICT, AND SETTING

Contents

Unit Planning

Selection and Workshop Resources

UNIT 2
PERSON TO PERSON: ANALYZING CHARACTER
AND POINT OF VIEW

Contents

Unit Planning

Selection and Workshop Resources

UNIT 3
THE BIG IDEA: UNDERSTANDING THEME

UNIT 4
WRITER'S CRAFT: SENSORY LANGUAGE, IMAGERY, AND STYLE

UNIT 5
WORD PICTURES: THE LANGUAGE OF POETRY

Contents

UNIT 8
KNOW THE FACTS: MAKE INFORMATION WORK FOR YOU

Contents

Unit Planning

Selection and Workshop Resources

UNIT 9
THE POWER OF RESEARCH: RESEARCH WORKSHOPS

The Program at a Glance

Teacher Resources

Time-saving, easy-to-use teacher resources make lesson planning and preparation simple.

Core Teacher Resources include:

Teacher's Edition

Teacher One Stop DVD-ROM with ExamView Test Generator

Resource Manager

MediaSmart DVD-ROM
Helps promote critical thinking through analysis of a variety of media

WriteSmart CD-ROM
An interactive writing-instruction tool with a rubric generator

Resource Manager

Teacher's Edition

PowerNotes DVD-ROM
Highly visual PowerPoint presentations and motivational video trailers introduce key lessons in the Student Edition.

ThinkCentral Online Assessment
- Diagnostic and Selection Tests
- Unit and Benchmark Tests
- Level Up Online Tutorials for Remediation

Assessment File
Provides comprehensive opportunities to assess student progress with an array of tests.

Assessment File

Best Practices Toolkit
Motivate students with engaging activities and over 200 graphic organizer transparencies.

Best Practices Toolkit

Professional Development for Language Arts DVD
Features video interviews with leading experts in differentiation, vocabulary, reading comprehension, and more.

xii Unit 1
Grade 6

Resource Manager

Student Resources

A complete program of technology and print resources provides support for differentiated student learning.

Core Student Resources include:

Student Edition

Student One Stop DVD-ROM

Interactive Reader

Adapted Interactive Reader

English Language Learner Adapted Interactive Reader

Adapted Interactive Reader: Audio Tutor

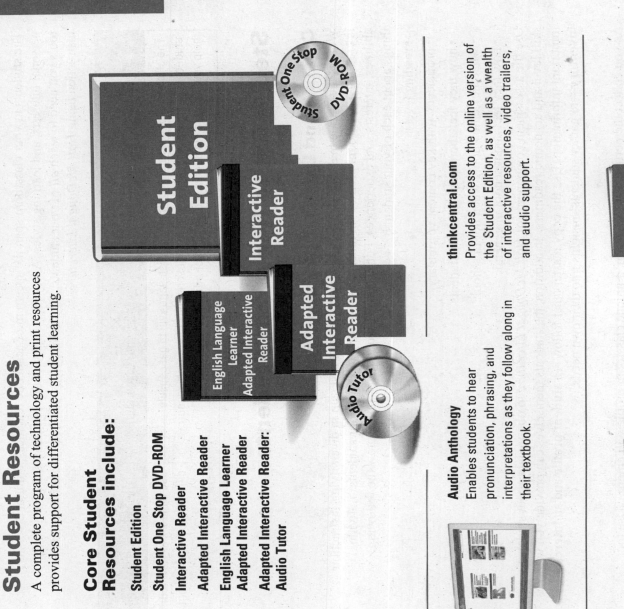

thinkcentral.com
Provides access to the online version of the Student Edition, as well as a wealth of interactive resources, video trailers, and audio support.

Audio Anthology
Enables students to hear pronunciation, phrasing, and interpretations as they follow along in their textbook.

Language Handbook
Supports systematic, student-friendly instruction in all aspects of grammar, usage, and mechanics.

Novels
Many novels, works of nonfiction, and plays promote independent learning and reading.

Planning for Differentiated Instruction

The students in your classroom span the spectrum of academic readiness, cultural diversity, personal interests, and learning styles. A key philosophy of this program is to give you the tools you need to teach *all* of your students. These three steps will help you differentiate instruction using *Holt McDougal Literature:*

STEP 1: Get to know your students.	STEP 2: Identify your resources.	STEP 3: Choose your lesson options.
The strategies below, along with the student copy masters that follow, will help you create a classroom profile.	Use page xviii to get capsule descriptions of program resources for adapting instruction.	Use page xix to view four different instructional paths.

Step 1. Get to Know Your Students

Creating and Using a Classroom Profile

What is the unique make-up of your classroom? A good first step in diversifying instruction is creating a classroom profile—in other words, getting to know your students' individual abilities, interests, and experiences. For example, you might want to know the following things about each of your students:

- reading level
- proficiency with key content vocabulary
- how they feel about themselves as students
- what they enjoy doing when not in school
- how they feel about school in general

Use the assessment components of *Holt McDougal Literature* to obtain data about students' skill level and academic readiness. In addition, the students themselves can provide you with important information. Use the copy masters that follow—a **student profile** and an **interest inventory**—to gather students' insights into their own needs.

As you collect the pertinent information, a unique classroom profile will emerge. Use this information, along with the program's differentiation resources, to create personalized instruction. For example, you may want to

- ensure access to advanced materials for students whose work is consistently strong
- scaffold instruction for those who need more help
- plan small group work that takes student interests, abilities, or work styles into account
- tap student motivation through writing prompts or activities built around topics of high student interest

Student Profile Survey

Directions These phrases describe ways that some people learn and what their preferences are. Write the phrases that best fit you in the "This Best Describes Me" column. Place the phrases that don't fit you in the "This Is Not Like Me" column. It isn't necessary to use all the phrases. Leave out the ones you are unsure about.

- Very logical
- Move around when I learn
- Great at planning
- Comfortable in the spotlight
- Sit still when I learn
- Very creative
- Prefer quiet when I work
- Like to do several things at a time
- Enjoy working with words
- Like art
- Prefer to work alone
- Not great at planning
- Enjoy working with ideas

- Prefer noise and activity when I work
- Enjoy working with numbers
- Like music
- Enjoy working with objects
- Prefer to be in the background
- Like science
- Prefer to decide on my own what to do
- Like collecting things
- Prefer to do one thing at a time
- Like the outdoors
- Prefer to work with people
- Like making things
- Prefer to be told how to do things

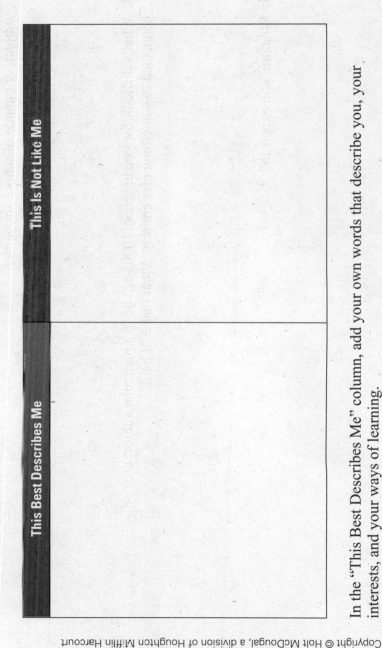

This Best Describes Me	This Is Not Like Me

In the "This Best Describes Me" column, add your own words that describe you, your interests, and your ways of learning.

Student Interest Inventory

Directions Give as much information as you can. It will help your teacher get to know you better.

1. What are your favorite interests outside of school? What do you enjoy about them?

2. What would others say are your strengths or talents?

3. What are some things you'd like to learn about? This can be in any school subject, or outside of school altogether.

4. What's difficult for you at school? This can be in a particular subject area or connected to something else entirely. What makes it hard?

5. What are you expert in?

STUDENT INTEREST INVENTORY, CONTINUED

6. What's your favorite

- book _____
- kind of music _____
- sport _____
- TV show _____
- movie _____
- video game _____
- radio station _____

7. Students use different methods to help them learn—like flashcards, memory devices, highlighting. What are some ways of learning that work for you?

8. What are some ways of learning that don't work well for you? Why?

9. In what areas would you like to improve? Why?

10. What else should I know about you as a person and a student that could help me teach you?

Resource Manager

Step 2: Identify Your Resources for Differentiation

Holt McDougal Literature provides a wide range of resources, highlighted below, to adapt instruction for your diverse classroom. In addition to activities that support individual learning behaviors, the program supplies comprehensive support for these three groups of learners:

- students learning English
- struggling readers and developing writers
- advanced learners

AUDIO ANTHOLOGY

Professional recordings of the selections provide extra support to less-proficient readers, students learning English, and auditory learners.

RESOURCE MANAGER

A variety of copy masters help you enhance and differentiate instruction. These include

- leveled comprehension questions
- translations into Spanish, Haitian Creole, and Vietnamese
- ideas for extension
- academic vocabulary practice
- writing support

INTERACTIVE READERS

The *Interactive Reader*, *Adapted Interactive Reader*, and *English Language Learner Adapted Interactive Reader* each provide the same core selections from the main anthology with reading and literary skills instruction, support for academic and selection vocabulary, and writing activities to support comprehension. Students can also use the *Adapted Interactive Reader Audio Tutor* to follow along as they read.

TEACHER'S EDITION

Comprehensive support for differentiation in the teacher's edition includes

- Targeted Passages—boxed passages of key parts of a selection for less-proficient readers and English learners
- Tiered Discussion Prompts—leveled questions for group discussion of key passages
- Teacher Notes—instructional strategies and activities for the guided reading of diverse learners

BEST PRACTICES TOOLKIT

The *Best Practices Toolkit* is a valuable collection of teacher tools, mini-lessons, copy masters, and transparencies that help you differentiate instruction.

WRITING WORKSHOPS

Highly visual and engaging, the *Writing Workshops* in the student's edition provide step-by-step modeling of the writing process.

3. Choose Your Lesson Options

You can teach a selection as presented in the anthology, or you may adapt the lesson flow as follows.

PATH 1—BEGIN WITH THE BIG QUESTION (ANTHOLOGY)

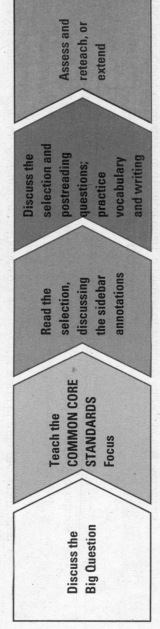

Discuss the Big Question → Teach the COMMON CORE STANDARDS Focus → Read the selection, discussing the sidebar annotations → Discuss the selection and postreading questions; practice vocabulary and writing → Assess and reteach, or extend

PATH 2—READ BEFORE TEACHING

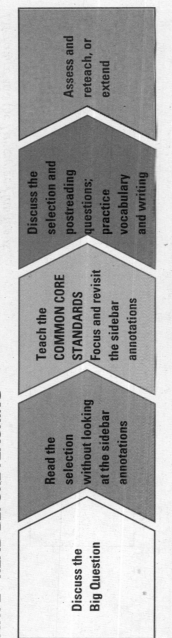

Discuss the Big Question → Read the selection without looking at the sidebar annotations → Teach the COMMON CORE STANDARDS Focus and revisit the sidebar annotations → Discuss the selection and postreading questions; practice vocabulary and writing → Assess and reteach, or extend

PATH 3—BEGIN WITH THE COMMON CORE STANDARDS

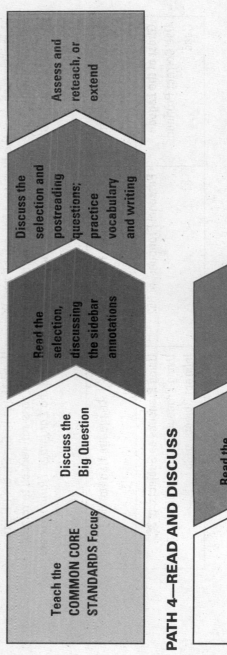

Teach the COMMON CORE STANDARDS Focus → Discuss the Big Question → Read the selection, discussing the sidebar annotations → Discuss the selection and postreading questions; practice vocabulary and writing → Assess and reteach, or extend

PATH 4—READ AND DISCUSS

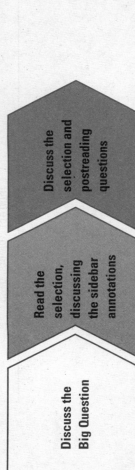

Discuss the Big Question → Read the selection, discussing the sidebar annotations → Discuss the selection and postreading questions

Integrating Grammar Instruction

Grammar Focus charts, provided in each unit of the *Resource Manager*, offer two methods of incorporating grammar instruction into your literature class. You may choose one approach or blend the two.

- *Systematic Grammar Instruction:* a framework for a year's worth of grammar instruction, based primarily on lessons in the *Language Handbook*
- *Integrated Grammar, Literature, and Writing:* opportunities for reinforcement and application of grammar concepts using the literature selections and Writing Workshops in the Student Edition

Systematic Grammar Instruction

The Systematic Grammar Instruction chart, a portion of which is shown below, serves as a pacing guide and provides references to all of the grammar resources of *Holt McDougal Literature* and the *Language Handbook*.

Week	Grammar Handbook (Student Edition)	Language Handbook
5 Complements	Complements, p. R60	Identifying Subject Complements, p. 69

Integrated Grammar, Literature, and Writing

This approach uses the literature selections and Writing Workshops in the Student Edition as opportunities to teach or reinforce specific grammar topics. Cross-references to related lessons in The Grammar Handbook in the Student Edition and the *Language Handbook* are also provided.

Teaching Opportunities	Grammar Handbook (Student Edition)	Language Handbook
Ghost of the Lagoon Use Correct Pronoun Case	Personal Pronouns, p. R52	Using Pronouns as Subjects, p. 36; Using Pronouns as Direct Objects and Indirect Objects, p. 38

Thematic Opportunities

If you prefer to group your lessons by themes instead of skills, choose from the thematic opportunities on the following six pages.

	Encounters with Nature
Big Question	**What in nature delights you?** Whether you live in the city or country, nature is a part of your life. What words would you choose to describe your attitude toward the natural world? The selections in this grouping explore people's impressions of and reactions to the natural world.
Selections in the Anthology	• from **Woodsong**, memoir by Gary Paulsen, pp. 114–125 Paulsen recalls his encounter with a bear and the lesson he learned from the majestic creature. • **"The Horse Snake,"** from the memoir *The Land I Lost*, by Huynh Quang Nhuong, pp. 126–137 Vietnamese villagers band together to battle a huge snake. • **"Fall,"** poem by Sally Andresen Stolte; and **"Change,"** poem by Charlotte Zolotow, pp. 600–607 The speakers in these poems describe changes in nature that occur during autumn. • **"A Message from a Caterpillar,"** poem by Lilian Moore; **"Fog,"** poem by Carl Sandburg; **"Two Haiku,"** poems by Bashō, pp. 608–613 The poems in this grouping present vivid impressions of nature.
Related Novels and Longer Works	*Listen!*, novel by Stephanie S. Tolan Charley's mother, a nature photographer, has died recently, and Charley herself is recovering from a car accident. Her interest in a wild dog named Coyote helps Charley recover physically, heal her spirit, and begin to see the natural world as her mother saw it. *Finding Day's Bottom*, novel by Candice Ransom Jane-Ery misses her father, who died a year ago, and dreams of leaving the Virginia mountains to find him in Richmond. A trip to the city with her Grandpap, however, helps her see the value of her rural life.
Wrap-Up	To assess understanding, have students respond to one of these culminating options. 1. Compose or select music that reflects a similar message about nature as one or more selections you read. Then play the composition as you read the selection to your class. 2. Create a collage that illustrates the theme of two or more of the selections you read. 3. Write a reflective essay that expresses your thoughts about the selections you read.

Leaving Legacies

Big Question	**What will be your legacy?** A *legacy* is an inheritance that is passed down from one generation to another. It might be a family tradition, a philosophy for living, or a social or cultural heritage. Legacies can contribute positively or negatively to those who receive them. What legacies have you inherited? What might those who come after you take from your life? The selections in this grouping show how legacies contribute to and influence people's lives.
Selections in the Anthology	• **"Jeremiah's Song,"** short story by Walter Dean Myers, pp. 220–233 A young boy learns to appreciate his grandfather's legacy—a treasury of stories passed down from their ancestors. • **"The First Emperor,"** from *The Tomb Robbers*, book excerpt by Daniel Cohen; **"Digging Up the Past: Discovery and Excavation of Shi Huandi's Tomb,"** magazine article by Helen Wieman Bledsoe, pp. 916–931 The tomb of the first emperor of China provides a wealth of information about China's past. • **"No Thought of Reward,"** speech by Mawi Asgedom, pp. 960–965 Asgedom describes his father's legacy, a philosophy for living well that is built on the idea of giving to others selflessly. • **"In a Neighborhood in Los Angeles,"** poem by Francisco X. Alarcón; **"For Gwen 1969,"** poem by Margaret Walker, pp. 864–871 The poems in this pairing present portraits of two strong and loving women and their legacies.
Related Novels and Longer Works	*Whirligig*, novel by Paul Fleischman Sixteen-year-old Brent must plant whirligigs in four corners of the United States to honor the life of a girl he killed in a car accident. What Brent learns will change him forever. *Freedom Riders: John Lewis and Jim Zwerg on the Front Lines of the Civil Rights Movement*, biography by Ann Bausum In the 1960s, a group of college students known as the Freedom Riders traveled the Deep South to challenge segregation. This book focuses on two members, one black and one white. *The Forbidden Schoolhouse: The True and Dramatic Story of Prudence Crandall and Her Students*, by Suzanne Jurmain Jurmain tells the story of Prudence Crandall, who started a secondary school for African American girls in the 1830s.
Wrap-Up	To assess understanding, have students respond to one of these culminating options. 1. Choose a person from the selections you read. What is his or her legacy? Write a letter in which the person explains the value of the inheritance. 2. Use a box to create a treasure chest. In the chest place items that represent the legacies passed on by people in the selections you read. Include a note card for each item that explains the legacy it represents. 3. Create a multimedia presentation that illustrates the legacy of a person you read about. As part of your presentation, show ways the legacy might influence the lives of future generations.

THEMATIC OPPORTUNITIES (CONTINUED)

	Bullies
Big Question	**How can you stop a bully?** It's hard to understand what causes someone to become a bully, but it is even tougher to face one. What harm can a bully cause? What is the best way to deal with a bully? The selections in this grouping examine the ways different people cope with bullies.
Selections in the Anthology	• **"Ghost of the Lagoon,"** short story by Armstrong Sperry, pp. 206–219 Mako fantasizes about killing Tupa, a great white shark known as the ghost of the lagoon. One day Mako gets a chance to be the hero of his dreams—or die trying. • **"Tuesday of the Other June,"** short story by Norma Fox Mazer, pp. 468–485 A bully is making life miserable for June. How long will she be able to endure the abuse dished out by the Other June? • **"The Problem with Bullies,"** feature article by Sean Price, pp. 486–491 Price examines the problem of bullying in American society today and describes a program designed to stop it. • **"The Red Guard,"** from the memoir *Red Scarf Girl* by Ji-li Jiang, pp. 274–287 In this memoir set in China during the Cultural Revolution, the Red Guards invade Ji-li Jiang's home to look for weapons and, in their search, destroy some of her prized possessions. • **"The Chenoo,"** Native American legend retold by Joseph and James Bruchac, pp. 712–723 When a woman comes face to face with a monster called the Chenoo, her kindness leads to an amazing transformation.
Related Novels and Longer Works	*Playing Dad's Song*, novel by D. Dina Friedman Gus is plagued by his family's single-mindedness, missing his father, and the taunts of the school bully, Ivan the Terrible. Taking oboe lessons with Mr. M begins to change the way Gus looks at himself, Ivan, and the world. *Hitler Youth*, nonfiction by Susan Campbell Bartoletti Hitler Youth tells the stories of young people's lives in Nazi Germany—the bullying leaders in Hitlerjügend (a Nazi organization for children and adolescents) and the boys and girls who dared to stand up against Hitler's horrific policies. *The Notorious Izzy Fink*, historical fiction by Don Brown For a poor kid in New York City at the turn of the century, life is tough, even for a street-wise boy like Sam. When Sam gets on the bad side of hooligan Izzy Fink and mob boss Monk Eastman, he has even more to worry about. Author notes address the historical accuracy of events and language in this book, which reflect the flavor of the times.
Wrap-Up	To assess understanding, have students respond to one of these culminating options. 1. Use situations and information from the selections you read to create a how-to manual for dealing with bullies. 2. Create a graphic representation of a person who was hassled by a bully in one of the selections you read. What traits did the person possess that helped him or her survive the tormentor? How did the experience affect him or her? 3. What leads someone to become a bully? Write a character analysis of one bully from these selections. Use details from the selection to support your opinions.

THEMATIC OPPORTUNITIES (CONTINUED)

True Friends

Big Question	**What do true friends do for each other?** It is said that a friend is someone who has "got your back," who supports you in time of need. You might say that's one of the most important jobs a friend has. What would you do to support a friend? Is it important to get anything in return? The characters in this grouping show what it means to be a true friend.
Selections in the Anthology	• **"The Good Deed,"** short story by Marion Dane Bauer, pp. 46–65 When Heather volunteers to read to Miss Benson as her summer project, her good deed turns into more than she bargains for. • **"Lob's Girl,"** short story by Joan Aiken, pp. 86–103 Nothing can break the bonds of love between a young girl and her loyal dog. • **"The Dog of Pompeii,"** short story by Louis Untermeyer, pp. 324–339 A blind boy named Tito and his dog Bimbo are best friends who work as a team to survive on the streets of Pompeii—until Mt. Vesuvius erupts. Will Bimbo be able to lead Tito to safety? • **"Good Hotdogs / Ricos Hot Dogs,"** poem by Sandra Cisneros pp. 642–654 For the speaker in this poem, hot dogs provide more than a tasty snack. They also bring back memories of a good friend • **Damon and Pythias,** Greek legend dramatized by Fan Kissen, pp. 724–735 A king learns that true friendship is worth more than power and riches when he condemns Pythias to death.
Related Novels and Longer Works	**Buddha Boy,** novel by Kathe Koja Justin is not happy when he is assigned to work with a new student the others call "Buddha Boy." But as the boys work together, Justin learns the value of friendship and the importance of being true to yourself. **Heartbeat,** novel in verse by Sharon Creech Annie is a talented runner whose life is changing. Her mother is having a baby, her grandfather is ill, and her best friend and running partner is acting strangely aloof. How can she support her friend with so much happening in her own life? **Where the Red Fern Grows,** novel by Wilson Rawls Rawls tells the story of a boy, his beloved dogs, and the adventures they share in the Ozark Mountains in the 1920s.
Wrap-Up	To assess understanding, have students respond to one of these culminating options. 1. Write an essay that explains the importance of support in the friendships you read about. Include details from the selections to support your opinions. 2. Create one or more scrapbook pages that highlight the stories of friendships you read about. 3. Imagine that you are one of the friends you read about. Perform a monologue in which you describe your closest friend and the value of that relationship.

THEMATIC OPPORTUNITIES (CONTINUED)

Accepting Challenges

Big Question	**What do you need to succeed?** Each of us encounters challenges in life. How we meet those challenges can influence the kind of person we become. What makes some people eager to accept a challenge? What helps some people succeed in reaching the goal, while others fail? The selections in this grouping introduce people who take advantage of what life has to offer.
Selections in the Anthology	• **"Scout's Honor,"** short story by Avi, pp. 360–377 An overnight camping trip turns into a memorable adventure for three boy scouts who try to earn a merit badge. • **"Matthew Henson at the Top of the World,"** biography by Jim Haskins, pp. 808–821 Stamina, determination, courage, and a spirit of adventure are a few of the traits that helped Matthew Henson become the first African American to reach the North Pole. • from **Over the Top of the World,** journal entries by Will Steger, pp. 822–826 Steger documents the obstacles he and his fellow explorers faced in their journey to and from the North Pole. • from **The Story of My Life,** autobiography by Helen Keller, pp. 832–839 In her own eloquent words, Keller recalls the challenges both she and her teacher, Anne Sullivan, faced in helping Helen connect to the world around her. • from **Spellbinder: The Life of Harry Houdini,** biography by Tom Lalicki, pp. 850–859 Harry Houdini became a world famous escape artist. This biography describes his journey to the top.
Related Novels and Longer Works	**Before We Were Free,** by Julia Alvarez Twelve-year-old Anita, a carefree girl growing up in the Dominican Republic in 1960, is shocked to learn that her family is part of a plot to overthrow the cruel dictator Trujillo. **Children of the Great Depression,** by Russell Freedman Russell Freedman examines the lives of children during the Great Depression of the 1930s and describes how these children survived their challenging circumstances. **The Clay Marble,** by Minfong Ho Fleeing the Khmer Rouge in Cambodia with her mother and brother, Dara makes important friends in the country's refugee camps and reveals her courage.
Wrap-Up	To assess understanding, have students respond to one of these culminating options. 1. Which person you read about do you most admire? Write an essay that explains how that person rose to face the challenges of life and what you learned from his or her experience. 2. Create a two-minute film for a children's television show that highlights a person you read about who worked hard to overcome challenges. Include a "take-away tip" that can help children face challenges in their own lives. 3. In meeting a challenge, a person has to make choices that will result in success or failure. With one or more classmates, perform a skit that highlights a turning point in the life of one person you read about and how a choice that was made affected his or her future.

THEMATIC OPPORTUNITIES (CONTINUED)

A Change in Attitude

Big Question	**How hard is it to change your way of thinking?** Some people make up their minds and never waver. Others are more open to new ways of thinking. Has an experience ever changed the way you thought about something? The selections in this grouping explore the idea of attitude adjustments.
Selections in the Anthology	• "**All Summer in a Day,**" short story by Ray Bradbury, pp. 66–77 Earth-born Margot yearns to see the sun, which shines briefly every seven years on Venus. Today is that special day, but Margot's classmates have other plans for her. • *The Prince and the Pauper,* novel by Mark Twain, dramatization by Joellen Bland, pp. 150–165 When young Edward, Prince of Wales and his poor look-alike, Tom Canty, trade places to experience a different way of life, both boys learn a lesson about the world. • "**Nadia the Willful,**" short story by Sue Alexander, pp. 348–359 A young girl breaks through her father's grief over the death of his son when she begins to recall their times together. • "**Ant and Grasshopper,**" fable by Aesop retold by James Reeves; "**The Richer, the Poorer,**" short story by Dorothy West pp. 382–393 The stories in this pairing examine attitudes toward work and the pleasures of life. • "**Same Song,**" poem by Pat Mora; "**Without Commercials,**" poem by Alice Walker, pp. 406–413 These poems speak to the dissatisfaction some people have with their appearance. • "**The All-American Slurp,**" short story by Lensey Namioka, pp. 442–456 A Chinese-American girl tries hard to fit in, but a dinner party teaches her that acceptance is a two-way street.
Related Novels and Longer Works	*A Small White Scar,* novel by K. A. Nuzum Will leaves home to compete in a rodeo, but his journey becomes complicated when his twin brother Denny, who has Downs Syndrome, tags along. The adventure serves to strengthen the brothers' bond and help Will and his father see both boys in a new light. *Best Foot Forward,* novel by Joan Bauer In this sequel to *Rules of the Road,* teenage Jenna helps Mrs. Gladstone overcome company problems while helping Tanner, a troubled teen, mature and change. *The Cay,* novel by Theodore Taylor Two castaways, a white boy and a West Indian man, learn to rely on each other in order to survive on an island in the Caribbean Sea during World War II.
Wrap-Up	To assess understanding, have students respond to one of these culminating options. 1. Choose a main character from the selections you read. Write a series of journal entries that explore the events and change in thinking that person experienced. 2. Create before and after portraits for each main character that show the change in thinking that person experienced by using thought bubbles or other graphics. 3. Choose a person from a selection you read. Perform a monologue in which your character describes the change in attitude or thinking that he, she, or another character experienced.

Lesson at a Glance

The Power of Ideas

WHY THIS UNIT?

In this Introductory Unit, students get a brief overview of the kinds of themes, literary genres, reading strategies, and writing skills they will study throughout the year. The unit gives them a preview of how their textbook is structured and how it approaches the study of literature and writing.

ABOUT THE WORKSHOPS

Student/Teacher's Edition Pages: 1–19

Summary The unit begins by introducing students to some of the "big questions" they will consider as they read each selection in the anthology. Then, in the Genres Workshop, students learn the defining characteristics of fiction, poetry, drama, nonfiction. The Reading Strategies Workshop outlines eight basic skills and strategies that will help students become active readers. The Academic Vocabulary Workshop teaches students ways to learn and reinforce the language that will help them succeed in school. The Writing Process Workshop reviews the basics of writing, from identifying audience, purpose, and format to following the steps of the writing process and using a rubric for self-assessment.

The Power of Ideas The unit captures students' attention by pointing out that literature explores the big questions that affect every person's life. It explains that questions can be explored in a variety of genres, and that students can tap into these questions through active, engaged reading. Finally, the unit invites students to use the power of literature to express their own ideas through writing.

LESSON RESOURCES

Student Copy Masters

🔴 Lesson resources are also available on the **Teacher One Stop DVD-ROM** and online at **thinkcentral.com**.

GENRES WORKSHOP

Note Taking

THE GENRES

Directions: Take notes about **the genres** of literature. First, fill in the key terms for these definitions, using information on page 4.

Key Terms

- Made-up stories are called

  [_____] fiction

- Texts about real people, places, and events are

  [_____]

- Stories that are meant to be performed are

  [_____]

- A type of literature in which words are carefully chosen and arranged to created specific effects is

  [_____]

- Communication that reaches many people is known as

  [_____]

Take notes on pages 5–10 by writing the definitions for these key terms about **genres.**
Tip: You don't need to copy the text word-for-word. Paraphrasing, putting things in your own words, will help you understand and remember the main ideas.

- (page 5) **Plot** is

  [_____]

- (page 6) **Stanzas** are

  [_____]

- (page 7) **Stage directions** are grouped lines of poetry

  [_____]

- (page 7) **Dialogue** is

  [_____]

- (page 8) A **biography** is

  [_____]

- (page 8) An **autobiography** is

  [_____]

- (page 8) An **essay** is

  [_____]

- (page 8) A **news article** is

  [_____]

- (page 8) A **consumer document** is

  [_____]

- (page 10) A **Web site** is

  [_____]

READING STRATEGIES WORKSHOP

Note Taking

BECOMING AN ACTIVE READER

Directions: Take notes about how to use the **skills and strategies for active reading** that are described on page 12. Fill in the missing elements of the chart.

Skills and Strategies for Active Reading
Preview
Does this relate to people & experiences in your own life?
Set a Purpose
Use Prior Knowledge
Predict
Picture what the writer describes.
Monitor
Make Inferences

Take notes on **Strategies That Work: Reading** (page 15), by completing this concept web. The web should have three main links that describe three important reading strategies. One link is already provided; create two more. Then add additional links that tell how to use each strategy.

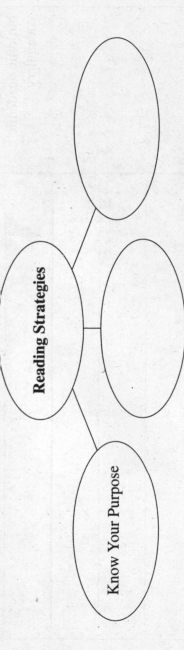

Reading Strategies

Know Your Purpose

ACADEMIC VOCABULARY WORKSHOP

Note Taking

WHAT IS ACADEMIC VOCABULARY?

Directions: Take notes about academic vocabulary by using the information on pages 16–19 to complete this chart.

ACADEMIC VOCABULARY	
Definition of academic vocabulary	
Benefits of learning academic vocabulary	
Three examples of academic vocabulary	1. _____ 2. _____ 3. _____
Three strategies for building academic vocabulary	1. _____ 2. _____ 3. _____

WRITING PROCESS WORKSHOP

Note Taking

EXPRESSING IDEAS IN WRITING

Directions: Take notes about **expressing ideas in writing** by outlining the important ideas on pages 16–18. It's fine to use abbreviations, short cuts, and paraphrasing.

I. Consider Your Options

A. *Purpose*

  1. Question: *Why am I writing?*

  2. Examples of purpose: *to entertain,* _____

    _____

B.

  1. Question: *Who are my readers?*

  2. Examples of readers: _____

    _____

C. _____

  1. Question: _____

  2. Examples of formats: _____

II. Continue the Process

A. *Planning / Prewriting* _____

  1. *Explore my ideas.*

  2. One way to prewrite: _____

B. _____

  1. *Turn prewriting into 1st draft.*

  2. Ways to draft: _____

C. _____

  1. Check writing against a _____

  2. Get feedback from a _____

D. Editing and Publishing

  1. Proofread your work for _____

  2. _____

Plot, Conflict, and Setting

Academic Vocabulary

A. Academic vocabulary is the language you use to talk about literature. Listen as your teacher reads each word and discusses its meaning and the example sentence.

Academic Vocabulary	Definition	Example Sentence
1. affect	to produce a response or reaction	One person's mood can **affect** everyone's.
2. analyze	to separate, or break into parts and examine	If I **analyze** the way an engine is put together, I will be able to fix cars.
3. evidence	specific information that supports a claim	Based on the **evidence**, the jury concluded that he was guilty.
4. impact	to have a direct effect on	The rain has had a good **impact** on our garden.
5. provide	to supply; make something available	If you **provide** me the ingredients, I will bake the cake.

B. Use an academic vocabulary word to complete each sentence.

1. To really understand something, you have to _____ how it was made.

2. Joining the speech team has had a great _____ on Terrence's self confidence.

3. The way you say something can _____ someone else's reaction.

4. The school will _____ the equipment and the uniforms for the team.

5. The _____ supported her claim of innocence.

C. Write the academic vocabulary words in your Reader/Writer Notebook. Practice using these words as you talk and write about the selections in this unit.

1. analyze   **2.** impact   **3.** affect   **4.** provide   **5.** evidence

UNIT 1

Additional Academic Vocabulary

A. Listen as your teacher reads each word and discusses its meaning and the example sentence.

Academic Vocabulary	Definition	Example Sentence
1. approach	to come closer or draw nearer; to go to someone with a plan or request	Our dog will always **approach** us with his tail wagging.
2. constitute	to make up; to set up, establish	All of your characteristics **constitute** your personality.
3. define	to tell the meaning of	You should **define** words that most people don't know.
4. economy	the managing of money; a system of producing, distributing, and consuming wealth	The bad **economy** has made it hard to start a new business.
5. participate	to take part in something with others	Sandra hopes to **participate** in chess, softball, and debate.

B. Write a word or words from the chart to replace each underlined word or phrase in the following sentences.

1. The winning team will take part in the state tournament.

_____

2. Sometimes you can tell the meaning of the word from the context.

_____

3. My mom always smiles when I come nearer.

_____

4. Banks, companies, the government and individuals all make up the system of wealth.

_____

Grammar Focus

These charts provide two methods of incorporating grammar instruction in your literature class. You may choose one approach, or blend the two.

Systematic Grammar Instruction: The Sentence and Its Parts I

Introducing the Unit: Students can start the academic year with an overview of the sentence and how it works.

Review	Grammar Handbook (See Student Edition)	Language Handbook
• *Complete Subjects and Predicates*	Quick Reference: The Sentence and Its Parts, p. R48	Identifying Complete Subjects and Predicates, p. 60

Week	Grammar Handbook (See Student Edition)	Language Handbook
1 Subjects	Quick Reference: The Sentence and Its Parts, p. R48	Identifying and Using Complete Subjects and Simple Subjects, p. 59
2 Predicates	Quick Reference: The Sentence and Its Parts, p. R48	Identifying Complete Predicates and Simple Predicates, p. 61
3 Compound Sentence Parts	Compound Subjects and Predicates, p. R60	Identifying Compound Subjects and Verbs, p. 63
4 Kinds of Sentences	Kinds of Sentences, p. R60	Identifying Simple and Compound Sentences, p. 75; Using Simple and Compound Sentences, pp. 76–77

Related Mechanics Topics	Grammar Handbook (See Student Edition)	Language Handbook
• End Marks	Quick Reference: End Marks, p. R49	Using End Marks, p. 112
• Capitalization	Quick Reference: Capitalization, p. R51	Capitalization, pp. 228–241 *Workbook:* pp. 178–189

Integrating Grammar, Literature, and Writing

Use activities provided in the literature selections and Writing Workshop to reinforce grammar concepts in the context of writing, revision, and author's style. You may extend or reinforce those lessons using Handbook lessons in the student edition or the Language Handbook.

Teaching Opportunities	Grammar Handbook (See Student Edition)	Language Handbook
The School Play Avoid Sentence Fragments	Correcting Fragments, p. R64	Identifying and Correcting Sentence Fragments, p. 84; Correcting Sentence Fragments
The Good Deed Avoid Run-On Sentences	Correcting Run-On Sentences, pp. R64–R65	Identifying and Correcting Run-on Sentences, pp. 87–88
All Summer in a Day Punctuate Dialogue Correctly	Quick Reference: Quotation Marks, p. R50	Punctuating Quotations and Titles, p. 122
Lob's Girl Punctuate Possessives Correctly	Quick Reference: Apostrophe, p. R50	Using Apostrophes to Show Possession, pp. 127–128
Woodsong Maintain Pronoun-Antecedent Agreement (Number)	Pronouns: Agreement with Antecedent, p. R52	Ensuring Agreement with Indefinite Pronouns, p. 19
The Horse Snake Create Compound Sentence	Compound Sentences, p. R63; Correcting Run-on Sentences, pp. R64–R65	Use Simple and Compound Sentences, pp. 76–77
Writing Workshop Descriptive Essay Present Participles, Consistent Verb Tense	Participles and Participial Phrases, p. R61; Verb Tense, p. R56	Using Different Verb Tenses, pp. 32–33

*Essential Course
of Study* EGOS **Lesson at a Glance**

Text Analysis
Workshop | What Makes
a Good Story?

OVERVIEW AND PURPOSE

The following key terms and concepts are
introduced in the Text Analysis Workshop for
Unit 1. They will be reviewed and reinforced
throughout the unit, and assessed on the
Unit 1 Test.

- Setting
- Characters
- Conflict
- Stages of plot (exposition, rising action,
  climax, falling action, resolution)

WORKSHOP LITERATURE

Trouble River
novel by Betsy Byars

"Zlateh the Goat"
short story by Isaac Bashevis Singer

"The Bracelet"
short story by Yoshiko Uchida

**"You're Not a Winner Unless Your
Picture's in the Paper"**
short story by Avi

"Boar Out There"
short story by Cynthia Rylant

LESSON RESOURCES

Student Copy Masters

These copy masters may be used to provide
note-taking support for students at lower
readiness levels.

- Note Taking, p. 9
- Note Taking, p. 10

Resource Manager

Note Taking:

PARTS OF A STORY

Use this page to take notes on page 28, Part 1: **Parts of a Story**. Fill in the information that's missing from the outline. Some parts are already filled in as note-taking examples. *Tip:* Notice that the examples omit unnecessary words like *the, a, or.* They also use abbreviations *(12-yr-old)* and symbols (=). It's fine to use short cuts like these when you take notes. The important thing is to record key ideas in a way that helps you understand and remember them.

I. SETTING

A. What Setting Is: _____

B. Examples of Settings:
   1. *rainy day on Venus* _____
   2. _____
   3. _____
   4. _____

II. CHARACTERS

A. What Characters Are: _____

B. Two Kinds of Characters:
   1. _____
   2. *minor characters = less important*

C. Examples of Characters
   1. *12-yr-old girl*
   2. _____
   3. _____
   4. _____

III. CONFLICT

A. What Conflict Is: _____

B. Three Types of Conflict:
   1. *Between characters*
      Example: *girl vs. friends*
   2. _____
      Example: _____
   3. _____
      Example: _____

TEXT ANALYSIS WORKSHOP: PART 2

Note Taking:

WHAT HAPPENS IN A STORY?

Use this page to take notes on page 30, Part 2: **What Happens in a Story?** First, fill in the key terms. You'll use a couple of them more than once. *Tip:* While you're taking notes, don't look back at your book unless you need to. Writing from memory helps "download" the key ideas into your permanent memory bank.

Key Terms

- The series of events in a story is known as the

- The beginning of a story is called the

- The most exciting part of a story is known as the

- The part of a story that reveals how everything turns out is the

- The part of a plot when the conflict becomes more difficult is the

- The part of a plot in which the tension eases is the

- Suspense builds during the

- The setting and the characters are introduced during the

In this space, draw a graphic that shows these five **stages of a plot**. Label each part. You can use the graphic on page 30 as an example, or create your own design.

Five Stages of a Plot

falling action   exposition   resolution   rising action   climax

rising action

Essential Course of Study **ECOS** Lesson at a Glance

The School Play
Gary Soto

WHY THIS SELECTION?

Gary Soto has written many books for and about the experiences of children, often based on his own experience growing up in California. "The School Play" is an entertaining and inviting story with which many students will identify. Its straightforward plot makes it an excellent vehicle for teaching this literary element.

ABOUT THIS SELECTION

Student/Teacher's Edition Pages: 34–45
Difficulty Level: Easy
Readability Scores: Lexile: 860; Fry: 7; Dale-Chall: 6.1

Summary "The School Play" is the story of sixth-grader Robert Suarez, who has a one-line part in a school play. Robert is nervous about forgetting his line, and his scene partner, Belinda, warns him not to make a mistake. He practices diligently, but on the day of the performance Robert loses his confidence. When he gets on stage, he mixes up the order of the words in his line. Yet, the play goes on, and everyone is more or less happy with how it turns out.

Engaging the Students This story offers students an opportunity to explore the key idea of fear. As students read the story, they can reflect on how they have coped with their own fears in the past.

COMMON CORE STANDARDS FOCUS

• Plot Elements
• Monitor

LESSON RESOURCES

Plan and Teach

Student Copy Masters

ⓘ Lesson resources are also available on the **Teacher One Stop DVD-ROM** and online at **thinkcentral.com**.

Resource Manager

Lesson Plan and Resource Guide

The School Play
Short Story by Gary Soto

Common Core Focus

RL 1 Cite evidence to support analysis of the text. **RL 3** Describe how a plot unfolds as well as how the characters respond as the plot moves toward a resolution. **RL 5** Analyze how a particular sentence fits into the structure of a text and contributes to the development of the setting or plot. **W 2** Write informative/explanatory texts to convey ideas. **L 1** Demonstrate command of the conventions of grammar. **L 4c** Consult thesauruses, both print and digital, to clarify meaning. **L 5c** Distinguish among the connotations (associations) of words with similar denotations (definitions).

Unless otherwise noted, resources can be found in the *Resource Manager.* **ⓘ** Lesson resources are also available on the **Teacher One Stop DVD-ROM** and online at **thinkcentral.com.** The Student Edition and selected copy masters are available electronically on the ✎ **Student One Stop DVD-ROM.**

Student/Teacher's Edition Pages	Additional Resources CM = Copy Master T = Transparency
Focus and Motivate	
☐ Big Question p. 34	☐ ⓘ PowerNotes DVD-ROM and **thinkcentral.com**
☐ Author Biography and Background Information p. 35	☐ ⓘ Literature and Reading Center at **thinkcentral.com**
Teach	
☐ Plot Elements p. 35	☐ ⓘ PowerNotes DVD-ROM and **thinkcentral.com**
☐ Monitor p. 35	☐ Monitor CM—English p. 23, Spanish p. 24 Ⓓ
☐ Vocabulary in Context p. 35	☐ Vocabulary Study CM p. 25 Ⓓ
	☐ ⓘ PowerNotes DVD-ROM and **thinkcentral.com**

Ⓓ = Resources for Differentiation

Student/Teacher's Edition Pages	Additional Resources CM=Copy Master T=Transparency
Practice and Apply: Guided Practice	
Selection and Teacher Notes	☐ *Audio Anthology* D
☐ "The School Play," pp. 36–42	☐ Summary CM—English and Spanish p. 19, Haitian Creole and Vietnamese p. 20 D
	☐ Reading Fluency CM pp. 31–32
	☐ **Best Practices Toolkit**
	☐ New Word Analysis p. E8 [T] D
	☐ Plot Diagram p. D12 [T] D
	☐ ThinkAloud Models and Audio Summaries at **thinkcentral.com**
Practice and Apply: After Reading	
☐ Selection Questions p. 43	☐ Reading Check CM p. 28
	☐ Plot Elements CM—English p. 21, Spanish p. 22 D
	☐ Monitor CM—English p. 23, Spanish p. 24 D
	☐ Question Support CM p. 29 D
	☐ Additional Selection Questions p. 15 D
	☐ Ideas for Extension pp. 16–17 D
☐ Vocabulary Practice p. 44	☐ Vocabulary Practice CM p. 26
☐ Academic Vocabulary in Speaking p. 44	☐ Academic Vocabulary CM p. 3
☐ Vocabulary Strategy: Denotations and Connotations p. 44	☐ Additional Academic Vocabulary CM p. 4
	☐ Vocabulary Strategy CM p. 27
	☐ *WordSharp* Interactive Vocabulary Tutor CD-ROM and online at **thinkcentral.com**
☐ Grammar in Context p. 45	☐ **Best Practices Toolkit**
☐ Writing Prompt p. 45	☐ Critical Review p. C27 [T] D
	☐ Avoid Sentence Fragments CM p. 30
	☐ Grammar Handbook— Student Edition p. R64

D = Resources for Differentiation

Student/Teacher's Edition Pages	Additional Resources CM = Copy Master T = Transparency
Assess and Reteach	
Assess	☐ **Diagnostic and Selection Tests**
	☐ Selection Tests A, B/C pp. 23–24, 25–26 **D**
	☐ **i** ThinkCentral Online Assessment
	☐ ⊘ ExamView Test Generator on the **Teacher One Stop DVD-ROM**
Reteach	
☐ Plot Elements	☐ Level Up Online Tutorials on **thinkcentral.com**
☐ Monitor	☐ Reteaching Worksheets on **thinkcentral.com**
☐ Denotation and Connotation	☐ Literature Lesson 5: Elements of Plot
☐ Avoid Sentence Fragments	☐ Reading Lesson 2: Monitoring
	☐ Vocabulary Lesson 17: Denotation and Connotation
	☐ Grammar Lesson 1: Avoiding Sentence Fragments

D = Resources for Differentiation

If you are following the *Essential Course of Study*, this selection may also be found in

- **Interactive Reader**
- **Adapted Interactive Reader**
- ⊘ **Adapted Interactive Reader: Audio Tutor**
- **English Language Learner Adapted Interactive Reader**

THE SCHOOL PLAY
Additional Selection Questions

Use to supplement the questions on SE page 43.

Differentiation Use these questions to provide customized practice with comprehension and critical thinking skills.

Easy

1. **Recall** How did Belinda get her reputation for being "one of the toughest girls since the beginning of the world"? (*She slaps boys and grinds their faces into the grass. Robert has also seen her stare down the janitor's pit bull.*)

2. *What do you FEAR most?*
   What is Robert's greatest fear? (*He is afraid that he will say his line incorrectly.*)

3. **Recall** What is the point of highest tension in the play? (*The highest tension occurs before Robert goes on stage and mixes up his line.*)

Average

4. **Analyze Plot Elements** How does Robert's experience with the beard in rehearsal foreshadow the events on the day of the play's performance? (*The beard is itchy and it bothers him. On the day of the performance, the beard feels hot and itchy when he ties it on. He sneezes, and in his confusion, he forgets his line.*)

5. **Make Inferences** How do you think Robert might react to Belinda's threats in the future? Have his feelings toward her changed? (*Some students may say that his reaction after the play shows that he isn't afraid of her, no matter what she might say.*)

Challenging

6. **Analyze Tone** Based on details in the story, Mrs. Bunnin might have a hearing problem. She doesn't hear Ruben when he asks if he can give the shirt to his father after the play (lines 27–30). She tells Robert and Belinda to speak louder during rehearsal, while it is quite obvious that Belinda, at least, is making a lot of noise. How does this character trait contribute to the tone and overall effect of the story? (*It creates a humorous tone. Mrs. Bunnin doesn't have a clue about what is going on between Belinda and Robert. It also underscores the fact that Mrs. Bunnin will not intervene.*)

7. *What do you FEAR most?*
   Most fears about social relationships often have a deeper level of meaning. What does Robert fear will happen if he makes a mistake in the play? What deeper anxiety causes that fear? (*Robert fears he will disappoint his mother and Mrs. Bunnin, get beaten up by Belinda, or be laughed at by the other kids. He fears rejection by the people he wants to please, showing that he wants to be liked.*)

8. **Evaluate Plot Elements** Robert thinks of the Donner Party in relation to his own experience on two occasions, the day before the performance when he is full after dinner, and after the performance when he remembers once being locked in a closet for five hours without food. Why do you think the author includes these details? (*He might have included them for contrast, to show both Robert and the story's readers that, in spite of his fears, Robert has a good life and that his bad experiences are relatively minor.*)

Ideas for Extension

Differentiation These activities provide students with a variety of options for demonstrating understanding of lesson concepts.

EXPLORATIONS AND ACTIVITIES

POSTER: SUMMARIZE MAIN IDEAS

Point out that, in the story, it appears that all of the students in the school are required to attend the performance. Suggest that the performance might be open to the students' family members, as well as to the general public.

If possible, show students examples of real play (or film) advertisements. Then have students work in small groups to create posters advertising the play about which they just read. They may illustrate their posters with images from the play as it is described in the story. They may also wish to describe the actors and their roles or use a catchy phrase to grab viewers' attention.

Have students present and display their posters.

DIAGRAM: COMPARE AND CONTRAST PLOTS

Distribute copies of another short story by Gary Soto from one of these collections: *Baseball in April*, *Help Wanted*, *Local News*, *Petty Crimes*. Remind students to monitor their understanding as they read, using one of the strategies they have learned.

Have pairs of students look for similarities and differences between the new story's plot and the plot of "The School Play." Ask them to decide which story has the most interesting exposition, the most suspenseful rising action, the most exciting climax, and the most satisfying falling action and resolution.

Lead a class discussion about students' conclusions.

UNDERSTANDING MEMORY: EXPLORE THEME

Have pairs of students explore how memory works by gathering a number of memory games and experiments from the Internet or elsewhere. Have them choose three of these games or experiments and lead an activity session with the entire class. Encourage them to use what they have learned to draw conclusions about the nature of memory.

Pre-AP Challenge: Have students conduct individual research on the nature and theory of memory. Students should research the relationship between short-term and long-term memory to further understand the ways in which humans remember (or forget!) various types of information.

This project will consist of two components. First, students should write a short research paper on memory, using at least two electronic or print sources. Second, they should create a poster charting their own memory pattern.

Students must include at least three personal examples for the procedural, semantic, and episodic memory systems. (For example: I use procedural memory when I ride a bike, tie my shoes, and so on.) Have students present and display their posters.

IDEAS FOR EXTENSION, CONTINUED

ROLE PLAY: EXPLORE CHARACTER

Ask students to plan an interview with one of the performers, a member of the audience, or Mrs. Bunnin. Before they begin, discuss what questions or insights this person might have about the performance and the events leading up to it. Then divide students into pairs and suggest that they write six to ten interview questions.

Have students role-play their interviews exploring these questions and insights. Then have the class evaluate the interview process. What kinds of questions resulted in the most interesting answers?

INQUIRY AND RESEARCH

THE DONNER PARTY AND WESTWARD EXPANSION

Divide the class into small groups and have each group research one aspect of westward expansion during the mid-1800s. These might include details about weather and landforms, conditions of travel, the numbers and kinds of people who made the trek, and significant routes.

Have each group make a poster showing what they have learned about the time period. The poster should include text and visuals. Encourage students to incorporate illustrations, images, maps, and charts to reinforce important ideas.

Have groups present their information and display their posters on the bulletin board.

WRITING

EXPRESS POINT OF VIEW: INTERNAL MONOLOGUE

Readers know about Robert's thoughts and feelings throughout the story, but they don't know what Belinda is like on the inside. They only know what she says and does. Is Belinda really as tough as she seems? Why does she act the way she does?

Have students plan and write an internal monologue that reveals what Belinda thinks and feels as she rehearses and then performs in the play. Encourage them to be creative but also realistic.

SUMMARIZE: JOURNAL REPORTS

Have students use the Internet to find one of the journals kept by the members of the Donner Party. Ask them to prepare a written report covering the journal's major points.

THE SCHOOL PLAY

Teacher Notes

Resource Manager

Review and Evaluate Outcome

What did I want students to know or be able to do?

How successful was the lesson?

Evaluate Process

- Differentiation
- Resources
- Strategies

What worked?

Reflect

What did not work? Why not?

The next time I teach "The School Play," what will I do differently? Why?

Plan Ahead

What must I do next?

THE SCHOOL PLAY

Summary

THE SCHOOL PLAY

Gary Soto

Setting: a present-day school classroom

Robert gets a small speaking part in a school play. The play is about the California explorers known as the Donner party. Robert knows his line very well. Still, he is nervous. He must deliver his line to Belinda, the classroom bully who is known for beating up boys. Belinda threatens to bury Robert's face in the ground if he messes up his line. After the class rehearses for weeks, the day of the performance finally arrives.

LA OBRA DE TEATRO ESCOLAR

Gary Soto

Escenario: un salón de clases en la actualidad

Robert obtiene una pequeño papel, con parlamento, en una obra de teatro de la escuela. La obra es sobre los exploradores de California conocidos como el grupo Donner. Robert se sabe de memoria su parlamento. Sin embargo, está nervioso. Debe decir su parlamento a Belinda, la bravucona del salón, quien tiene fama de golpear a los niños. Belinda amenaza a Robert con enterrarle la cara en el suelo si se equivoca en su parlamento. Después de que la clase ensaya durante semanas, por fin llega el día de la presentación.

Summary

JWÈT LEKÒL LA

Gary Soto

Espas ak tan: yon salklas lekòl la jodi a

Robert jwenn yon ti tan pou l pale nan yon jwèt lekòl la. Jwèt la se osijè eksploratè Kalifòni ki rele gwoup Donner. Robert konnen de kòd li yo trè byen. Men l timid kanmenm. Li dwe bay Belinda kòd li yo. Belinda se mechan ki nan klas la ki abitye bat tigason. Belinda menase pou l fwote figi Robert nan tè si li mete kòd li yo andezòd. Apre klas la fin fè repetisyon, jou pou pèfòmans lan resi rive.

VỞ KỊCH TẠI TRƯỜNG HỌC

Gary Soto

Bối cảnh: một lớp học thời nay

Robert nhận vai thoại trong một vở kịch ở trường. Vở kịch nói về những nhà thám hiểm California mang tên nhóm Donner. Robert rất thuộc hai dòng thoại của mình. Tuy vậy, cậu vẫn cảm thấy rất lo lắng. Cậu phải đọc lời thoại với Belinda, một cậu học sinh ngỗ nghịch nổi tiếng hay đánh bạn. Belinda dọa sẽ vùi mặt Robert xuống đất nếu cậu đọc sai lời thoại của mình. Sau vài tuần tập dượt trên lớp, cuối cùng ngày biểu diễn đã đến.

Name _____ Date _____

COPY MASTER

THE SCHOOL PLAY
Text Analysis

PLOT ELEMENTS

Everything in a story happens for a reason. The series of events is the story's **plot.** The plot usually follows a pattern.

- **Exposition** introduces the characters and **setting.** It may also hint at what the **conflict,** or problem, will be.

- **Rising action** shows how the conflict develops.

- The most exciting part, or turning point of the story, is the **climax.** The outcome of the conflict is decided at this time.

- Tension eases during the **falling action,** and events unfold as a result of the climax.

- The **resolution** is the final point in the plot, in which the reader learns how everything turns out.

Directions: On the back of this sheet, make a list of important events from "The School Play." Then record the events on the following diagram to identify what happens at each stage of the plot.

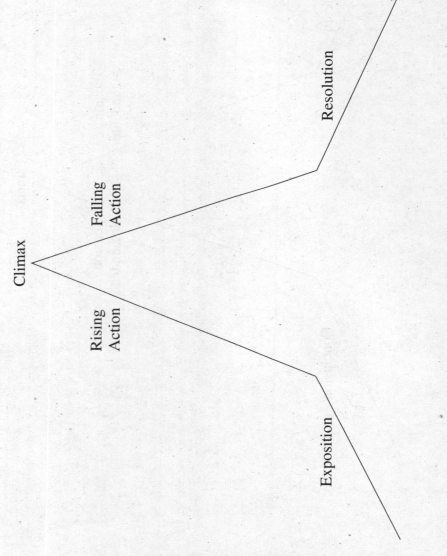

LA OBRA DE TEATRO ESCOLAR

Text Analysis

PLOT ELEMENTS

En un cuento todo sucede por una razón. La serie de sucesos es la **trama** del cuento. La trama sigue por lo general un patrón.

- El **planteamiento** presenta a los personajes y el **escenario.** También puede insinuar cuál será el **conflicto,** o problema.

- La **tensión ascendente** muestra cómo se desarrolla el conflicto.

- La parte más emocionante, o momento decisivo del cuento, es el **clímax.** El desenlace del conflicto se determina en este momento.

- El suspenso se aligera durante la **tensión descendente** y los sucesos se explican como resultado del clímax.

- La **conclusión** es el punto final de la trama, en la cual el lector se entera del desenlace.

Instrucciones: En la parte de atrás de esta hoja, haz una lista de los sucesos importantes de "La obra de teatro escolar." Luego anota los sucesos en el diagrama que aparece abajo, para identificar qué sucede en cada etapa de la trama.

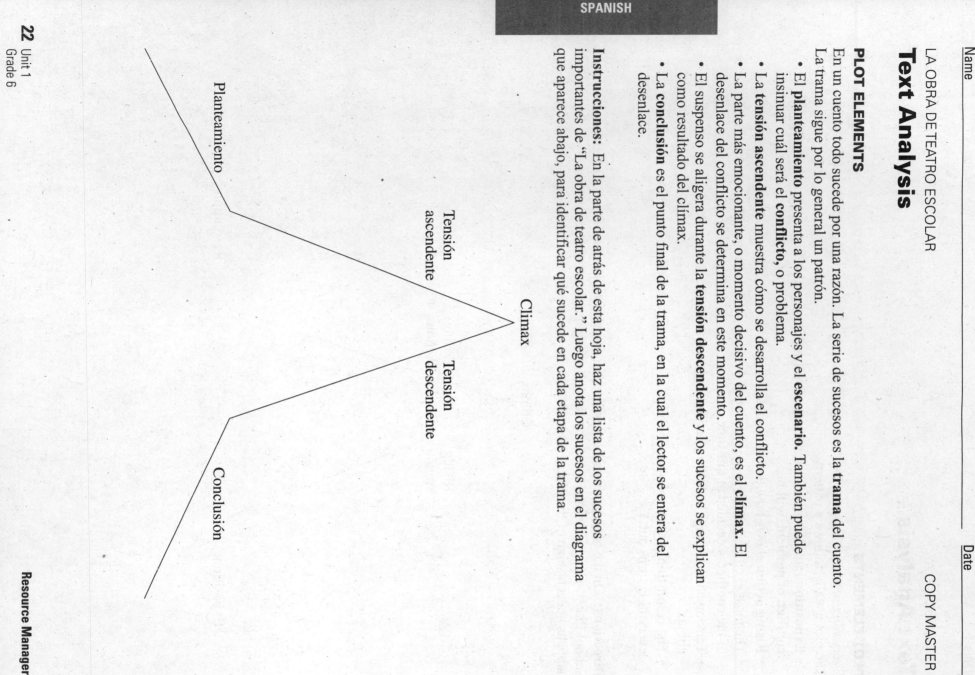

Planteamiento

Tensión
ascendente

Climax

Tensión
descendente

Conclusión

Name _____ Date _____

_____ COPY MASTER

THE SCHOOL PLAY

Reading Strategy

MONITOR

You can improve your comprehension if you **monitor** your reading by pausing occasionally to check your understanding. You can also ask yourself questions about what you are reading.

Directions: As you read "The School Play," use this chart to record questions about what is happening. An example has been done for you.

My Questions	Answers
What is inside the cardboard box?	costumes and props, a fake beard

SPANISH

LA OBRA DE TEATRO ESCOLAR

Reading Strategy

MONITOR

Puedes mejorar tu comprensión si **monitoreas** tu lectura haciendo pausas de vez en cuando para revisar tu comprensión. También puedes hacerte preguntas sobre lo que estás leyendo.

Instrucciones: Mientras lees "La obra de teatro escolar", usa esta tabla para anotar preguntas sobre lo que sucede. Te damos un ejemplo.

Mis preguntas	Respuestas
¿Qué hay en la caja de cartón?	disfraces y accesorios, una barba postiza

COPY MASTER

THE SCHOOL PLAY

Vocabulary Study

CONTEXT CLUES

A. Directions: Cover up or fold under the right-hand column. As your teacher reads each sentence, listen for the boldfaced word. Discuss possible meanings for the word. Then check your answers by reading the definition in the right-hand column.

Word	How It Is Used	Definition
narrative	Uncle Harry's **narrative** of his trip to Brazil was very interesting. He told us about some amazing adventures.	a story
prop	The actor wanted to wear the sunglasses in the play, but at the last minute they broke, and he had to find another **prop** to use.	an object an actor uses in a play
relentless	The winter storm was **relentless**. It had been snowing for two days, and there was no end in sight.	refusing to stop or give up
smirk	Jocelyn finished her math test effortlessly. She tried not to **smirk** as she saw the other students struggle to answer the questions.	to smile in an insulting way

B. Directions: Write a sentence using each word. If possible, use your sentences to tell a story.

_____

_____

_____

_____

_____

_____

Name _____ Date _____

Vocabulary Practice

narrative	relentless	prop	smirk

A. Directions: Fill in each set of blanks with the correct word from the word list. The boxed letters will spell something an actor might receive at the end of a performance.

1. In a play about pirates, this is what the treasure chest is.

□ □ __

2. This is what people often do while they are saying, "I told you so!"

□ __ __

3. This is what a person shares when telling about her day at school.

__ __ __

4. This can describe teasing when the teaser just won't quit.

__ __ __ □ □

5. Mystery word: __ __ __ __

B. Directions: Complete each analogy with one of the words in the box. In an analogy, the last two words must be related in the same way that the first two are related.

6. KITCHEN : UTENSIL :: drama : _____

7. CHEER : TEASE :: smile : _____

8. CALM : RELAXED :: persistent : _____

C. Writing Option: Pretend you are the director of *The Last Stand*. Write some advice you might give Robert to help him play his part. Use at least **two** of the vocabulary words.

_____

_____

_____

_____

_____

Name _____ Date _____

THE SCHOOL PLAY

Vocabulary Strategy

DENOTATIONS AND CONNOTATIONS

A word's **denotation** is its literal, dictionary meaning. A word's **connotation** is the shades of meaning it has beyond its dictionary definition. The connotation includes the way people feel when they hear the word—negative, positive, or neutral. For example, the word smirk does mean "smile." But *smirk* also carries negative connotations of smugness or conceitedness.

A. Directions: Use a dictionary to find the denotative meanings of both words in each pair. Circle the word that has a negative connotation.

1. her (loud, brassy) voice

2. his (arrogant, proud) manner

3. his (skinny, slender) appearance

4. her (fawning, flattering) speech

5. his (carefree, indifferent) attitude

B. Directions: Choose **two** of the word pairs from exercise A. Write a sentence for each word in the pair. Try to show the difference in connotation between the two words.

6. _____

_____

7. _____

_____

8. _____

_____

9. _____

_____

Resource Manager

THE SCHOOL PLAY

Reading Check

Directions: Recall the characters and events in the selection. Then answer the questions in sentences or phrases.

1. What part does Robert have in the play?

   _____

   _____

2. Describe Belinda.

   _____

   _____

3. Why is Robert worried about his lines? How does he prepare for the performance?

   _____

   _____

4. What would Robert's dream job be? Why?

   _____

   _____

5. After the play, how does Robert feel? What does Belinda think?

   _____

   _____

THE SCHOOL PLAY

Name _____ Date _____

THE SCHOOL PLAY

Question Support

TEXT ANALYSIS
For questions 1–3, see page 43 of the Student Edition.

Directions: Answer the questions.

4. Monitor Write two questions that helped you understand the story.

_____

_____

5. Compare and Contrast On the line following each name, write the letter of the words that best describe Robert or Belinda on the day of the play.

Robert _____   Belinda _____

a. relieved   **b.** loud   **c.** nervous   **d.** timid   **e.** angry   **f.** satisfied

6. Make Inferences Does the audience enjoy the play? How can you tell?

_____

_____

7. Examine Plot Elements Match each event in the story in the first column to the stage of the plot listed in the second column. Write the letter of the plot stage on the line.

____ Mrs. Bunnin calls Robert's work "almost perfect."   **a.** Exposition
____ The cast receives their costumes.   **b.** Rising Action
____ Robert delivers his lines on stage.   **c.** Climax
____ Robert finds a lucky dollar.   **d.** Falling Action
____ Robert practices his lines at home.   **e.** Resolution

8. Analyze Character's Effect on Plot Robert shows some other qualities besides fear as the story develops. Underline two qualities he shows.

a. intelligence   **b.** anger   **c.** humor   **d.** persistence

Explain how these two qualities help Robert resolve a conflict.

_____

_____

Name _____ Date _____

Grammar in Context

AVOID SENTENCE FRAGMENTS

A **sentence fragment** lacks a subject (whom or what the sentence is about), a predicate (what the subject is or does), or both. It cannot stand as a complete sentence. Often, a fragment can be combined with the sentence before it to make a complete sentence.

Original: Robert was nervous. About his part in the play.
Revised: Robert was nervous about his part in the play.

A. Directions: Rewrite this paragraph, correcting the sentence fragments.

Our school put on a play. Called *The Last Stand.* It was performed by the students in Mrs. Bunnin's class. It was about a group of people from Illinois and nearby states. Headed for California. Alonso played the narrator. And he told about the historic background of the Donner party. Some of the other students in the class. Played trees and snowflakes. Belinda Lopez played a pioneer woman, and Robert Suarez played a pioneer man. They got their roles by scoring high. On their spelling tests!

_____
_____
_____
_____
_____
_____
_____
_____
_____
_____
_____

Name _____ Date _____

COPY MASTER

THE SCHOOL PLAY

Reading Fluency

TRACKING ORAL READING RATE AND ACCURACY

Directions: In "The School Play," Robert takes part in a play about the Donner party. The passage that follows offers more information about these brave pioneers. Use this passage with the activity on page 32. Follow the directions on that page.

As pioneers traveled west from the original thirteen colonies, they

faced many life-threatening dangers. One of the greatest dangers

was the weather, especially the cold and snowy winter weather.

As a result, the pioneers planned their trips so that they would

reach their new homes before winter set in.

One famous group of pioneers that ran into trouble was the

Donner party. The Donners left Springfield, Illinois, in April

of 1846. They met up with other travelers at Independence,

Missouri. From there they continued west across the Great Plains

and the Rocky Mountains. Their goal was to reach Sutter's Mill,

California. Unfortunately, they tried a new shortcut through

the Sierra Nevada Mountains. This shortcut proved slow and

impassable. As a result, the party was caught in a bad snowstorm.

Several rescue parties were sent to help, but many pioneers died

before the rescue party reached them. Of the 87 men, women,

and children in the party, only 41 survived. Sadly, the pioneers

were only one day away from their goal when they were hit by the

storm that killed half their party. (181 words)

Resource Manager

THE SCHOOL PLAY

Reading Fluency

TRACKING ORAL READING RATE AND ACCURACY

When you read aloud, your goal is to help the listener understand the text. To do this, read the words accurately and with expression. Use a normal speaking rate.

Directions to the Reader:

- Use this page with the passage on page 31. Read the passage in a natural tone of voice to your partner for one minute. He or she will tell you when to start and stop.

- Read the same passage three more times. Your goal is to increase your speed each time, while still reading each word accurately.

- Your partner will calculate your score, which shows how you compare to others at your grade level. Answer the questions below the chart to evaluate your progress.

Directions to the Checker:

- Tell your partner when to begin reading. As your partner reads, follow along. Lightly underline each word your partner skips or mispronounces. Jot down words he or she adds.

- After one minute, say "stop" and circle the last word your partner read. Share the marks you made with your partner.

- To calculate the reading fluency score, subtract the number of errors your partner made from the number of words read in a minute. Count as an error any words your partner left out, added, or mispronounced. If your partner substituted one word for another (*home*, for example), that substitution counts as an error as well. Put a checkmark in the table to show the reading score.

- Then erase the marks on the passage and tell your partner to begin again.

	Number of Words Read Correctly Per Minute	1–77	79–98	99–106	107–112	113–124	125–133	134–145	146–155	156–161	162–168	169–185
			10th percentile	20th percentile	25th percentile	30th percentile	40th percentile	50th percentile	60th percentile	70th percentile	75th percentile	80th percentile	90th percentile
Reading 1												
Reading 2												
Reading 3												
Reading 4												

Directions: Write your answer to the following questions on the back of this sheet.

1. How did reading the passage several times affect your speed and accuracy?

2. Summarize the effect of repeated readings on your understanding of the passage.

Lesson at a Glance

The Good Deed

Marion Dane Bauer

WHY THIS SELECTION?

This story by award-winning author Marion Dane Bauer is an excellent example of a subject with which many students will identify— the problems that result from wrong first impressions. Many students will relate to the main character's internal conflict as she struggles between the impulses of jealousy and compassion.

ABOUT THIS SELECTION

Student/Teacher's Edition Pages: 46–65

Difficulty Level: Average

Readability Scores: Lexile: 790; Fry: 5; Dale-Chall: 5.3

Summary To earn a scouting badge, Heather is assigned to help sight-impaired Miss Benson. On her first visit, Risa, a young neighbor of Miss Benson's, barges in. Heather soon becomes jealous of the girl. Eventually, however, she learns more about Risa's difficult situation, and the girls start to become friends.

Engaging the Students This story offers students an opportunity to explore the key idea of forming and giving an impression. The main character, Heather, forms an initial impression of Risa that later proves to be incorrect. All students will have had similar experiences. They will also have had the experience of others forming wrong impressions of them. As students read the story, they will have an opportunity to reflect on those experiences.

COMMON CORE STANDARDS FOCUS

- Conflict and Climax
- Connect

LESSON RESOURCES

Plan and Teach

Student Copy Masters

ⓘ Lesson resources are also available on the **Teacher One Stop DVD-ROM** and online at thinkcentral.com.

Lesson Plan and Resource Guide

The Good Deed
Short Story by Marion Dane Bauer

Common Core Focus

RL 3 Describe how the characters respond as the plot moves toward a resolution. **RL 9** Compare and contrast texts in different genres in terms of their approaches to similar topics. **L 1** Demonstrate command of the conventions of grammar. **W 2** Write informative/ explanatory texts to convey ideas. **L 1** Demonstrate command of the conventions of grammar. **L 4b** Use common affixes as clues to the meaning of a word. **L 6** Gather vocabulary knowledge when considering a word important to comprehension or expression.

Unless otherwise noted, resources can be found in the *Resource Manager.* **ⓘ** Lesson resources are also available on the **Teacher One Stop DVD-ROM** and online at **thinkcentral.com.** The Student Edition and selected copy masters are available electronically on the **Student One Stop DVD-ROM.**

Student/Teacher's Edition Pages	Additional Resources CM = Copy Master T = Transparency
Focus and Motivate	
☐ Big Question p. 46	
☐ Author Biography p. 47	☐ ⓘ Literature and Reading Center at <u>thinkcentral.com</u>
Teach	
☐ Conflict and Climax p. 47	
☐ Connect p. 47	☐ Connect CM—English p. 45, Spanish p. 46 **D**
☐ Vocabulary in Context p. 47	☐ Vocabulary Study CM p. 47 **D**

D = Resources for Differentiation

Student/Teacher's Edition Pages	Additional Resources CM = Copy Master T = Transparency
Practice and Apply: Guided Practice	
Selection and Teacher Notes ☐ "The Good Deed," pp. 48–61 ☐ "The Pasture," p. 62	✎ **Audio Anthology CD** D ☐ Summary CM—English and Spanish p. 41, Haitian Creole and Vietnamese p. 42 D ☐ Reading Fluency CM p. 53 ☐ ⓘ Audio Summaries at <u>thinkcentral.com</u> 🔧 **Best Practices Toolkit** ☐ Reciprocal Questioning p. A3 D ☐ Venn Diagram p. A26 [T] ☐ Sensory Notes p. B9 [T] D ☐ Character Map p. D8 [T] D
Practice and Apply: After Reading	
☐ Selection Questions p. 63	☐ Reading Check CM p. 50 ☐ Conflict and Climax CM—English p. 43, Spanish p. 44 D ☐ Connect CM—English p. 45, Spanish p. 46 D ☐ Question Support CM p. 51 D ☐ Additional Selection Questions p. 37 D ☐ Ideas for Extension pp. 38–39 D
☐ Vocabulary Practice p. 64 ☐ Academic Vocabulary in Writing p. 64 ☐ Vocabulary Strategy: Suffixes p.64	☐ Vocabulary Practice CM p. 48 ☐ Academic Vocabulary CM p. 3 ☐ Additional Academic Vocabulary CM p. 4 ☐ Vocabulary Strategy CM p. 49 ☐ ⓘ *Word Sharp*: Interactive Vocabulary Tutor CD-ROM and online at <u>thinkcentral.com</u> ☐ ⓘ *Word Sharp*: Interactive Vocabulary Tutor CD-ROM and online at <u>thinkcentral.com</u>
☐ Grammar in Context p. 65 ☐ Writing Prompt p. 65	🔧 **Best Practices Toolkit** ☐ Compare–Contrast (by Subject) p. C26 [T] ☐ Avoid Run-On Sentences CM p. 52 ☐ Grammar Handbook—Student Edition p. R64 ☐ ⓘ **GrammarNotes DVD-ROM** at <u>thinkcentral.com</u> ☐ ⓘ Interactive Revision Lessons on **Write*Smart* CD-ROM** and online at <u>thinkcentral.com</u>

D = Resources for Differentiation

Resource Manager

Resource Manager

Student/Teacher's Edition Pages	Additional Resources CM = Copy Master T = Transparency
Assess and Reteach	
Assess	☐ **Diagnostic and Selection Tests** ☐ Selection Tests A, B/C pp. 27–28, 29–30 **D** ☐ **1** ThinkCentral Online Assessment ☐ **●** ExamView Test Generator on the **Teacher One Stop DVD-ROM**
Reteach ☐ Conflict and Climax ☐ Suffixes ☐ Avoid Run-On Sentences	☐ **Level Up Online Tutorials** on **thinkcentral.com** ☐ **Reteaching Worksheets** on **thinkcentral.com** ☐ Literature Lesson 6: Conflict ☐ Vocabulary Lesson 1: Word Parts: Base Words, Prefixes, Suffixes, and Roots ☐ Vocabulary Lesson 5: Noun Suffixes ☐ Grammar Lesson 2: Avoiding Run-Ons

D = Resources for Differentiation

THE GOOD DEED

Additional Selection Questions

Differentiation Use these questions to provide customized practice with comprehension and critical thinking skills.

Easy

1. **Recall** What motivates Heather to do her "good deed"? (*She visits Miss Benson so that she can get another Girl Scout badge.*)

2. **Recall** What does Heather think has happened to the missing book? What has actually happened to it? (*She thinks Risa stole the book. In fact, Miss Benson gave it to Risa.*)

3. ***Can first IMPRESSIONS be trusted?***
   What impression does Miss Benson's kitchen give? What does it say about Miss Benson? (*The kitchen is warm and inviting, as is Miss Benson.*)

Average

4. **Analyze Conflict** Which internal conflict causes Heather the most discomfort? How is the conflict resolved? (*Answers will vary. One conflict and resolution is that Heather feels bad about losing Miss Benson's book and then learns that Risa found the book.*)

5. **Analyze Conflict** Why does Heather hide the book from Risa? (*She does not want Risa to "horn in" on her good deed. She is jealous of Risa.*)

6. **Speculate** How do you think Risa feels when she walks into her apartment and finds Heather? (*She probably feels surprised, confused, and protective of her brothers.*)

Challenging

7. ***Can first IMPRESSIONS be trusted?***
   Heather concludes that Risa is a poor reader, a liar, and a thief. Which conclusions are drawn from evidence and which from impressions? (*Heather observes that Risa is a poor reader. She assumes that Risa is a liar and a thief because her first impression is so negative.*)

8. **Evaluate Character** Risa doesn't tell Miss Benson that Heather hid the book. Would Heather have made the same decision? Explain. (*Risa isn't jealous. She doesn't want to get Heather in trouble. Heather probably would not have made the same decision.*)

9. **Evaluate Symbol** What does Miss Benson's blindness represent in the story? Explain. (*The blindness is symbolic of a closed mind. Heather has a hard time seeing people for who they really are. In some ways she is blinder than Miss Benson.*)

Ideas for Extension

Differentiation These activities provide students with a variety of options for demonstrating understanding of lesson concepts.

EXPLORATIONS AND ACTIVITIES

SMALL GROUP DISCUSSION: EXPLORE THEME

Share the following quotation with students:

"The chief handicap of the blind is not blindness, but the attitude of seeing people towards them." —Helen Keller

For students who are not familiar with Helen Keller's story, give a brief summary. Explain that she was profoundly handicapped by her blindness (and deafness), but that the positive attitude and persistence of a dedicated teacher helped her break through so that she was able to communicate with the outside world.

Have small groups discuss the quotation. Suggest that they explore answers to the following questions:

- Why is Helen Keller critical of "seeing people"?
- What attitudes might "seeing people" have toward people who are blind or vision impaired?
- What is Helen Keller implying about the potential abilities of the blind and vision impaired?

Have the class meet as a whole to discuss their conclusions.

IMPROVISE SKETCH: ANALYZE INTERNAL AND EXTERNAL CONFLICT

Review with students the distinction between internal and external conflict, drawing on examples from the story. Have them brainstorm other internal conflicts for Heather and Risa. Then have them improvise a sketch based on these conflicts. Encourage students to hypothesize about the kinds of external conflicts that might arise from the internal conflicts.

INQUIRY AND RESEARCH

TECHNOLOGY FOR THE VISUALLY IMPAIRED

Ask students to discuss the ways in which technology—from printed materials to computers and the Internet—contributes to their ability to communicate with the world. Discuss how being visually impaired might be an impediment to gaining full access to the information and ideas available from these sources.

Have students work in small groups to research one of the technologies mentioned in the Background note on page 49 in the Teacher's Edition. Encourage them to look for information about the cost and training involved with these technologies.

Have students make a presentation to the class on one of these technologies in the form of a poster, computer presentation, or summary report.

IDEAS FOR EXTENSION, CONTINUED

Pre-AP Challenge: Have students research Books on Tape or other organizations that record books for the blind and visually impaired. Suggest that they contact one of these organizations and volunteer to record a book (or help with some part of the process of preparing the recording).

WRITING

DESCRIBE CHARACTERS: PERSONAL LETTER

Heather and Risa meet and the conflict between them develops within the context of the "good deed"—Heather's initial motivation for going to see Miss Benson. But how does Miss Benson feel? Is she aware of the conflict between the girls? What is her history, and what is her life like today?

Have students write a letter written by Miss Benson to a friend or family member, in which she describes and draws conclusions about Heather and Risa. Students may wish to include some of the details of the story's "eye bouquets" in their letters.

Have volunteers share and comment on each other's letters. Identify points on which the letter writers agree, and ask them what details in the story led them to their conclusions.

EXPLORE TOPICS: STORY IDEA

Marion Dane Bauer says that many of her ideas come from outside sources, such as newspaper articles, overheard conversations, and talks with friends. She then filters the information through her own thoughts and feelings to come up with a story.

Have students look in the newspaper for an idea for a story. Suggest that they choose an article that speaks to them strongly on an emotional or intellectual level. Then have them write an outline or a draft of a story based on the article.

Teacher Notes

Review and Evaluate Outcome
What did I want students to know or be able to do?
How successful was the lesson?

Evaluate Process
• Strategies
• Resources
• Differentiation
What worked?
What did not work? Why not?

Reflect
The next time I teach "The Good Deed," what will I do differently? Why?

Plan Ahead
What must I do next?

THE GOOD DEED

Summary

THE GOOD DEED

Marion Dane Bauer

Setting: a present-day apartment house

As an assignment for Girl Scouts, Heather has to do a good deed for someone in need. She has to read to a blind lady named Miss Benson. When Heather visits Miss Benson for the first time, she also meets Risa. Risa lives across the hall from Miss Benson. She has three little brothers and a mother who works. Heather picks a book to read from the shelf in Miss Benson's bedroom. It is a book of children's stories. Risa listens carefully and moves her mouth. Miss Benson asks Risa to read, but Risa refuses. Instead, she makes Miss Benson a picture with words by describing, in great detail, lilacs that Miss Benson hadn't seen in years. Miss Benson is impressed, but Heather is annoyed. She feels as though Risa is taking over her good deed. Instead of returning the book to the shelf, she puts it in the wastebasket. When she visits Miss Benson a few days later, the book is gone. Could Risa have taken it?

LA BUENA OBRA

Marion Dane Bauer

Escenario: un edificio de apartamentos en la actualidad

Como tarea de las Niñas Exploradoras, Heather tiene que hacer una buena obra para alguien necesitado. Debe leer en voz alta a una mujer ciega llamada Miss Benson. Cuando Heather visita a Miss Benson, cruzando el pasillo. Tiene tres hermanos pequeños y una mamá que trabaja. Heather toma de la repisa de la recamara de Miss Benson un libro para leer. Es un libro de cuentos para niños. Risa escucha con atención y mueve la boca. Miss Benson le pide a Risa que lea, pero ella se niega. En lugar de eso, hace a Miss Benson una imagen con palabras al describir, con gran detalle, unas lilas que Miss Benson no había visto en años. Miss Benson está impresionada, pero Heather está molesta. Siente como si Risa se apropiara de su buena obra. En vez de poner el libro de vuelta en el estante, lo pone en la papelera. Cuando visita a Miss Benson algunos días después, el libro ya no está. ¿Podría haberlo tomado Risa?

Summary

THE GOOD DEED

BON ZAK

Marion Dane Bauer

Espas ak tan: yon kay ki gen apatman jodi a

Pou yon asiyasyon pou Eskout Fi yo, Heathèr gen pou fè yon bon zak pou yon moun ki nan bezwen. Li dwe li pou yon dam ki avèg ki rele Miss Benson. Lè Heater vizite Miss Benson pou premye fwa, li rankontre Risa tou. Risa ap viv akote antre kay Miss Benson. Li gen twa ti frè epi manman l ap travay. Heather chwazi yon liv pou li nan etajè ki nan chanm Miss Benson. Se yon liv osijè istwa timoun. Risa koute avèk atansyon epi li fè jès avèk bouch li. Miss Benson mande Risa pou l li, men Risa refize fè sa. Olye sa, li fè yon desen pou Miss Benson avèk mo li dekri avèk gwo detay lila Miss Benson pa t wè depi plizyè ane. Miss Benson enpresyone, men Heather kontrarye. Li santi se kòm si Rita ap ranplase l pou bon zak li a. Olye pou li retounen mete liv la nan etajè a, li mete li nan kòbèy papye a. Lè l ap vizite Miss Benson nan kèk jou annapre, liv la pa la. Èske se Risa ki pran liv la?

MỘT VIỆC TỐT

Marion Dane Bauer

Bối cảnh: một căn nhà chung cư thời nay

Theo yêu cầu bài tập dành cho Hướng đạo sinh nữ, Heather phải làm một việc tốt cho ai đó đang gặp khó khăn. Cô phải đọc sách cho một phụ nữ bị mù là cô Benson. Khi Heather lần đầu tiên đến thăm cô Benson, cô cũng gặp Risa. Risa sống ở căn hộ bên kia sảnh căn hộ của cô Benson. Cô có ba em trai và một người mẹ đang đi làm. Heather lấy một cuốn sách trên giá trong phòng ngủ của cô Benson để đọc. Đó là một tuyển tập truyện thiếu nhi. Risa chăm chú nghe và mấp máy môm. Cô Benson bảo Risa đọc, nhưng Risa từ chối. Thay vào đó, cô vẽ cho cô Benson một bức tranh có lời mình họa mô tả hết sức chi tiết những cây từ đinh hương mà cô Benson đã nhiều năm không nhìn thấy. Cô Benson rất ấn tượng, nhưng Heather thì cảm thấy khó chịu. Cô có cảm giác Risa đang làm mất việc tốt của cô. Thay vì trả cuốn sách lại trên giá, cô vứt cuốn sách vào sọt rác. Vài ngày sau cô đến thăm cô Benson thì cuốn sách đã bị mất. Liệu có phải Risa đã lấy cuốn sách?

Name _____

Date _____

THE GOOD DEED

Text Analysis

CONFLICT AND CLIMAX

An **external conflict** is a character's struggle against an outside force. An **internal conflict** takes place inside a character's mind. These conflicts lead toward a **climax,** the point in the story when we find out how the conflicts will be resolved, or worked out.

Directions: Use the graphic organizers to record examples of the external and internal conflicts Heather faces in "The Good Deed." One example has been done for you. Then answer the questions below the graphic organizers.

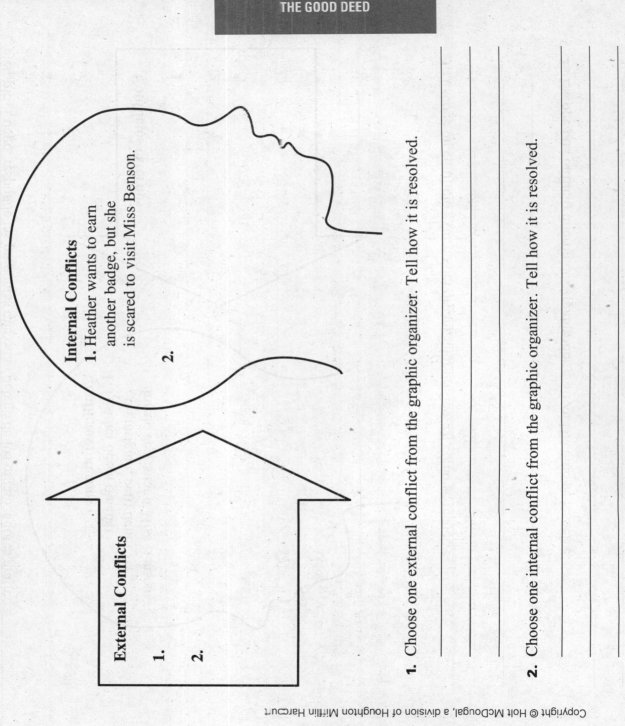

Internal Conflicts
1. Heather wants to earn another badge, but she is scared to visit Miss Benson.

2.

External Conflicts

1.

2.

1. Choose one external conflict from the graphic organizer. Tell how it is resolved.

_____
_____
_____

2. Choose one internal conflict from the graphic organizer. Tell how it is resolved.

_____
_____
_____

LA BUENA OBRA

Text Analysis

CONFLICT AND CLIMAX

Un **conflicto externo** es la lucha de un personaje contra una fuerza exterior. Un **conflicto interno** tiene lugar en la mente del personaje. Estos conflictos llevan al **clímax**, es decir, el punto de la historia en donde descubrimos la manera en la que se resolverán los conflictos.

Instrucciones: Usa los organizadores gráficos para anotar ejemplos de los conflictos externos e internos a los que se enfrenta Heather en "La buena obra". Te damos un ejemplo. Luego, responde las preguntas que están debajo de los organizadores gráficos.

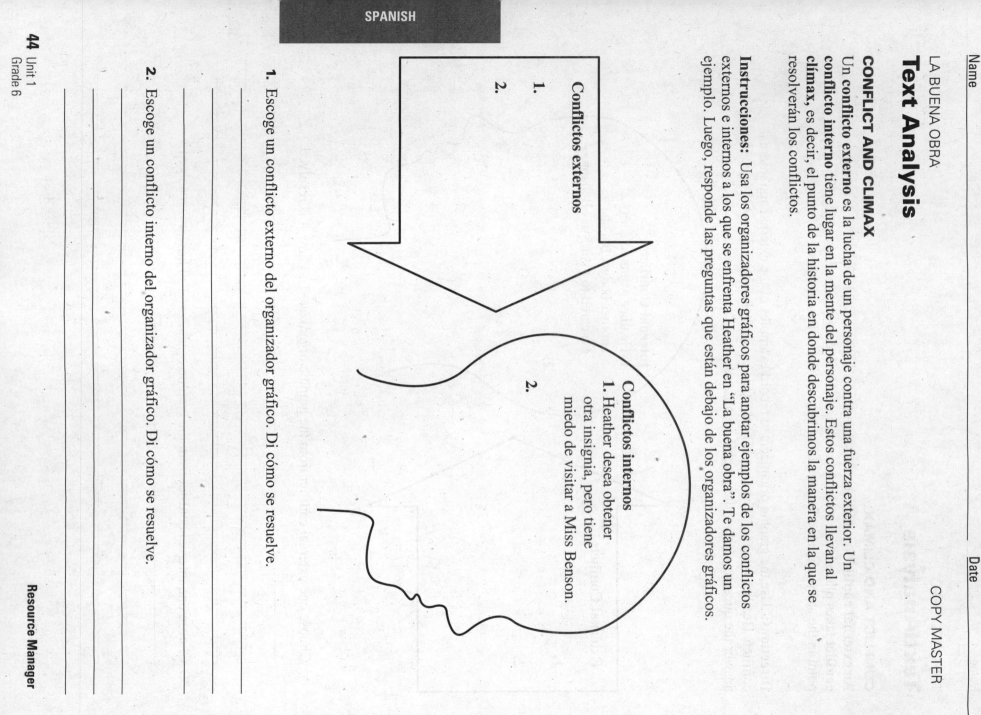

Conflictos externos

1.

2.

Conflictos internos

1. Heather desea obtener otra insignia, pero tiene miedo de visitar a Miss Benson.

2.

1. Escoge un conflicto externo del organizador gráfico. Di cómo se resuelve.

_____

_____

2. Escoge un conflicto interno del organizador gráfico. Di cómo se resuelve.

_____

_____

Name _____ Date _____

THE GOOD DEED

Reading Strategy

CONNECT

When you read a story, you may **connect** your own experiences and feelings to those of the characters in the story. By connecting, you can better understand why the characters act and feel the way they do.

Directions: As you read "The Good Deed," use this chart to record the connections you make. An example has been done for you.

What Is Happening?	My Connection
Heather is scared to talk to Miss Benson.	I was nervous to meet my pen pal at the Senior Center for the first time.

COPY MASTER

LA BUENA OBRA

COPY MASTER

Reading Strategy

CONNECT

Cuando lees un cuento, puedes **conectar** tus experiencias y sentimientos con los de los personajes del cuento. Al hacer conexiones puedes entender mejor por qué los personajes actúan y sienten de la forma en que lo hacen.

Instrucciones: Mientras lees "La buena obra", usa esta tabla para anotar las conexiones que hagas. Te damos un ejemplo.

¿Qué sucede?	Mi conexión
Heather tiene miedo de hablar con Miss Benson.	Tenía nervios al reunirme por primera vez con mi amigo por correspondencia en el Centro de personas de la tercera edad.

SPANISH

THE GOOD DEED

Vocabulary Study

WORDS IN CONTEXT

A. Directions: As your teacher reads each item, listen for the boldfaced word. Discuss possible meanings of the word, and write on the chart what you think the word means. After reading "The Good Deed," confirm or adjust your definitions.

1. Heather worries that Risa will make a false **accusation,** blaming her for the disappearance of the book.

2. The boys' clothing is **generic.** It is as ordinary and plain as the boys themselves.

3. Being sight **impaired** limits Miss Benson in some ways, but the fact that she can't see does not affect her positive attitude toward life.

4. **Incredibly,** Heather finds herself becoming sympathetic toward Risa; she would never have believed it was possible.

5. Unlike Heather, who tends to be polite and respectful when meeting new people, Risa is **pert** and unpleasantly rude.

6. Heather has a hard time coming up with an original eye bouquet for Miss Benson—one that doesn't use **trite** language such as "green as grass" or "blue as the sky."

Vocabulary Word	Predicted Meaning	Meaning in Selection
1. accusation		
2. generic		
3. impaired		
4. incredibly		
5. pert		
6. trite		

Vocabulary Practice

accusation	generic	impaired	incredibly	pert	trite

A. Directions: Complete each sentence with the correct word from the box. The boxed letters will spell out what Heather tried to do.

1. If you have a bad cold, your sense of smell might be ____ ____ — ____ ____ [ ] ____ ____

2. If your cousin were cute and lively, you might say that she was ____ [ ] ____ ____

3. If your friend told a corny story that was full of clichés, you might call it ____ — ____ [ ] ____

4. If you hang up all your clothes in your closet, people might use this word to describe how neat your room is. ____ — ____ [ ] — ____ [ ]

5. Mystery word: ____ — ____ ____

B. Directions: Use a thesaurus or synonym finder to find two synonyms for each word.

6. generic _____

7. pert _____

8. accusation _____

C. Writing Option: Imagine that Heather and Risa became friends. On a separate sheet of paper, write a letter that Heather might send Risa, reminding her of how they met. Use at least **three** of the vocabulary words from the box.

Vocabulary Strategy

SUFFIXES

A **suffix** is a word part that appears at the end of a root or base word. A suffix often changes the base word's part of speech.

Suffixes	Meanings
-er, -or	person or thing that
-ance, -ence, -ion, -tion, -ation	act or condition of

A. Directions: Underline the base word in each boldfaced word. Then use your knowledge of the word and the information in the chart to write the meaning of the boldfaced word.

1. The **generator** provided us with electricity. _____

2. Our **discussion** ended in agreement. _____

3. We took notes on each **occurrence.** _____

4. Use the bottle **opener** carefully. _____

5. The twins' **resemblance** is amazing. _____

B. Directions: Make a new word by adding one of the suffixes listed above. Use a dictionary if you need to.

6. introduce _____

7. act _____

8. write _____

9. assist _____

10. concentrate _____

11. absent _____

Reading Check

THE GOOD DEED

Directions: Recall the events in Marion Dane Bauer's short story. Then answer the questions in phrases or sentences.

1. Why does Heather visit Miss Benson?

_____

_____

2. What does Heather think about Risa at the beginning of the story?

_____

_____

3. What does Heather notice about Risa's reading skills?

_____

_____

4. What does Heather learn about Risa's family?

_____

_____

5. What good deeds does Heather do throughout the story?

_____

_____

Name _____ Date _____

COPY MASTER

THE GOOD DEED

Question Support

TEXT ANALYSIS

For questions 1–3, see page 63 of the Student Edition.

Directions: Answer the questions.

4. Connect Look at the chart you made.

Name one event from the story that you made a connection with. _____

_____

Tell how this connection helped you understand the characters' actions. _____

_____

5. Identify Conflicts Heather has external conflicts—conflicts with outside forces. She also has internal conflicts—conflicts inside her own mind. Give one example of each.

Conflict with outside force: _____

_____

Conflict in her own mind: _____

_____

6. Identify Climax Look back at lines 356–361. What does Heather realize about Risa?

_____

Why is this realization the climax in the story?

_____

_____

7. Evaluate Underline **one** word or phrase in parentheses and complete the following sentence.

Heather (does/does not) do a good deed because _____

_____

8. Connect Literary Works Reread the poem on page 62. Is the speaker in the poem more like Heather or more like Miss Benson? Why do you think so?

_____

_____

Resource Manager

Grammar in Context

AVOID RUN-ON SENTENCES

A **run-on sentence** is two or more sentences written as one sentence. To correct run-on sentences, use a **period** to make two separate sentences, or use a **comma** and a **coordinating conjunction** (*and, but,* or *or*) to divide the parts of the run-on.

Original: Heather was jealous of Risa it showed in everything she did.
Revised: Heather was jealous of Risa. It showed in everything she did.

Directions: Rewrite the following sentences, making changes in punctuation and, if necessary, capitalization to correct the run-on sentences. Add coordinating conjunctions where needed.

1. I knew Risa stole the book from Miss Benson I didn't know how to prove it.

   _____

   _____

2. I went over to Risa's apartment, she was reading one of the stories to her brothers.

   _____

   _____

3. Risa hid the book behind her back she didn't answer when I asked why she took it.

   _____

   _____

4. I went back over to Miss Benson's apartment I told her who had the book.

   _____

   _____

5. I thought Miss Benson would yell at Risa she let Risa keep the book.

   _____

   _____

Reading Fluency

PHRASING

One key to better fluency is proper **phrasing,** or using pauses to group words into meaningful chunks. To improve your phrasing, look for commas, semicolons, periods and other punctuation marks as you read. These marks often hint at natural places to pause, take a breath, or come to a complete stop.

A. Directions: Read silently the excerpt from "Good Trouble for Lucy," by Nelly Rosario. Note how the slash marks indicate natural places to stop or take a breath. Practice reading the passage aloud one or two times.

I know all the numbers about Abuela. / She died a year ago in 1987, / the 27th of the seventh month of the year /—that's July. / Her feet were a tiny size 5, / my size minus three. / I got big feet, / she used to tell me. And then she would laugh and say that the bigger my foot, / the prettier my shoes.

B. Directions: Draw slash marks to show where you might stop or pause for breath in another passage from the story. Practice reading the passage, and then read it to your partner. Ask your partner if your phrasing seems natural. Discuss how you might improve your phrasing.

Abuela doesn't like to wear her teeth and wig to the doctor's. Then he can feel extra sorry for her. But I know Abuela's strong and smart, even without her costume.

"No, Abuela, you have to count yourself."

"But you're the one who's supposed to know!" she yells because to her ears, I sound far away.

Am I not learning anything in a school Papi cleans around the clock to pay for? I am, Abuela, I am. The doctor is laughing even though he doesn't understand Spanish. This is why Papi sends me to the doctor with Abuela. He complains he has to work. I know he sends me because he can't deal with Abuela. Me, I do whatever for Abuela, crazy or not. (124 words)

"Good Trouble for Lucy" by Nelly Rosario. Copyright © 2003 by Nelly Rosario. Reprinted by permission of the author.

THE GOOD DEED

Essential Course of Study ECOS Lesson at a Glance

ALL SUMMER IN A DAY

RAY BRADBURY

WHY THIS SELECTION?

Ray Bradbury is one of the most popular and prolific writers in the science fiction genre. His stories are timeless and compelling for young people. "All Summer in a Day" provides a vehicle for teaching the relationship between plot and setting and explores relevant issues such as peer acceptance and the difficulty of being different.

ABOUT THIS SELECTION

Student/Teacher's Edition Pages: 66–77
Difficulty Level: Easy
Readability Scores: Lexile: 950; Fry: 7+; Dale-Chall: 5.2

Summary On futuristic Venus, it rains constantly and the sun appears only once every seven years. Margot, who has lived on Earth, misses the sun terribly. The other children dislike her, and on the day the sun is expected, they lock her in a closet. Everyone but Margot goes outside and revels in the sunshine. Only after the children return underground do they remember Margot and regret what they have done.

Engaging the Students The key idea of this story reflects the universal experience of change. The impact of a changing world can be severe, as it is in this story, or mild and therefore more easily adjusted to.

COMMON CORE STANDARDS FOCUS

- Plot and Setting
- Make Inferences

LESSON RESOURCES
Plan and Teach

Student Copy Masters

ⓘ Lesson resources are also available on the **Teacher One Stop DVD-ROM** and online at <u>thinkcentral.com</u>.

Resource Manager

Lesson Plan and Resource Guide

All Summer in a Day
Short Story by Ray Bradbury

Common Core Focus

RL 1 Cite textual evidence to support inferences drawn from the text. **RL 3** Describe how the characters respond as the plot moves toward a resolution. **RL 5** Analyze how a particular sentence fits into the structure of a text and contributes to the development of the setting or plot. **L 2** Demonstrate command of the conventions of punctuation. **L 4c** Consult thesauruses, both print and digital, to clarify meaning. **W 3** Write narratives to develop imagined events.

Unless otherwise noted, resources can be found in the *Resource Manager*. ℹ Lesson resources are also available on the **Teacher One Stop DVD-ROM** and online at **thinkcentral.com**. The Student Edition and selected copy masters are available electronically on the ✎ **Student One Stop DVD-ROM.**

Student/Teacher's Edition Pages	Additional Resources CM = Copy Master T = Transparency
Focus and Motivate	
☐ Big Question p. 66	☐ ℹ **PowerNotes DVD-ROM** and online at **thinkcentral.com**
☐ Author Biography and Background Information p. 67	☐ ℹ Literature and Reading Center at **thinkcentral.com**
Teach	
☐ Plot and Setting p. 67	☐ ℹ **PowerNotes DVD-ROM** and online at **thinkcentral.com**
☐ Make Inferences p. 67	☐ Make Inferences CM—English p. 67, Spanish p. 68 ᴰ ☐ ℹ **PowerNotes DVD-ROM** and online at **thinkcentral.com**
☐ Vocabulary in Context p. 67	☐ Vocabulary Study CM p. 69 ᴰ ☐ ℹ **PowerNotes DVD-ROM** and online at **thinkcentral.com**

ᴰ = Resources for Differentiation

Student/Teacher's Edition Pages	Additional Resources CM = Copy Master T = Transparency
Practice and Apply: Guided Practice	
Selection and Teacher Notes	
☐ "All Summer in a Day," pp. 68–74	✎ **Audio Anthology CD** Ⓓ
	☐ Summary CM—English and Spanish p. 63, Haitian Creole and Vietnamese p. 64 Ⓓ
	☐ Reading Fluency CM pp. 75–76
	🔧 **Best Practices Toolkit**
	☐ Two-Column Chart p. A25 [T] Ⓓ
	☐ Cause-and-Effect Chain p. B16, B39 [T] Ⓓ
	ⓘ ThinkAloud Models and Audio Summaries at **thinkcentral.com**
Practice and Apply: After Reading	
☐ Selection Questions p. 75	☐ Reading Check CM p. 72
	☐ Plot and Setting CM—p. 65, Spanish p. 66 Ⓓ
	☐ Make Inferences CM—English p. 67, Spanish p. 68 Ⓓ
	☐ Question Support CM p. 73 Ⓓ
	☐ Additional Selection Questions p. 59 Ⓓ
	☐ Ideas for Extension pp. 60–61 Ⓓ
☐ Vocabulary Practice p. 76	☐ Vocabulary Practice CM p. 70
☐ Academic Vocabulary in Speaking p. 76	☐ Academic Vocabulary CM p. 3
☐ Vocabulary Strategy: Find the Best Synonym p. 76	☐ Additional Academic Vocabulary CM p. 4
	☐ Vocabulary Strategy CM p. 71
	☐ *WordSharp* Interactive Vocabulary Tutor CD-ROM and online at **thinkcentral.com**
☐ Grammar in Context p. 77	☐ Punctuate Dialogue Correctly CM p. 74
☐ Writing Prompt p. 77	

Ⓓ = Resources for Differentiation

Student/Teacher's Edition Pages	Additional Resources CM = Copy Master T = Transparency
Assess and Reteach	

Assess	☐ **Diagnostic and Selection Tests**
	  ☐ Selection Tests A, B/C pp. 31–32, 33–34 **D**
	  ☐ ❶ ThinkCentral Online Assessment
	  ☐ ✎ ExamView Test Generator on the **Teacher One Stop DVD-ROM**

Reteach
☐ Plot and Setting
☐ Make Inferences
☐ Best Synonym
	☐ ❶ Level Up Online Tutorials on **thinkcentral.com**
	☐ ❶ Reteaching Worksheets on **thinkcentral.com**
	  ☐ Literature Lesson 9: Setting and Its Roles
	  ☐ Reading Lesson 8: Making Inferences
	  ☐ Vocabulary Lesson 18: Synonyms and Antonyms

D = Resources for Differentiation

If you are following the *Essential Course of Study*, this selection may also be found in

- **Interactive Reader**
- **Adapted Interactive Reader**
- ✑ **Adapted Interactive Reader: Audio Tutor CD**
- **English Language Learner Adapted Interactive Reader**

ALL SUMMER IN A DAY

Additional Selection Questions

Use to supplement the questions on SE page 75.

Differentiation Use these questions to provide customized practice with comprehension and critical thinking skills.

Easy

1. **Recall Setting** How is Venus different from Earth? (*On Venus, it rains all the time and the sun appears for only one hour every seven years; on Earth, the sun shines often.*)

2. **Recall** What do the children do when the sun appears? (*They run and play outdoors.*)

3. *What if your whole WORLD changed?*
   How is Margot's world different from that of the other children? (*Her world includes her memories of living on Earth, warmed by the sun. Because of those memories, living on Venus is painful for her.*)

Average

4. **Analyze Plot and Setting** Could the setting of the story be changed? Why or why not? (*Answers will vary. Students may say that the story's plot is dependent on the setting.*)

5. **Make Inferences** Margot's parents are thinking of returning to Earth, even though it would mean a loss of money for the family. What can you infer about why people are paid so much more to live and work on Venus? (*Living circumstances on Venus are difficult, so people are paid more as an incentive to move there.*)

Challenging

6. *What if your whole WORLD changed?*
   Margot is in the same physical location at the end of the story as she is at the beginning—underground. Her world, however, is completely changed. Explain. (*The children's cruelty cannot be forgotten. Also, since she missed her one chance to see the sun, she probably has little or nothing to look forward to.*)

7. **Evaluate Setting** How well did the author succeed in transporting you to the world of the story? (*Students should give details of setting to support their answers.*)

8. **Synthesize** What larger theme is implied in this story about people who are different from or do not share similar experiences with others? (*People who are different are often isolated, punished, and/or abused.*)

9. **Make Inferences** Reread lines 66–71. Why do the children dislike Margot? How does her experience set her apart from the others? (*The children are envious of Margot. She has had an experience that they have never had and that they want. They may think she feels superior to them because she has seen the sun and remembers what it feels like. She has memories of a whole different world that they may never know or experience.*)

Ideas for Extension

Differentiation These activities provide students with a variety of options for demonstrating understanding of lesson concepts.

EXPLORATIONS AND ACTIVITIES

STORYBOARD: ANALYZE SETTING AND PLOT

Have students reread "All Summer in a Day" and take notes about the story's most vivid images—for example, the dark tunnels and schoolroom, the raining world, and the sun-drenched hour.

Next, challenge students to create a storyboard for a silent film based on the story. Have them work in small groups to choose at least six scenes from the story that they think could tell the story if they were represented visually. Then have them sketch the panels.

Invite students to display their storyboards and give feedback.

READERS THEATER: EXAMINE STYLE

Explain that Ray Bradbury has written hundreds of stories and many novels, plays, poetry collections, and essays. Students can find a list of these publications at www.raybradbury.com/books/books.html.

Plan a class "Ray Bradbury Day." Assign small groups to prepare and perform readings of Bradbury's poetry, stories, or scenes from his plays. Discuss common elements of his style based on students' performances.

BRAINSTORM: EXPLORE GENRE

Review the elements of science fiction, including setting (past or future, often in an imaginary place or space), the role of technology and science, the creation of a believable world or a fantasy world with familiar elements, and universal themes of human nature and community.

Then ask students to work in small groups to brainstorm the plot of a science fiction story or play. Remind them of the elements of plot and encourage them to identify conflicts—both internal and external—that will be resolved by the end of the story.

Have students create a sequence chart outlining their idea. Ask them to present their charts to the class and have students discuss what they like about each concept.

LIST: EXPLORE KEY CONCEPT

Have students review the descriptions of setting and life on Venus according to Ray Bradbury. Ask them what would motivate people to leave Earth to live in such a place.

Have students work in small groups to develop a list of reasons that people would leave their familiar world to settle in a new one.

Have groups share their lists and discuss whether they would be willing to live in dramatically different conditions in space or on another planet.

Pre-AP Challenge: Have students imagine that they are about to leave Earth forever—that they will spend the rest of their lives in a space colony. Have them discuss the following question: What object or characteristic of your life on Earth would you need to bring or replicate in order to survive in your new home?

IDEAS FOR EXTENSION, CONTINUED

INQUIRY AND RESEARCH

EXTREME ENVIRONMENTS

Discuss the extreme environments in which scientists and explorers make their temporary or permanent homes. Examples include Antarctica, Mt. Everest, underground, and space. Students will probably have read books or other accounts and will have seen movies, documentaries, and news reports about such environments.

Form small groups, and assign each student an extreme environment—Antarctica, for example, or the space station. Then have students research the physical and psychological effects of living in such an environment. Encourage them to gather general information as well as examples of how individuals fare under these circumstances. Have them find photographs and illustrations of people, habitations, and physical environments.

Each student should give a report to the group summarizing what he or she has learned. Have students in the class ask questions about the reports. Then have them discuss whether or not they would be tempted to live and work in an extreme environment and why.

WRITING

EXAMINE AUTHOR'S PERSPECTIVE: MONOLOGUE

Have students review the biographical information about Ray Bradbury on page 67. Suggest that they go online to gather more information, including intriguing facts and anecdotes from the various stages of his life. The website www.raybradbury.com includes this information as well as a number of quotations and a videotaped interview.

Ask students to write a monologue for an actor playing Ray Bradbury on stage. Have them incorporate the above information and also include notes to the director and actor. Make sure they determine a purpose before they begin writing.

Finally, have volunteers perform some or all of the monologues before the class.

SUMMARIZE: DIARY ENTRY

Readers know where Margot has been and what happens to her before she is put in the closet. But what else happens?

Ask students to imagine they are Margot, and have them write a diary entry about what happened earlier in the day. Be sure that they include details from the story about Margot's interactions with the other children and her own thoughts and feelings as she waited for the rain to stop. Have her describe her hour in the closet and how she felt after the children let her out.

Students can expand this activity by composing diary entries describing Margot's earlier experiences—both on Earth and on Venus.

DESCRIBE SETTING: POEM

Ask students to think about the impression that the setting of this story creates. Have them jot down words and phrases that they would use to describe the setting and how it makes them feel. Encourage students to include powerful verbs as well as sensory details. Then ask students to write a poem about the setting of Venus as it is developed in this story.

Teacher Notes

Review and Evaluate Outcome

What did I want students to know or be able to do?

How successful was the lesson?

Evaluate Process

What did not work? Why not?

- Differentiation
- Resources
- Strategies

What worked?

Reflect

The next time I teach "All Summer in a Day," what will I do differently? Why?

Plan Ahead

What must I do next?

ALL SUMMER IN A DAY

Summary

ALL SUMMER IN A DAY

Ray Bradbury

Setting: the planet Venus, the future

Margot's classmates do not like her because she is different. The other children were all born on Venus, where it has rained for seven years. Margot moved to Venus from Earth, and is the only child who remembers what the sun was like. Scientists predict that the sun is about to shine on Venus for only one hour. Margot really wants to see it. In preparation for the event, the class reads about the sun and writes essays and poems about it. None of Margot's classmates believe her memories of the sun. As a cruel trick, they lock her in a closet just as the sun is about to appear.

TODO EL VERANO EN UN DÍA

Ray Bradbury

Escenario: el planeta Venus en el futuro

Los compañeros de clase de Margot no la quieren porque es diferente. Todos los demás niños nacieron en Venus, donde ha llovido durante siete años. Margot se mudó de la Tierra a Venus y es la única de los niños que recuerda cómo es el Sol. Los científicos predicen que el sol brillará en Venus sólo durante una hora. Margot en verdad quiere verlo. Como preparación para el suceso, la clase lee sobre el Sol y escribe ensayos y poemas sobre él. Ninguno de sus compañeros cree en los recuerdos que Margot tiene del Sol. Como una broma cruel, la encierran en un armario justo cuando el Sol está por aparecer.

Summary

TOUT LETE A NAN YON JOU

Ray Bradbury

Espas ak tan: planèt Venis, fiti

Kamarad klas Margo pa renmen li paske li diferan. Tout lòt timoun yo te fèt sou Venis, kote lapli tonbe pandan setan. Margot soti sou Latè pou li ale nan Venis, epi li se sèl pitit ki sonje ak kisa solèy la sanble. Syantis yo prevwa solèy la pral briye sou Venis pandan inèdtan sèlman. Margot vle wè sa toutbon. Nan preparasyon pou evènman an, klas la li kèk bagay osijè solèy epi yo ekri redaksyon ak powèm sou li. Okenn kamarad klas Margot pa kwè nan souvni li genyen sou solèy. Tankou yon move trik, yo fèmen li nan yon amwa nan moman solèy la pral parèt.

MÙA HÈ CHỈ TRONG MỘT NGÀY

Ray Bradbury

Bối cảnh: sao Kim, trong tương lai

Các bạn cùng lớp Margot không thích cô bé vì cô rất khác thường. Những đứa trẻ khác đều sinh ra ở sao Kim, một hành tinh đã mưa suốt bảy năm nay. Margot đến sao Kim từ Trái đất, và cô bé là đứa trẻ duy nhất còn nhớ được mặt trời ra sao. Các nhà khoa học dự đoán rằng mặt trời sắp sửa chiếu sáng sao Kim nhưng chỉ trong một giờ. Margot rất muốn chứng kiến sự kiện đó. Để chuẩn bị cho sự kiện này, cả lớp đọc về mặt trời, viết bài luận và làm thơ về mặt trời. Không bạn nào trong lớp Margot tin ký ức về mặt trời của cô bé. Các bạn cô đã bày ra một trò chơi độc ác là nhốt cô bé vào tủ ngay khi mặt trời chuẩn bị mọc.

Text Analysis

PLOT AND SETTING

The **plot** of a story is the series of events that make up the story, including the conflict and its resolution. The **setting** of a story tells where and when the story takes place.

Directions: In the first column of the chart below, list plot events from the story set on Bradbury's Venus. Then in the second column, describe how the plot events might be different if the story were set on Earth. One example has been recorded for you.

Setting: Bradbury's Venus	Setting: Earth
Plot event: The children tried to remember what the sun was like.	If the story were set on Earth, the children would not have completely forgotten what the sun was like.
Plot event:	
Plot event:	
Plot event:	

What statement can you make about the importance of setting to the plot of a story?

_____

_____

TODO EL VERANO EN UN DÍA

Text Analysis

PLOT AND SETTING

El escenario de un cuento indica dónde y cuándo tiene lugar el cuento.

Instrucciones: En la primera olumna de la siguiente tabla, lista los elementos de la prosa de la historia en Bradbury's Venus. Luego, en la segunda columna, describe cómo es que los sucesos de la trama podrían ser diferentes si la historia tuviera lugar en la Tierra. Obseva el ejemplo que hicimos para ti.

Escenario: Bradbury's Venus	Escenario: La Tierra
Suceso de la trama: Los niños tartan de recordar cómo era el sol. The children tried to remember what the sun was like.	Si la historia hubiera tenido lugar en la Tierra, los niños no habrían olvidado cómo es el Sol.
Suceso de la trama:	
Suceso de la trama:	
Suceso de la trama:	

¿Qué declaración puedes hacer sobre la importancia de establecer la trama de la historia?

_____

ALL SUMMER IN A DAY

Reading Skill

MAKE INFERENCES

As you read, you put together clues from the story and your own knowledge to **make inferences**, or guesses, about how the characters feel and what might happen.

Directions: As you read "All Summer in a Day," use the chart to record the inferences you make about the characters' feelings and actions. One example has been done for you.

Clues from the Story	+	My Knowledge	=	Inference
Margot is not part of the group.	+	Not being part of a group can make you feel sad.	=	Margot feels sad.
	+		=	
	+		=	
	+		=	
	+		=	

TODO EL VERANO EN UN DÍA

Reading Skill

MAKE INFERENCES

Mientras lees, reúnes pistas del cuento y tus conocimientos para **hacer inferencias**, o deducciones, sobre cómo se sienten los personajes y qué podría suceder.

Instrucciones: Mientras lees "Todo el verano en un día", usa la tabla para anotar las inferencias que haces sobre los sentimientos y el comportamiento de los personajes. Te damos un ejemplo.

Pistas del cuento	+	Mis conocimientos	=	Inferencia
Margot no es parte del grupo.	+	No ser parte de un grupo puede hacer que te sientas triste.	=	Margot se siente triste.
	+		=	
	+		=	
	+		=	
	+		=	

Name _____

Date _____

COPY MASTER

ALL SUMMER IN A DAY

Vocabulary Study

WORD QUESTIONING

A. Directions: As your teacher reads each sentence, listen for the boldfaced word. On a separate sheet of paper, work together to create a word map for the word like the one shown. Fill in as much information as you can.

1. Since Evelyn wasn't quite sure how to use the exercise **apparatus** at the gym, someone had to show her.

2. Geordie had never seen such **immense,** or massive, snowdrifts; even during last year's record-breaking blizzard.

3. **Savor** each moment. For once it is gone, it can never be enjoyed again.

4. Trying not to **slacken** her pace, Jory continued walking in time with the beat.

5. The children ran **tumultuously** into the playground, shouting and bumping into each other.

6. Even though it had been jumped on hundreds of times, the mattress was still **resilient** and springy.

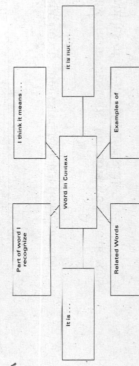

I think it means . . . .

It is not . . .

Examples of

Word in Context

Part of word I recognize

Related Words

It is . . . .

B. Directions: Use the boldfaced words to write a brief essay about how life might be different in the distant future.

_____

_____

_____

_____

_____

_____

_____

Resource Manager

Unit 1 **69**

Grade 6

Vocabulary Practice

apparatus	immense	resilient	savor	slacken	tumultuously

A. Directions: Fill in each blank with the correct word from the box.

1. Pots and pans are part of a cook's _____

2. Springs under a mattress make a bed more _____

3. It takes longer to eat if you _____ every bite, but it is a
   healthier, more pleasant way to dine.

4. Because frightened people often behave _____
   are important and practical.

5. When the lines on a sail _____ the sail begins to flap
   and the boat slows.

6. To a mouse, even a small dog may seem _____

B. Directions: Decide which word from the box is suggested by each description.
Then write the word on the line.

7. In the science lab, we used to have only one microscope, but now we have dozens
   of them, plus test tubes, glass slides, bottles of chemicals, and scales.
   _____

8. The advice, "Stop and smell the roses," warns us that we miss many of life's
   delights if we rush about and that we should take the time we need to enjoy them.
   _____

C. Writing Option: How do you think the children of Bradbury's Venus would
react if they could spend one summer afternoon at an ordinary playground on Earth?
Describe their afternoon. Use at least **two** of the words in the box.

_____

_____

_____

_____

_____

Vocabulary Strategy

FIND THE BEST SYNONYM

A **synonym** is a word with the same, or nearly the same, meaning as another word. Not all synonyms mean exactly the same thing. You must choose the word that has the best shade of meaning for the sentence context.

| hike | peaceful | rivals | immense | remark | suspicious |

A. Directions: Choose the word from the box that is the synonym for the underlined word in each sentence.

1. Ian was <u>doubtful</u> about the upcoming class trip to Washington.

_____

2. He was expecting his friends, Michael and Juan, to make a smart <u>comment</u> when he suggested that they postpone the trip.

_____

3. The boys were best friends but also <u>competitors</u> with each other at the same time.

_____

4. One day, the boys took a <u>walk</u> through the woods, where they saw a bridge.

_____

5. The bridge seemed <u>big</u> from afar.

_____

6. This <u>tranquil</u> sight seemed to put them at ease with each other.

_____

B. Directions: One the line, write the synonym that best complements the meaning of the sentence.

7. An entire pride of lions growled _____ as we drove into the preserve.
    a. fiercely   **b.** wildly   **c.** angrily

8. The beautiful sunset was so _____ that we wanted to take a picture of it.
    a. brilliant   **b.** bright   **c.** colorful

Reading Check

Directions: Recall the characters and events in the selection. Then answer the questions in sentences or phrases.

1. What is the planet Venus like, according to the story? Describe its vegetation and its weather.

_____

_____

2. Why are the children living on Venus?

_____

_____

3. Why is Margot so unhappy on Venus?

_____

_____

4. Why do the other children lock Margot in the closet?

_____

_____

5. Suppose another hour of sunlight was on the way. How do you think Margot's classmates would behave toward her?

_____

_____

Name _____ Date _____

ALL SUMMER IN A DAY

Question Support

TEXT ANALYSIS

For questions 1–3, see page 75 of the Student Edition.

Directions: Answer each question.

4. Make Inferences Review the inferences you made as you read the story. Were any of your ideas wrong? If so, write one inference that you had to change.

_____

_____

5. Identify Cause and Effect Complete the following sentence.

Margot was unhappy because _____

_____

6. Analyze Setting Write two ways that a sunny day on Earth is different from a sunny day on Venus.

_____

_____

7. Examine Conflict An **external conflict** is a struggle between a character and an outside force. An **internal conflict** happens when a character is at odds with his or her feelings. Reread lines 182–196. Then underline one word in parentheses and complete the following sentence.

The children are experiencing an (external/internal) conflict as they walk to the closet

because _____

_____

8. Analyze Plot and Setting Underline one of the phrases in parentheses and complete the following sentence.

The plot and setting of "All Summer in a Day" (seem realistic/do not seem realistic) to me because _____

_____

Name _____

Date _____

COPY MASTER

ALL SUMMER IN A DAY

Grammar in Context

PUNCTUATE DIALOGUE CORRECTLY

Keep these rules in mind when you write **dialogue:**

• Put quotation marks before and after a speaker's exact words.
• Place punctuation marks such as commas and periods *inside* the quotation marks.
• If a speaker tag comes before the quotation, set a comma after the speaker tag.
• If a speaker tag follows the dialogue, set a comma after the quotation (*inside* the closing quotation mark) and a period after the speaker tag.

Original: It's like a penny she said once, eyes closed.
Revised: "It's like a penny," she said once, eyes closed.

A. Directions: Rewrite the following sentences. Correct the misplaced punctuation marks and insert any missing marks.

1. "It's been raining for years" the girl said.

2. "Let's go outside the teacher said."

3. The boy said "What are you waiting for?"

4. The sun looks like a penny Margot said

B. Directions: Insert punctuation where needed in this dialogue.

—Juan said I don't like science fiction.

—Why not asked Teresa.

—I don't think it is realistic enough he responded. Who could believe people walking around on Saturn?

—But if the story tells you something about the way people really think and feel Teresa suggested isn't that realistic enough?

Name _____ Date _____

COPY MASTER

Reading Fluency

REPEATED READINGS

To get the most from your reading, it helps to read a passage several times. As you read, group words into meaningful phrases that sound like natural speech. Vary the rise and fall of your voice to emphasize important words or ideas. Do not read too fast or too slow.

Directions to the Reader:

1. In a normal voice, practice reading the passage about the planet Venus.
2. Then read the passage aloud four times as your checker listens.
3. Talk with your checker about ways you can do better.

Directions to the Checker:

1. Follow along while your partner reads, timing the reading. Underline each word the reader mispronounces or skips. Jot down words he or she adds.
2. Share the marked words with the reader. Record them in the chart.
3. Erase the marks you made. Repeat these steps three times.

Reading	1	2	3	4
Time				
Words Missed				

For many years, people knew little about the planet Venus. Dark

clouds covered it. It was hard to see, even through powerful

telescopes. In the late 1900s, both Russia and the United States

sent spaceships to Venus. As a result, people learned new things

about Venus.

It turns out that in many ways Venus is quite different from

Earth. Earth has one moon. Venus has none. On Earth a day is

shorter than a year. On Venus one day lasts longer than a year.

(This is because Venus circles the Sun faster than it spins around.)

Venus spins clockwise, while Earth spins the opposite way. Many

READING FLUENCY CONTINUED

plants and animals live on Earth, but there is no known life on

Venus. In fact, Venus is a very dry planet that appears to have no

water. It may be that this is a result of a runaway Greenhouse

Effect. Some people are afraid that Earth may end up hot and dry

like Venus if we do not take care. (167 words)

Essential Course of Study EGOS Lesson at a Glance

Reading for Information | Settling in Space

WHY THESE SELECTIONS?

The idea of living in space, or on another planet, continues to be a source of great fascination for humans. These articles and illustrations provide facts to inform students about the plausibility of both concepts.

ABOUT THESE SELECTIONS

Student/Teacher's Edition Pages: 78–85

Difficulty Level: Challenging

Readability Scores: Lexile: 1020; Fry: 8; Dale-Chall: 7.4

Summary The three selections explore the possibility of living in space. The first article gives facts about the intense heat and sulfuric acid rain of Venus's climate that would deter human habitation. The second article describes life in an orbital space colony, the way one would be built, and its size. The illustrations present artists' views of how these colonies might look.

COMMON CORE STANDARDS FOCUS

- Synthesize Ideas Across Texts
- Find the Main Idea

LESSON RESOURCES

Plan and Teach

Student Copy Masters

ⓘ Lesson resources are also available on the **Teacher One Stop DVD-ROM** and online at **thinkcentral.com.**

Lesson Plan and Resource Guide

Settling in Space
Magazine Article by Alan Dyer, Online Article by Alan Globus, Illustrations

Common Core Focus

RI 1 Cite textual evidence to support what the text says explicitly. **RI 2** Determine a central idea of a text and how it is conveyed through details. **RI 7** Integrate information presented in different media or formats to develop a coherent understanding of a topic. **W 2** Write informative/explanatory texts to examine a topic.

Unless otherwise noted, resources can be found in the *Resource Manager*. **ⓘ** Lesson resources are also available on the **Teacher One Stop DVD-ROM** and online at **thinkcentral.com**. The Student Edition and selected copymasters are available electronically on the **●Student One Stop DVD-ROM.**

Student/Teacher's Edition Pages	Additional Resources CM = Copy Master T = Transparency		
Focus and Motivate			
☐ What's the Connection? p. 78	☐ **Best Practices Toolkit**		
	☐ Anticipation Guide p. A14 [T]		
	☐ **ⓘ PowerNotes DVD-ROM** and online at thinkcentral.com		
Teach			
☐ Synthesize Ideas Across Texts, p. 78	☐ Synthesize Ideas Across Texts CM—English p. 85, Spanish p. 87 **ⓓ**		
	☐ **ⓘ PowerNotes DVD-ROM** and online at thinkcentral.com		

ⓓ = Resources for Differentiation

Student/Teacher's Edition Pages	Additional Resources CM = Copy Master T = Transparency
Practice and Apply: Guided Practice	
Selection and Teacher Notes	☐ **Audio Anthology CD** D
"Weather That's Out of This World," p. 79	☐ Summary CM—English and Spanish p. 83, Haitian Creole and Vietnamese p. 84 D
"Space Settlements," pp. 80–83	☐ **Best Practices Toolkit**
"Space Colony" p. 84 (illustrations)	☐ Read Aloud/Think Aloud p. A34 [T] D
	☐ ThinkAloud Models and Audio Summaries at **thinkcentral.com**
Practice and Apply: After Reading	
☐ Selection Questions p. 85	☐ Reading Check CM p. 89
	☐ Synthesize Ideas Across Texts CM—p. 85, Spanish p. 87 D
	☐ Question Support CM p. 90 D
	☐ Additional Selection Questions p. 80 D
☐ Read for Information: Synthesize Ideas Across Texts p. 85	☐ Synthesize Ideas Across Texts CM—English p. 86, Spanish p. 88
Assess and Reteach	
Assess	**Diagnostic and Selection Tests**
	☐ Selection Tests A, B/C pp. 35–36, 37–38 D
	☐ ThinkCentral Online Assessment
	☐ ExamView Test Generator on the **Teacher One Stop DVD-ROM**
Reteach	☐ Level Up Online Tutorials on **thinkcentral.com**
☐ Synthesize Ideas Across Texts	☐ Reteaching Worksheets on **thinkcentral.com**
☐ Find the Main Idea	☐ Reading Lesson 14: Synthesizing Information
	☐ Reading and Information Texts Lesson 4: Recognizing Main Ideas and Details

D = Resources for Differentiation

If you are following the *Essential Course of Study*, this selection may also be found in

• **Interactive Reader**
• **Adapted Interactive Reader**
• **Adapted Interactive Reader: Audio Tutor CD**
• **English Language Learner Adapted Interactive Reader**

SETTLING IN SPACE

Additional Selection Questions

Use to supplement the questions on SE page 85.

Differentiation Use these questions to provide customized practice with comprehension and critical thinking skills.

Easy

1. **Recall** Why is Venus hotter than Mercury despite its greater distance from the Sun? (*Unlike Mercury, Venus has an atmosphere. This atmosphere, which is mostly carbon dioxide gas, traps the heat coming from the Sun.*)

2. **Recall** How would a space colony be able to raise enough food for its inhabitants? (*Carefully controlled growing conditions would increase the crop yield. Therefore, the area needed to be set aside for agriculture would be much less than what would be required for the same number of people on Earth.*)

Average

3. **Use Text Features** "Space Settlements" is made up of several sections. Identify each section by its **subheading** and summarize its main ideas. (*The subheading and main ideas are as follows: "What is an Orbital Space Colony" is an introduction; "What will Life be Like?" sums up the similarities and differences between life on a space colony and life on Earth." "How Will We Build One?" sums up the needs for materials, energy, transportation, communications, life support, and radiation protection. "How Big Will the Colonies Be?" explains that they will house ten or twenty thousand people and, perhaps someday, millions.*)

4. **Analyze Science Articles** Reread lines 16–21 in "Weather That's Out of This World!" and lines 16–19 in "Space Settlements." What strategies do the writers use in these passages to help readers understand the information more clearly? (*The first writer makes comparisons, explaining that the atmosphere on Venus is like a blanket, or the glass in a greenhouse, trapping heat. This writer also gives examples to illuminate his point. The second writer includes definitions of technical terms, explaining that toruses are donut shapes and pseudo-gravity is false gravity.*)

Challenging

5. **Evaluate Science Articles** Science articles must be relatively short. How do both writers meet the limitations of the form and still accomplish their purpose? (*Both writers narrow their focus. The first writer chooses to explain only the weather of Venus. He does not try to include information about any other aspect of life on Venus. The second writer chooses four main ideas about space colonies to develop in detail. He does not try to address objections or answer all the questions that readers might have about the space colony concept.*)

6. **Synthesize Ideas Across Texts** These two articles and Bradbury's "All Summer in a Day" all deal with conditions in outer space. Would you say that they express any similar attitudes towards outer space? Explain. (*The three pieces all regard outer space as something of interest to human beings and something that can be explored and learned about. Both "Space Settlement" and "All Summer in a Day" deal with space as a place that will one day be settled by humans.*)

SETTLING IN SPACE

Teacher Notes

Review and Evaluate Outcome

What did I want students to know or be able to do?

How successful was the lesson?

Evaluate Process

What worked?
- Strategies

- Resources

- Differentiation

What did not work? Why not?

Reflect

The next time I teach "Settling in Space" what will I do differently? Why?

Plan Ahead

What must I do next?

Resource Manager

SETTLING IN SPACE

Summary

SETTLING IN SPACE

The magazine article tells about the weather on Venus. It is the hottest planet, and it rains constantly. However, the rain is not water; it is acid. Venus is not a great place to live.

The online article tells about space colonies. A space colony would be a giant spacecraft. It would always travel through space, while the people inside would live much like people on earth live today. However, some things would be different there than on Earth. Air and water would be manufactured. Nothing could be thrown away. Food would be grown in special rooms. Space stations with colonies would be much larger than today's space stations. Right now space colonies are just an idea, but someday they may be real.

The illustrations help you visualize what life in a space colony might be like.

ASENTARSE EN EL ESPACIO

Este artículo de revista habla sobre el clima en Venus. Es el planeta más caliente y llueve todo el tiempo. Sin embargo, la lluvia no es agua; es ácido. Venus no es un buen lugar para vivir.

El artículo en Internet habla sobre las colonias espaciales. Una colonia espacial sería una nave espacial gigante. Siempre viajaría por el espacio, mientras que las personas en el interior vivirían casi como la gente vive ahora en la Tierra. Sin embargo, algunas cosas serían diferentes que en la Tierra. Se tendrían que producir el aire y el agua. No podría desecharse nada. Se cultivarían los alimentos en cuartos especiales. Las estaciones espaciales con colonias serían mucho más grandes que las estaciones espaciales actuales. Por ahora, las colonias espaciales son sólo una idea, pero algún día podrían ser realidad.

Las ilustraciones te ayudan a visualizar cómo podría ser la vida en una colonia espacial.

SETTLING IN SPACE

Summary

KOLONIZASYON NAN LESPAS

Atik magazin nan pale osijè tan an sou Venis. Se planèt ki pi cho, epi lapli tonbe ladan souvan. Men, lapli a se pa dlo; se asid. Venis pa yon gwo kote pou moun viv.

Atik ki sou entènèt la pale osijè koloni ki nan lespas yo. Yon koloni espasyal se ta yon veso espasyal ki gwo anpil. Li ta vwayaje atravè lespas, pandan moun ki andedan li yo ta tankou moun k ap viv sou tè a jodi a. Men, kèk bagay ta diferan ladan pase sou Latè. Lè a ak dlo a pa ta natirèl. Ou pa ka voye anyen jete. Manje ta devlope nan chanm espesyal. Estasyon espasyal ki gen koloni yo ta pi gwo pase estasyon espasyal ki genyen jodi a. Kounye a, koloni espasyal yo se sèlman yon lide, men yon jou, yo ka vin reyèl.

Desen yo ap ede w imajine kisa lavi nan yon koloni espasyal kapab ye.

ĐỊNH CƯ TRONG KHÔNG TRUNG

Bài báo này nói về thời tiết trên sao Kim. Đó là hành tinh nóng nhất, và có mưa thường xuyên. Tuy nhiên nước mưa không phải nước mà là axít. Sao Kim không phải là nơi sống lý tưởng.

Bài báo trực tuyến này nói về những khu định cư trong không trung. Một khu định cư trong không trung có thể là một chiếc tàu vũ trụ khổng lồ. Chiếc tàu luôn bay trong vũ trụ, còn những người trên tàu sống tương tự như mọi người sống trên trái đất ngày nay. Tuy nhiên, có một số điều khác biệt so với Trái đất. Người ta sản xuất ra không khí và nước. Không thứ gì có thể vứt đi được. Thực phẩm được nuôi trồng trong những phòng đặc biệt. Các trạm không gian với các khu định cư sẽ lớn hơn rất nhiều so với những trạm không gian hiện nay. Hiện tại các khu định cư trong không trung mới chỉ là ý tưởng, nhưng một ngày nào đó có thể trở thành sự thật.

Những minh họa này giúp các bạn hình dung được cuộc sống tại một khu định cư trong không trung.

SETTLING IN SPACE
Skill Focus

SYNTHESIZE IDEAS ACROSS TEXTS

When you read several texts on the same topic, you connect the ideas you find in each piece. You can then synthesize this information by putting it all together.

Directions: As you read the selections, use this chart to take notes on the main ideas and supporting details in the two articles. Some notes have been recorded for you.

Selection	Main Ideas	Supporting Details
"Weather That's Out of This World"	• Venus's weather is much worse than Earth's weather.	• The temperature on Venus can melt lead. • Acid rain constantly falls on Venus.
"Space Settlements"		
"Artists' Views of a Space Colony"		

SETTLING IN SPACE

Read for Information

SYNTHESIZE IDEAS ACROSS TEXTS

The three texts you just read provide different ideas about living in space.

Directions: Write a paragraph to explain what you learned about living in space from these texts. Use the chart that you created as you read to synthesize, or combine what you learned, into a paragraph.

_____

_____

_____

_____

_____

_____

_____

_____

_____

_____

_____

_____

_____

_____

_____

_____

_____

_____

_____

ASENTARSE EN EL ESPACIO

Skill Focus

SYNTHESIZE IDEAS ACROSS TEXTS

Cuando lees diversos textos del mismo tema, conectas las ideas que encuentras en cada selección. Entonces puedes sintetizar esta información al recopilarla toda.

Instrucciones: Mientras lees las selecciones, usa esta tabla para tomar apuntes sobre las ideas principales y detalles de apoyo que hay en los dos artículos. Algunos apuntes se han dado ya.

Selección	Ideas principales	Detalles de apoyo
"¡El tiempo que está fuera de este mundo" frente al tiempo de otros planetas	• El clima de Venus es much peor que el clima de la Tierra.	• La temperatura de Venus puede derretir plomo. • La lluvia ácida cae constantemente en Venus.
"Colonias espaciales"		
"Vistas de los artistas de una colonia espacial"		

Resource Manager

SPANISH

ASENTARSE EN EL ESPACIO

Read for Information

SYNTHESIZE IDEAS ACROSS TEXTS

Los tres textos que acabas de leer proporcionan ideas distintas sobre la vida en el espacio.

Instrucciones: Escribe un párrafo que explique lo que aprendiste de estos textos sobre la vida en el espacio. Usa la tabla que creaste mientras leías, para sintetizar, o combinar lo que aprendiste en un solo párrafo.

Name _____ Date _____

COPY MASTER

SETTLING IN SPACE
Reading Check

Directions: Recall the information in each article. Then answer the questions in phrases or sentences.

1. According to "Weather That's Out of This World!" why is the rain on Venus dangerous?

   _____

   _____

2. According to "Weather That's Out of This World!" what makes Venus the hottest planet in the solar system?

   _____

   _____

3. According to "Space Settlements," how will living on Earth and living in an orbital space station be alike?

   _____

   _____

4. According to "Space Settlements," why does Earth look like one large, flat surface?

   _____

   _____

5. According to "Space Settlements," why will materials for space stations have to come from the moon, asteroids, and comets near Earth?

   _____

   _____

Resource Manager

Question Support

TEXT ANALYSIS

For questions 1–2, see page 85 of the Student Edition.

Directions: Answer the questions.

3. **Find the Main Idea** In the chart, write the names of the sections of "Space Settlements." Then write the main idea of each section. The first one is done for you.

Subheading	Main Idea		
"What Is an Orbital Space Colony?"	It is a giant spacecraft that people live on.		

4. **Analyze Characteristics of Form** How can you tell that "Space Settlements" is a science article? Name two ways.

_____

_____

_____

5. **Synthesize Ideas Across Texts** Think about what you know about neighborhoods on Earth and what you learned about orbital space colonies in the articles you read. Look at the pictures of an orbital space colony. How are they like neighborhoods on Earth? How are they different?

_____

_____

_____

Lesson at a Glance

Lob's Girl

Joan Aiken

WHY THIS SELECTION?

This story by noted young adult author Joan Aiken will appeal to readers because of its likeable and sympathetic characters, engrossing plot, and surprise ending.

ABOUT THIS SELECTION

Student/Teacher's Edition Pages: 86–103
Difficulty Level: Challenging
Readability Scores: Lexile: 960; Fry: 11; Dale-Chall: 6.1

Summary Lob, a German shepherd, becomes passionately attached to young Sandy Pengelly. Recognizing this, Lob's owner gives the dog to Sandy. For nine years, she and Lob are constant companions. Then one night Sandy is hit by a truck. As she lies in a coma in the hospital, Lob turns up. His whine rouses Sandy and sets her on the road to recovery. Only later is it revealed that Lob was killed in the accident and is already buried at sea.

Engaging the Students This story offers students an opportunity to explore the key idea of loyalty. When Lob meets Sandy, he gives her his heart, journeying from great distances to return to her. As students read the story, they will think about how the power of loyalty can overcome obstacles.

COMMON CORE STANDARDS FOCUS

• Foreshadowing
• Identify Sequence

LESSON RESOURCES

Plan and Teach

ⓘ Lesson resources are also available on the **Teacher One Stop DVD-ROM** and online at <u>thinkcentral.com</u>.

Resource Manager

Lesson Plan and Resource Guide

Lob's Girl
Short Story by Joan Aiken

Common Core Focus

RL 1 Cite textual evidence to support what the text says explicitly. **RL 5** Analyze how a particular sentence fits into the structure of a text and contributes to the development of the plot. **W 2** Write informative/explanatory texts to convey ideas. **L 2** Demonstrate command of the conventions of punctuation. **L 4b** Use common affixes as clues to the meaning of a word. **L 5** Demonstrate understanding of figurative language in word meanings. **L 6** Acquire and use accurately academic words.

Unless otherwise noted, resources can be found in the *Resource Manager*. ❶ Lesson resources are also available on the **Teacher One Stop DVD-ROM** and online at **thinkcentral.com**. The Student Edition and selected copy masters are available electronically on the 🔖 **Student One Stop DVD-ROM.**

Student/Teacher's Edition Pages	Additional Resources CM = Copy Master T = Transparency
Focus and Motivate	
☐ Big Question p. 86	
☐ Author Biography and Background Information p. 87	☐ ℹ️ Literature and Reading Center at **thinkcentral.com**
Teach	
☐ Foreshadowing p. 87	
☐ Identify Sequence p. 87	☐ Identify Sequence CM—English p. 103, Spanish p. 104 Ⓓ
☐ Vocabulary in Context p. 87	☐ Vocabulary Study CM p. 105 Ⓓ

Ⓓ = Resources for Differentiation

Student/Teacher's Edition Pages	Additional Resources CM = Copy Master T = Transparency
Practice and Apply: Guided Practice	
Selection and Teacher Notes	☐ **Audio Anthology CD** [D]
☐ "Lob's Girl," pp. 88–100	☐ Summary CM—English and Spanish p. 99, Haitian Creole and Vietnamese p. 100 [D]
	☐ Reading Fluency CM pp. 111–112
	Best Practices Toolkit
	☐ Context Clues (Restatement) p. E18 [T] [D]
	☐ Think-Pair-Share p. A18 [T]
	☐ Cause-and-Effect Chain pp. B16, B39 [T]
	[i] Audio Summaries at **thinkcentral.com**
Practice and Apply: After Reading	
☐ Selection Questions p. 101	☐ Reading Check CM p. 108
	☐ Foreshadowing CM—English p. 101, Spanish p. 102 [D]
	☐ Identify Sequence CM—English p. 103, Spanish p. 104 [D]
	☐ Question Support CM p. 109 [D]
	☐ Additional Selection Questions p. 95 [D]
	☐ Ideas for Extension pp. 96–97 [D]
☐ Vocabulary Practice p. 102	☐ Vocabulary Practice CM p. 106
☐ Academic Vocabulary in Writing p. 102	☐ Academic Vocabulary CM p. 3
☐ Vocabulary Strategy: Literal and Figurative Meanings p. 102	☐ Additional Academic Vocabulary CM p. 4
	☐ Vocabulary Strategy CM p. 107
	Best Practices Toolkit
	☐ Cluster Diagram p. B18 [T]
	[i] *WordSharp* Interactive Vocabulary Tutor CD-ROM and **thinkcentral.com**
☐ Grammar in Context p. 103	**Best Practices Toolkit**
☐ Writing Prompt p. 103	☐ Spider Map p. B22 [T] [D]
	☐ Punctuate Possessives Correctly CM p. 110
	☐ Grammar Handbook—Student Edition p. R50

[D] = Resources for Differentiation

Resource Manager

Student/Teacher's Edition Pages	Additional Resources CM = Copy Master T = Transparency

Assess and Reteach

Assess

☐ **Diagnostic and Selection Tests**

  ☐ Selection Tests A, B/C pp. 39–40, 41–42 **D**

  ☐ **ThinkCentral Online Assessment**

  ☐ ExamView Test Generator on the **Teacher One Stop DVD-ROM**

Reteach

☐ Foreshadowing

  ☐ Level Up Online Tutorials on **thinkcentral.com**

  ☐ Reteaching Worksheets on **thinkcentral.com**

  ☐ Literature Lesson 8: Foreshadowing and Suspense

☐ Identify Sequence

  ☐ Reading Lesson 6: Recognizing Sequence and Chronological Order

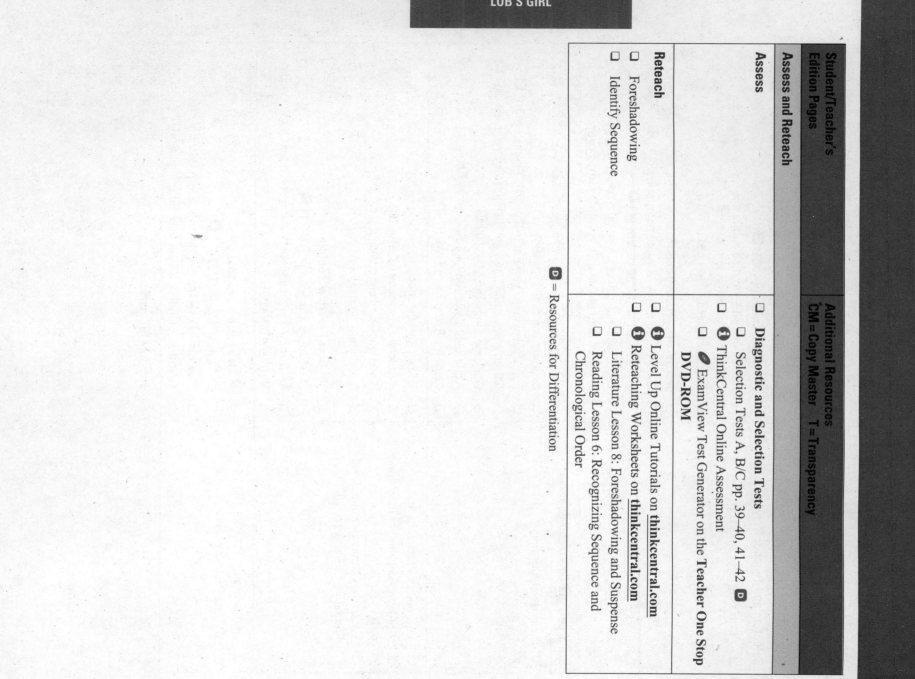

D = Resources for Differentiation

Additional Selection Questions

Differentiation Use these questions to provide customized practice with comprehension and critical thinking skills.

Easy

1. *How powerful is LOYALTY?*
   How would you describe Lob's loyalty toward Sandy? (*Lob is devoted to her. He is a constant and faithful companion who is loving and reliable.*)

2. **Understand Foreshadowing** How does foreshadowing contribute to a story? (*It creates suspense and excitement. Readers become involved in the story and want to read further.*)

3. **Recall** Why is Mr. Pengelly relieved when Mr. Dodsworth says he will give Lob to them? (*Lob is a pedigree. The Pengellys cannot afford to buy Lob from Mr. Dodsworth.*)

Average

4. **Analyze Foreshadowing** In what way do Lob's two journeys from Liverpool foreshadow his final journey back to Sandy? (*The two journeys from Liverpool show immense determination and strength on Lob's part. They suggest that he will do whatever it takes to be with Sandy.*)

5. **Identify Sequence** What might have happened if Mrs. Pearce had not arrived at the hospital when she did? (*Lob may not have been able to see and save Sandy.*)

Challenging

6. **Evaluate** Why is the story entitled "Lob's Girl" instead of "Sandy's Dog"? (*Lob is the protagonist in the story. His choice of Sandy as his girl drives the story's action.*)

7. *How powerful is LOYALTY?*
   Is loyalty always a positive quality? Explain. (*No. Sometimes, feeling loyalty to one person can cause problems for others. For example, Lob's loyalty to Sandy disrupts the lives of the Pengellys and causes many problems for Mr. Dodsworth.*)

8. **Evaluate Foreshadowing** Mr. Dodsworth is described as "put out" (line 127) when he arrives in Cornwall to take Lob home and "weary" (line 141) when he answers the phone. Could Mr. Dodsworth's attitude towards Lob's disappearance foreshadow events to come? (*Yes. Both of these examples show that Lob is causing problems for Mr. Dodsworth. His frustration with the situation may force him to look for an alternative.*)

9. **Analyze Sequence** The author chooses to narrate the events in chronological sequence, although some events, such as Sandy's accident and Lob's burial, occur without the readers' knowledge. How does this pattern of organization affect the story? (*Not knowing the outcome of the conflicts ahead of time helps to create suspense. The sequential order helps readers follow what happens and makes the story more realistic.*)

Ideas for Extension

Differentiation These activities provide students with a variety of options for demonstrating understanding of lesson concepts.

EXPLORATIONS AND ACTIVITIES

DESIGN MODEL: CHARACTER

Have students imagine that the Pengellys want to expand their memorial to Lob by adding a sculpture next to or near the stone in their garden. The sculpture might depict just Lob or Lob and Sandy or another related image.

Have students work alone or in pairs to design a plan for a sculpture that would honor Lob and illustrate his character traits. Have students present their designs to the class. Ask students to discuss how each design illustrates Lob's character traits.

MURAL: INTERPRET KEY CONCEPT

Discuss all of the ideas about loyalty that this story inspires. Have students consider questions such as these: What is loyalty? How does someone show loyalty? How does loyalty affect people and events? Can someone be loyal to more than one person or cause?

Then assign small groups a segment of wall space. Have them design and create a mural on large sheets of paper that expresses their ideas about loyalty through images and text. Encourage students to draw from the story as well as everyday life.

Have the class tour the murals and discuss what they learn about loyalty from the art.

ORAL PRESENTATION: THEME

Discuss with students how this story might be seen as a testament to the heroic nature of dogs. Tell students that although Lob is fictional, throughout history, real dogs have performed some truly amazing acts.

Divide students into small groups. Ask them to do research on a real dog that was extraordinary, such as Balto, Greyfriars Bobby, Owney (the postal service dog), and Stubby, a war hero.

Have students share the facts they learn in an oral presentation.

Pre-AP Challenge: Have students use the facts that they learn to write a short story that illustrates the important qualities of their dog. Have students share their stories with the class.

BRAINSTORM: EXPLORE ALTERNATE CONCLUSIONS

Discuss the effect of the surprise twist at the end of the story. Then ask students to think of other ways in which the author could have chosen to conclude her tale.

Have students work in small groups to brainstorm alternate conclusions. They may choose to pick up from the time Dr. Travers finds Sandy or provide a different version of Lob's appearance at the hospital.

Ask students to present their ideas in a sequence chart. Have the class discuss the merits of each alternate conclusion.

IDEAS FOR EXTENSION, CONTINUED

DIALOGUE: EXAMINE VIEWPOINTS

Have students reread lines 352–371. Ask students to consider how the three characters feel and what they say after Lòb disappears again.

Have students work in groups of three to sketch out the gist of the conversation among the characters in a graphic organizer or script format. Remind students to keep the speech and ideas consistent with the text.

Have students rehearse and then perform their dialogues for the class. Have the class discuss which conversations seem most probable.

INQUIRY AND RESEARCH

CORNWALL AND LIVERPOOL

Tell students that although Sandy's village in Cornwall and the city of Liverpool are both on the sea, they have very different characters.

Divide students into several small groups. Have some of the groups research the county of Cornwall and others look up information about the city of Liverpool. Groups might cover topics such as industry, landmarks, tourist attractions, history, current economic status, population, and culture. Ask each group to write a brief essay about the information they find. Students can include illustrations, maps, or other graphics in their essays.

Have students who researched the same area then collaborate to produce a brochure on their region or city. Have students use the brochures to compare and contrast the two settings of the story.

WRITING

EVALUATE CHARACTER: EULOGY

Have students imagine that a short service honoring Lob is held after Sandy recovers. What might Sandy include in her eulogy for her dog? Ask students to write the speech that Sandy might give on this occasion. Suggest that they brainstorm Lob's characteristics and think about what he meant to Sandy. Students should write their eulogy from Sandy's perspective.

EXAMINE PERSPECTIVES: LETTER

Ask students to think about the way Mr. Dodsworth feels after he hears of Lob's death. Then have students write a letter of condolence that Mr. Dodsworth might have sent to Sandy. Have them keep first-person point of view throughout.

LOB'S GIRL

Teacher Notes

Review and Evaluate Outcome

What did I want students to know or be able to do?

How successful was the lesson?

Evaluate Process

What worked?

- Strategies

- Resources

- Differentiation

What did not work? Why not?

Reflect

The next time I teach "Lob's Girl," what will I do differently? Why?

Plan Ahead

What must I do next?

Summary

LOB'S GIRL

Joan Aiken

Setting: Cornwall, England, twentieth century

Sandy is a five-year-old girl who lives in a fishing village in Cornwall, England. One day on the beach, she meets a German shepherd named Lob. Although Lob belongs to someone else, he soon has a special attachment to Sandy. Mr. Dodsworth, Lob's owner, realizes that Lob would rather be with Sandy and gives the dog to her family. When Sandy is a teenager, she is struck by a speeding truck. She is in a coma and the doctors are unable to help her. When Sandy's grandmother arrives at the hospital, she sees Lob waiting outside. She convinces the hospital staff to let her take Lob inside to see Sandy.

LA CHICA DE LOB

Joan Aiken

Escenario: Cornualles, Inglaterra, siglo XX

Sandy es una niña de cinco años que vive en un pueblo pesquero en Cornualles, Inglaterra. Un día en la playa, conoce a un perro pastor alemán llamado Lob. Aunque Lob pertenece a otra persona, enseguida desarrolla un apego especial hacia Sandy. El Sr. Dodsworth, dueño de Lob, se da cuenta que Lob prefiere estar con Sandy y lo regala a la familia de la niña. Cuando Sandy es adolescente, la golpea un camión que va a exceso de velocidad. Queda en coma y los doctores no pueden hacer nada por ella. Cuando la abuela de Sandy llega al hospital, ve a Lob esperando afuera. Convence al personal del hospital de que permitan entrar a Lob para que vea a Sandy.

Summary

TIFI LOB LA

Joan Aiken

Espas ak tan: Cornwall, Angletè, ventyèm syèk

Sandy se yon tifi senkan k ap viv nan yon vilaj kote yo fè lapèch nan Cornwall, Angletè. Yon jou, pandan li sou plaj la, li rankontre yon Bèje alman ki rele Lob. Malgre Lob se pou yon lòt moun, li gentan gen yon atachman espesyal pou Sandy. Msye Dodsworth, ki se mèt Lob, reyalize Lob ta pito rete avèk Sandy epi li ba li chyen an pou fanmi li. Lè Sandy vin yon adolesan, yon kamyon ki t ap fè vitès frape li. Li vin tonbe nan koma epi doktè yo pa annmezi pou ede li. Lè granm Sandy rive nan lopital la, li wè Lob ap tann deyò a. Li konvenk pèsonèl lopital la pou kite li mennen Lob andedan an pou wè Sandy.

CÔ BẠN CỦA LOB

Joan Aiken

Bối cảnh: Cornwall, Anh, thế kỷ 20

Sandy là một cô bé năm tuổi sống trong một làng chài ở Cornwall, Anh. Một hôm trên bãi biển, cô gặp chú chó chăn cừu Đức tên Lob. Mặc dù Lob đã thuộc về người khác, nhưng chú đã nhanh chóng thấy có cảm tình với Sandy. Ông Dodsworth, chủ của Lob, nhận thấy Lob nên ở với Sandy và tặng chú cho gia đình cô bé. Khi Sandy đang tuổi thanh niên, cô bị một chiếc xe tải chạy với tốc độ cao đâm phải. Cô bị hôn mê và các bác sĩ không thể giúp cô. Khi bà Sandy đến thăm cô ở bệnh viện, bà gặp Lob đang đợi bên ngoài. Bà thuyết phục nhân viên bệnh viện cho Lob vào gặp Sandy.

Name _____ Date _____

LOB'S GIRL

Text Analysis

FORESHADOWING

Sometimes writers build excitement and curiosity by providing a hint about something that will happen later in the story. This hint is known as **foreshadowing.** Foreshadowing may appear in

- what the characters say ("*I wish we could play with him every day*")
- what the characters do (*Don came home very late and grim-faced.*)
- descriptions of setting (*narrow, steep, twisting hillroad*)

Directions: Use the diagram to record hints from "Lob's Girl" that foreshadow what happened to Lob. Complete the diagram by telling what happened to him. One example has been done for you.

Hints

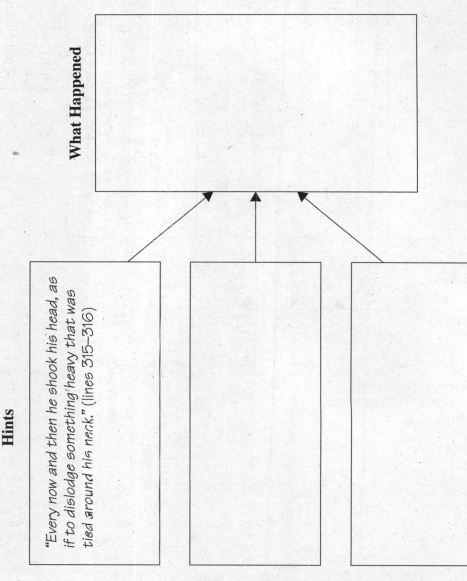

"*Every now and then he shook his head, as if to dislodge something heavy that was tied around his neck.*" (lines 315–316)

What Happened

LA CHICA DE LOB

Text Analysis

FORESHADOWING

Los escritores suelen generar emoción y curiosidad al proporcionar una pista sobre algo que sucederá más adelante en el cuento. Esta pista se conoce como **presagio**. Los presagios pueden aparecer en

- lo que dicen los personajes ("*Ojalá pudiéramos jugar con él todos los días*").
- lo que hacen los personajes (*Don llegó a casa muy tarde y con una expresión sombría*.).
- las descripciones del escenario (*camino por la colina angosto, empinado y sinuoso*).

Instrucciones: Usa el diagrama para anotar pistas de "La chica de Lob" que presagien lo que le sucedió a Lob. Completa el diagrama diciendo qué le sucedió. Te damos un ejemplo.

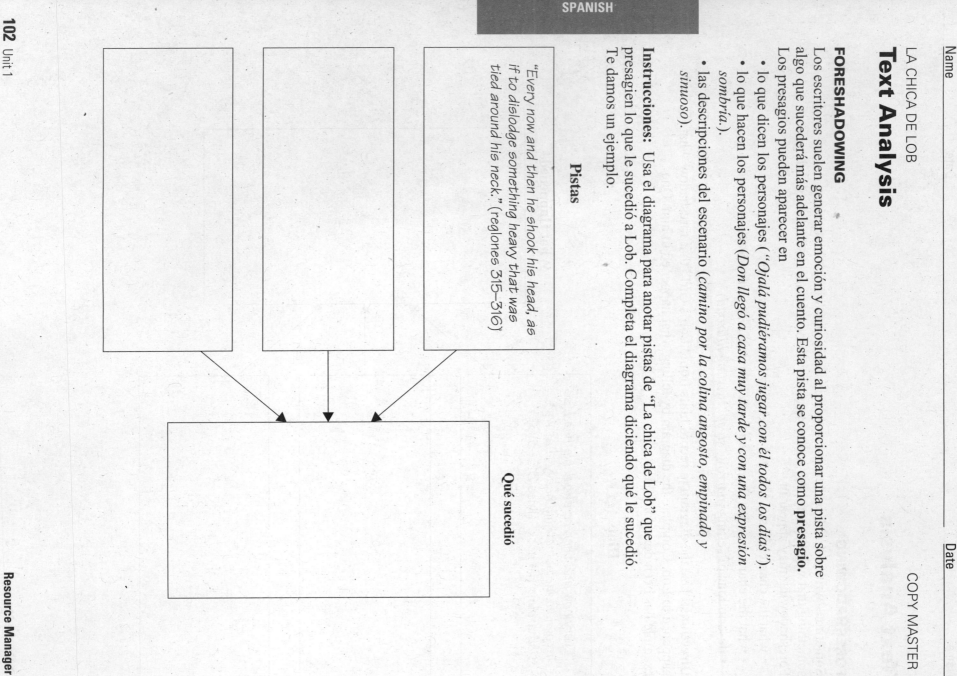

Pistas

"Every now and then he shook his head, as if to dislodge something heavy that was tied around his neck." (reglones 315–316)

Qué sucedió

Name _____

Date _____

LOB'S GIRL

Reading Skill

IDENTIFY SEQUENCE

Events in a story are presented in a specific order, or **sequence.** Certain words and phrases such as *the next day, then,* and *by that afternoon* can help you identify the sequence of events.

Directions: As you read "Lob's Girl," record the sequence of events on this timeline. Write the clue words and phrases that signal the order of events.

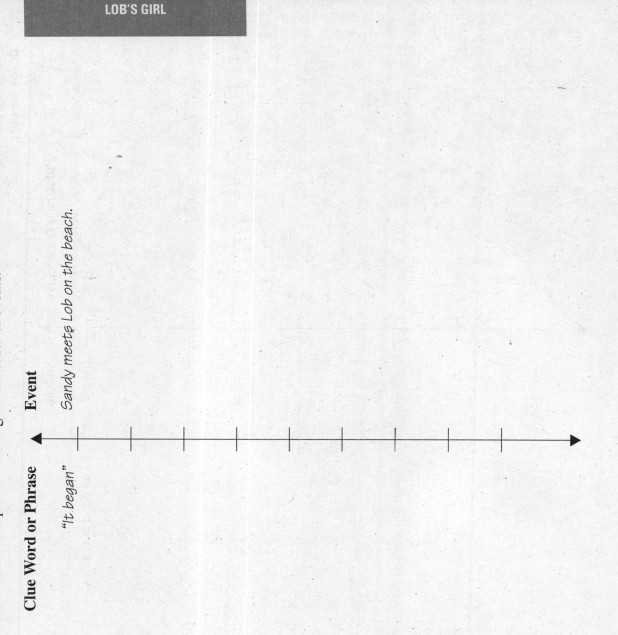

Clue Word or Phrase   **Event**

"It began"   *Sandy meets Lob on the beach.*

Resource Manager

LA CHICA DE LOB

Reading Skill

IDENTIFY SEQUENCE

Los sucesos de un cuento se presentan en un orden específico, o **secuencia**. Ciertas palabras o frases como *al día siguiente, luego* o *esa tarde* pueden ayudarte a identificar la secuencia de sucesos.

Instrucciones: Mientras lees "La chica de Lob", anota la secuencia de sucesos en esta línea cronológica. Escribe las palabras y las frases clave que señalen el orden de los sucesos.

Palabra o frase clave

"It began"

Suceso

Sandy conoce a Lob en la playa.

Name _____ Date _____

COPY MASTER

Vocabulary Study

CLOZE PRACTICE

agitated	atone	decisively	erupt	melancholy	reluctant

A. Directions: As your teacher reads each set of sentences, listen for the boldfaced word. Then discuss the possible meaning of the word.

1. The dog became **agitated**, barking and whining loudly.
   Some people are **agitated** and nervous at the sight of a big dog.

2. He felt he was innocent of wrongdoing and shouldn't have to **atone** for anything.
   To **atone** for her bad temper, she made her brother his favorite cookies.

3. Her answer was spoken **decisively**, which ended all argument.
   Lob chose Sandy **decisively** and without hesitation.

4. Lob had so much energy that he seemed to **erupt** into a room.
   Her excitement at the thought of keeping Lob threatened to **erupt** into tears.

5. The gloomy weather made her feel even more **melancholy.**
   The beach appeared **melancholy** and deserted after the summer tourists left.

6. She dragged her feet, **reluctant** to arrive at her aunt's house.
   The dog was **reluctant** to get into the bathtub; he fought with all his strength until we gave up.

B. Directions: Listen as your teacher reads the story. Then complete the story, using words from the box.

"No! No! No!" I said 1. _____ "I do not want that

2. _____ color on my bedroom walls. I want a shade that is bright and sunny, not one that makes me feel depressed." The salesclerk backed off.

She looked quite taken aback at my 3. _____ state. "Don't worry,"

I told her. "I won't 4. _____ again. I feel much better now." To

5. _____ for my outburst, I tried to be especially nice about the next colors she chose. I felt 6. _____ to commit to anything, though, and told her I'd come back another day.

Vocabulary Practice

| agitated | atone | decisively | erupt | melancholy | reluctant |

A. Directions: Fill in each set of blanks with the correct word from the box. Then use the boxed letters to complete the sentence.

1. How you might feel on a rainy day.

___ ___ ___ [ ] ___

2. How you might feel if people were annoying you.

[ ] ___ ___ ___

3. What you should do if you've done something mean to your friend.

___ ___ [ ] ___ ___

4. How you might answer a question if you knew you had the right answer.

___ ___ [ ] ___ ___

5. How you feel if you didn't want to do something.

___ ___ ___ ___ ___

6. What you might do if you were suddenly angry.

___ ___ [ ] ___ ___

7. Lob was an unusually perceptive _____

B. Directions: Circle the word in each group that is closest in meaning to the boldfaced word.

8. **agitated**
   a. reliable
   b. deceived
   c. restless
   d. baffled

9. **decisively**
   a. cruelly
   b. purposefully
   c. awkwardly
   d. splendidly

10. **erupt**
   a. explode
   b. force
   c. delight
   d. refuse

Name _____ Date _____

LOB'S GIRL

Vocabulary Strategy

LITERAL AND FIGURATIVE MEANINGS

The **literal** meaning of a word is its most common definition. The **figurative** meaning of a word is an expanded meaning that has emerged from the basic definition. For example, the literal meaning of *erupt* is "to explode from a volcano with fire and noise." Now *erupt* is also used figuratively to refer to a person or animal "exploding" with emotion.

A. Directions: For each boldfaced word, write its literal and figurative meaning.

1. The bright sun **bathed** me with warmth.

   Literal meaning: _____

   Figurative meaning: _____

2. The news of her marriage was **fodder** for all of the gossips in town.

   Literal meaning: _____

   Figurative meaning: _____

3. A **blanket** of snow soon covered the sleeping farm.

   Literal meaning: _____

   Figurative meaning: _____

4. A **burst** of wind ripped the pages from my hands.

   Literal meaning: _____

   Figurative meaning: _____

B. Directions: Write two sentences using the word *mule*. Use the literal sense of *mule* in one sentence and the figurative sense in the other.

5. _____

_____

6. _____

_____

LOB'S GIRL

Reading Check

Directions: Recall the characters and events in the selection. Then answer the questions in sentences or phrases.

1. What role did Lob play in the Pengelly family?

_____

_____

2. Why do you think Lob and Sandy became such close companions?

_____

_____

3. From Lob's point of view, describe what happened on the night of the accident.

_____

_____

4. What do you think really happened in the hospital the night Granny came to visit?

_____

_____

5. What do you think life was like for Sandy once she left the hospital and returned home?

_____

_____

Name _____

Date _____

LOB'S GIRL

Question Support

TEXT ANALYSIS
For questions 1–3, see page 101 of the Student Edition.

Directions: Answer the questions.

4. Make Inferences Reread lines 84–96. How does Sandy feel?

_____

5. Identify Sequence When did Don find Lob?

_____

6. Analyze Foreshadowing Read these hints from the story. What do they tell you about Lob's fate?

"...twins were crying bitterly. Lob was nowhere to be seen." (line 250) _____

"'...that dog has walked the length of England—*twice*—to be with that girl.'" (lines 309–310) _____

7. Analyze Setting

Describe the setting on the day Sandy meets Lob. _____

_____

Describe the setting on the day of Sandy's accident. _____

_____

Why are these settings important to the plot? _____

_____

8. Evaluate Plot Underline one of the two phrases in parentheses and complete the sentence.

The plot of "Lob's Girl" (is realistic/is not realistic) because _____

_____

_____

Name _____   Date _____

Grammar in Context

PUNCTUATE POSSESSIVES CORRECTLY

The possessive form of a noun shows ownership or relationship. When forming a possessive noun, be sure to put the **apostrophe** in the correct place. A misplaced apostrophe can be confusing. Follow these guidelines for punctuating possessive nouns correctly.

- **Singular nouns:** Add an apostrophe and *s*, even if the word ends in *s* (*Don's boat*)
- **Plural nouns ending in *s*:** Add an apostrophe (*the seagulls' cries*)
- **Plural nouns not ending in *s*:** Add an apostrophe and an *s* (*the children's pails*)

Original: Sandys' family couldn't explain how she recovered so quickly.
Revised: Sandy's family couldn't explain how she recovered so quickly.

Directions: Correct the possessive nouns in these sentences. Rewrite the sentences.

1. Lobs's collar seemed heavy and damp.

   _____

2. The two nurses's chatter could be heard upstairs.

   _____

3. No one could repair Sandys injuries.

   _____

4. Originally, Lob was Mr. Dodsworths's dog.

   _____

5. The twins's shriek made Lob lick their faces harder.

   _____

6. Sandy could see the fishermens' boats far out at sea.

   _____

Name _____ Date _____

LOB'S GIRL

Reading Fluency

TRACKING ORAL READING RATE AND ACCURACY

Directions: In "Lob's Girl," the ghost of a faithful dog helps an injured child. In this passage from *The Stranger*, a mysterious and ghostly young woman startles a driver on a dangerously stormy night. Use this passage with the activity on page 112. Follow the directions on that page.

Late one Saturday night, a young man was driving home on a

deserted stretch of road. He could hear the rain beating against

the roof of his car. What a night to be out! He shivered and

wished he were safe at home.

Suddenly, as he rounded a curve, his headlights lit up a young

woman standing by the side of the road. Her hair and white dress

were soaked from the rain. She looked so alone. He couldn't

just leave her there.

The young man skidded to a stop, then backed up until he

could see her face in the window. He leaned over and opened the

door. "Would you like a ride?"

She nodded and he reached out his hand to help her into the

car. He shivered at her touch—her hand was so cold! She smiled

at him and said, "Can you take me home? I only live a mile away."

Now that she was sitting beside him, he could see how

beautiful she was. Dark hair framed her face, and her eyes seemed

unusually large and sad. (182)

—Sue Baugh, from *The Stranger*

Reading Fluency

TRACKING ORAL READING RATE AND ACCURACY

When you read aloud, your goal is to help the listener understand the text. To do this, read the words accurately and with expression. Use a normal speaking rate.

Directions to the Reader:

- Use this page with the passage on page 111. Read the passage in a natural tone of voice to your partner for one minute. He or she will tell you when to start and stop.
- Read the same passage three more times. Your goal is to increase your speed each time, while still reading each word accurately.
- Your partner will calculate your score, which shows how you compare to others at your grade level. Answer the questions below the chart to evaluate your progress.

Directions to the Checker:

- Tell your partner when to begin reading. As your partner reads, follow along. Lightly underline each word your partner skips or mispronounces. Jot down words he or she adds.
- After one minutes, say "stop" and circle the last word your partner read. Share the marks you made with your partner.
- To calculate the reading fluency score, subtract the number of errors your partner made from the number of words read in a minute. Count as an error any words your partner left out, added, or mispronounced. If your partner substituted one word for another (*home*, for example), that substitution counts as an error as well. Put a checkmark in the table to show the reading score.
- Then erase the marks on the passage and tell your partner to begin again.

Number of Words Read Correctly Per Minute	1–68 10th percentile	69–91 20th percentile	92–98 25th percentile	99–104 30th percentile	105–115 40th percentile	116–127 50th percentile	128–137 60th percentile	138–148 70th percentile	149–153 75th percentile	154–160 80th percentile	161–177 90th percentile
Reading 1											
Reading 2											
Reading 3											
Reading 4											

Directions: Write your answer to the following questions on the back of this sheet.

1. How did reading the passage several times affect your speed and accuracy?

2. Summarize the effect of repeated readings on your understanding of the passage.

Text Analysis

IDENTIFY GENRE FEATURES

A novel is a long work of fiction. An **historical novel** is a work of fiction that is set in a particular time in history. It often mixes references to real events, people, and places with fictional plots and characters.

Directions: As you read the excerpt from *Bud, Not Buddy*, watch for examples of the genre feature listed in the first column of the chart. Then record those examples in the second column. Some examples have been done for you.

Genre Features	Examples
Reference to Real Events	Line for food during the Great Depression of the 1930s
References to Real Places	mission
Fictional plot	

Essential Course of Study ECOS Lesson at a Glance

Media Study | *from Lemony Snicket's, a* Series of Unfortunate Events

WHAT'S THE CONNECTION?

This Media Study reinforces the unit focus on plot, conflict, and setting. The creators of a feature film have a unique set of tools to help them create setting and plot. Students learn how moviemakers use visual and sound effects to create a vivid setting and to build suspense as characters struggle to resolve a conflict.

ABOUT THE MEDIA STUDY

Student Edition/Teacher's Edition Pages: 110–113

Summary In this film clip, the three Baudelaire children are locked in a car that is parked on a train track. Suspense builds as they see a train approaching in the distance. Using Klaus's knowledge of trains and Violet's genius for invention, the children quickly devise a way to pull the track switcher. Just as the train is about to crash into the car, it is diverted onto another track and the children are saved.

Engaging the Students Throughout the Media Study, students explore the key concept of how moviemakers can use visual and sound effects to make a viewer's heart pound with excitement.

Lesson Plan and Resource Guide

Media Study: *from* Lemony Snicket's
A Series of Unfortunate Events

Common Core Focus

RI 4 Determine the meaning of words and phrases, including technical meanings. **SL 1** Engage effectively in collaborative discussions (one-on-one, in groups). **SL 2** Interpret information presented in media.

Unless otherwise noted, resources can be found in the *Resource Manager.* ⓘ Lesson resources are also available on the **Teacher One Stop DVD-ROM** and online at <u>thinkcentral.com</u>. The Student Edition and selected copymasters are available electronically on the ⌛ **Student One Stop DVD-ROM.**

Student/Teacher's Edition Pages	Additional Resources CM=Copy Master T=Transparency
Focus and Motivate	
☐ Big Question p. 110	☐ Summary CM—p. 119, p. 120 ⓓ
Teach	
☐ Media Literacy: Setting and Conflict in Movies p. 111	☐ ⌛ **MediaSmart DVD-ROM** ☐ Introduction, First Viewing, Media Lessons
Practice and Apply: Guided Practice	
☐ Viewing Guide and Teacher Notes p. 112	☐ Viewing Guide CM p. 121 ☐ Close Viewing CM p. 122 ☐ Media Activity CM p. 123 ☐ Ideas for Extension p. 117 ⓓ ☐ ⌛ **MediaSmart DVD-ROM** ☐ Guided Analysis
Assess and Reteach	
Assess	
☐ Write or Discuss p. 113 ☐ Produce Your Own Media p. 113	☐ Produce Your Own Media CM p. 124 ☐ ⌛ **MediaSmart DVD-ROM** ☐ ⓘ MediaScope at <u>thinkcentral.com</u>
Reteach	
☐ Setting and Conflict in Movies	

ⓓ = Resources for Differentiation

MEDIA STUDY: *from* LEMONY SNICKET'S A SERIES OF UNFORTUNATE EVENTS

Ideas for Extension

Differentiation These activities provide students with a variety of options for demonstrating understanding of lesson concepts.

EXPLORATIONS AND ACTIVITIES

EXPERIMENT WITH TECHNIQUES: SOUND EFFECTS

Have small groups view the clip from *Lemony Snicket's A Series of Unfortunate Events* and list specific sound effects that they notice (such as Violet's tearing the strap from the car seat and Sunny's biting the head off the elf). Then have them brainstorm ways they could make these sounds and choose some of their best ideas to try out. Have groups record their sound effects and play them for the class. Discuss which ones are most realistic.

Pre-AP Challenge: Remind students that dialogue is another sound element that can be used to create various effects in a movie. The way an actor says a particular line might make viewers laugh, feel sad, or wonder what will happen next. Ask pairs to select a brief section of dialogue from a story or play. Have students rehearse and present two readings of the dialogue, using their voices to give two different impressions of the plot or of the characters' relationship.

INQUIRY AND RESEARCH

GLOSSARY OF VISUAL AND SOUND TECHNIQUES

Tell students that making a feature film requires the work of many experts using specialized techniques. Explain that they will research some of the terms associated with visual and sound techniques and compile a glossary.

Display a list of terms and have students or pairs select some to research. Possible terms include *establishing shot, reaction shot, point of view shot, medium shot, close-up shot, extreme close-up shot, high-angle shot, low-angle shot, animation, soundtrack, sound effects,* and *voiceover.* Encourage students to add other terms that they encounter during their research. Have them write a definition of each term and provide examples and illustrations as appropriate.

Compile students' glossary entries in a binder. Keep the binder in the classroom or place it in the school library as a resource for the whole school.

WRITING

ANALYZE VISUAL AND SOUND TECHNIQUES: MOVIE REVIEW

Ask students to think of a movie that they think shows especially good—or especially bad—use of visual and sound techniques. Have them write a review in which they explain why the movie's visuals and sound are effective or ineffective. Encourage them to use terminology from the Media Study (*close-up shots, dialogue,* and so on) to analyze the movie.

Teacher Notes

Review and Evaluate Outcome	
What did I want students to know or be able to do?	
Which Teaching Option did I use? _____ Teaching Option 1: The Basics (1–2 days) _____ Teaching Option 2: In-Depth Study (2–3 days) How successful was the lesson?	
Evaluate Process	
What worked? • Strategies • Resources What did not work? Why not?	
Reflect	
The next time I teach this Media Study, what will I do differently? Why?	
Plan Ahead	
What must I do next?	

Summary

FROM **LEMONY SNICKET'S A SERIES OF UNFORTUNATE EVENTS (FILM)**

Violet, Klaus, and Sunny Baudelaire are three very intelligent orphans. Their parents died in a fire, leaving the children a lot of money. The three Baudelaire children are sent to live with their new guardian, Count Olaf, who is only interested in stealing the money for himself.

In this clip from the 2004 film, Count Olaf locks Violet, Klaus, and Sunny in his car, which is parked on a set of train tracks. Violet discovers a book about inheritance laws and a train schedule in the backseat. They realize that a train is going to arrive in just a few minutes. Violet and Klaus try to unlock the car, but Olaf has taken the keys. Klaus tells Violet that they need to pull the train switch. Using items she finds inside the car, Violet is able to pull the switch and reroute the train.

You can analyze the clip to see how different camera shots, sound effects, and dialogue portray a conflict and draw you in to a setting.

DE LEMONY SNICKET: UNA SERIE DE EVENTOS DESAFORTUNADOS (PELÍCULA)

Violet, Klaus y Sunny Baudelaire son tres huérfanos muy inteligentes. Sus padres murieron en un incendio, dejándoles mucho dinero. Los tres niños Baudclaire son van a vivir con su nuevo tutor, el Conde Olaf, quien sólo está interesado en quedarse con su dinero.

En este fragmento de la película de 2004, el Conde Olaf encierra a Violet, Klaus y Sunny en su carro, el cual está estacionado sobre las vías del tren. Violet descubre un libro de las leyes sobre la herencia y un horario de trenes en el asiento trasero. Se dan cuenta que un tren llegará en unos cuantos minutos. Violet y Klaus intentan abrir el carro, pero Olaf se llevó las llaves. Klaus le dice a Violet que necesitan jalar la palanca de cambio de vías. Usando cosas que encuentra dentro del carro, Violet logra jalar la palanca y hacer que se desvíe el tren.

Puedes analizar el fragmento para ver cómo las diferentes tomas, los efectos de sonido y el diálogo retratan un conflicto y te transportan a un escenario.

Resource Manager

Summary

DAPRE YON SERI EVÈNMAN MALERE SNIKET LEMONY (FILM)

Violet, Klaus, ak Sunny Baudelaire se twa òfelen ki trè entèlijan. Paran yo te mouri nan yon ensandi, epi yo kite timoun yo avèk anpil lajan. Yo voye twa pitit Baudelaire yo al viv avèk nouvo gadyen yo, Count Olaf, ki enterese sèlman nan vòlè lajan an pou li.

Nan klip sa a dapre film 2004 la, Count Olaf fèmen Violet, Klaus, ak Sunny nan oto li, ki estasyone sou yon ray tren. Violet dekouvri yon liv konsènan lwa sou eritaj ak yon orè tren dèyè kousen an. Yo reyalize yon tren pral rive nan kèk minit sèlman. Violet ak Klaus eseye louvri oto a, men Olaf te pran kle yo. Klaus di Violet yo bezwen redi entèripté tren an. Avèk atik Violet jwenn annndan oto a, li anmezi pou redi entèripté tren an epi pou detounene tren an.

Ou ka analize klip la pou wè kouman kout kamera diferan, efè son, ak dyalòg prezante yon konfli epi mennen ou nan yon espas.

trich từ NHỮNG SỰ KIỆN BẤT HẠNH CỦA LEMONY SNICKET (PHIM)

Violet, Klaus, và Sunny Baudelaire là ba đứa trẻ mồ côi rất thông minh. Cha mẹ chúng đã mất trong một vụ hỏa hoạn, để lại cho chúng rất nhiều tiền. Ba đứa trẻ nhà Baudelaire được đưa tới sống với người bảo trợ mới của chúng, Bá tước Olaf, người chỉ muốn lấy cắp tiền bỏ vào túi ông ta.

Trong đoạn phim năm 2004 này, Bá tước Olaf khóa Violet, Klaus, và Sunny trong xe chiếc xe hơi đang đỗ trên đường ray xe lửa. Violet phát hiện ra một cuốn sách về luật thừa kế và lịch trình xe lửa trên băng ghế sau. Lũ trẻ nhận thấy rằng chỉ vài phút nữa thôi là xe lửa sẽ tới. Violet và Klaus cố gắng mở cửa xe, nhưng Olaf đã cầm chìa khóa. Klaus bảo Violet rằng chúng cần phải kéo ghi xe lửa. Với những đồ tìm thấy trong xe, Violet có thể kéo ghi xe lửa và đổi hướng đoàn tàu.

Bạn có thể phân tích cuốn băng để thấy sự khác biệt mà các cảnh quay, hiệu ứng âm thanh và đối thoại thể hiện mâu thuẫn và đặt bạn vào trong bối cảnh.

Media Literacy: Setting and Conflict in Movies

VIEWING GUIDE

Filmmakers use different visual and sound techniques to bring a story to life. **Camera shots, music, sound effects,** and **dialogue** all help reveal the setting and conflict to an audience.

Directions: Watch the clip. Jot down one example for each film technique listed in the chart. In the third column, explain how the examples you listed make the scene's conflict seem exciting.

Film Techniques	Examples	How do these techniques make the conflict exciting?
Camera Shots • Long shots *(provide a wide view of the scene)*		
• Medium shots *(show one or more characters from the waist up)*		
• Close-up shots *(show the details of a person or object)*		
Sound • Music		
• Sound effects		
• Dialogue *(what the characters say and how they say it)*		

Media Literacy: Setting and Conflict in Movies

CLOSE VIEWING

The setting of a film is the time and place in which the events occur. Dangerous
settings can create more **conflict** for characters.

Directions: As you watch the clip, use the chart to record how each element of the
setting increases the amount of danger the Baudelaire children face.

Element of the Setting	How does this element add to the conflict?
Count Olaf's car	
The train tracks	
Mr. Poersquos car	

What do Violet, Klaus, and Sunny find in the setting that solves the conflict in the
scene?

_____

_____

Name _____ Date _____

Media Literacy: Setting and Conflict in Movies

MEDIA ACTIVITY

The director of *Lemony Snicket's A Series of Unfortunate Events* uses a unique setting to add a sense of excitement and create more conflict for the three main characters. You can use film and sound techniques to evaluate the use of setting and conflict in other movies.

Directions: Think of another movie you have seen recently that included a dangerous setting. Write its title in the chart and briefly describe the setting and conflict. Then explain how the setting affected what you understood about the conflict.

Title: _____

Setting: _____

Conflict: _____

How the Setting Affected My Understanding of the Conflict: _____

Name _____ Date _____

COPY MASTER

Media Literacy: Setting and Conflict in Movies

PRODUCE YOUR OWN MEDIA

Storyboards are tools directors use to plan how they will film a movie. Each frame of the storyboard includes a sketch and a short description of what will be seen on camera. The descriptions tells what kind of camera shot will be used, what action is taking place, and what sounds will be heard during a specific scene.

Directions: Imagine you're a director and you've been asked to make a movie based on one of the stories from this unit. Write down the name of the story in the space provided. Work with a partner to create a storyboard for the most exciting scene from the story you choose. Use the back of the sheet if you need to create more drawings.

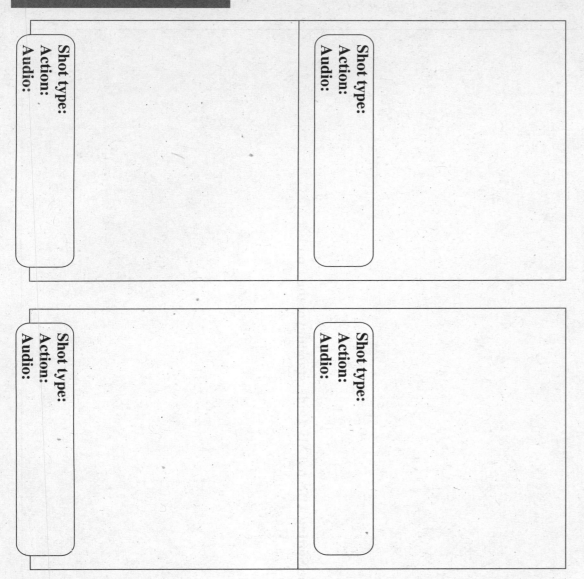

Shot type:
Action:
Audio:

Shot type:
Action:
Audio:

Shot type:
Action:
Audio:

Shot type:
Action:
Audio:

Woodsong

Gary Paulsen

Lesson at a Glance

WHY THIS SELECTION?

Gary Paulsen is a well-respected writer of young adult books. His strong connection to nature is evident in this excerpt from his widely read memoir *Woodsong*.

ABOUT THIS SELECTION

Student/Teacher's Edition Pages: 114–125

Difficulty Level: Average

Readability Scores: Lexile: 1040; Fry: 10; Dale-Chall: 5.4

Summary This excerpt describes author Paulsen's encounter with a bear in the Minnesota wilderness. Attempting to drive the bear from his trash, Paulsen hurls a stick at it. The bear is provoked and approaches Paulsen threateningly. Knowing he cannot escape, Paulsen stands still. Suddenly, the bear retreats, giving Paulsen time to retrieve his gun. But as he aims, Paulsen realizes that he is no better than the animal he seeks to kill. He then lowers his weapon.

Engaging the Students This excerpt offers students an opportunity to explore the key idea of respect. Through an intense encounter with a bear, Gary Paulsen is reminded of the need to treat nature with regard. As students read the memoir, they are encouraged to think about their own relationship with nature and the need to respect it.

COMMON CORE STANDARDS FOCUS

- Narrative Nonfiction
- Identify Author's Purpose

LESSON RESOURCES

ⓘ Lesson resources are also available on the **Teacher One Stop DVD-ROM** and online at <u>thinkcentral.com</u>.

Resource Manager

Lesson Plan and Resource Guide

from Woodsong
Memoir by Gary Paulsen

Common Core Focus

RI 4 Determine the meaning of words and phrases as they are used in the text. **RI 6** Determine an author's purpose and explain how it is conveyed in the text. **RI 10** Read and comprehend literary nonfiction. **W 2** Write informative/explanatory texts to convey ideas. **L 1c** Recognize and correct inappropriate shifts in pronoun number and person. **L 4b** Use Latin affixes and roots as clues to the meaning of a word.

Unless otherwise noted, resources can be found in the *Resource Manager:* ❶ Lesson resources are also available on the **Teacher One Stop DVD-ROM** and online at **thinkcentral.com**. The Student Edition and selected copymasters are available electronically on the ✐ **Student One Stop DVD-ROM**.

Student/Teacher's Edition Pages	Additional Resources CM = Copy Master T = Transparency
Focus and Motivate	
☐ Big Question p. 114	
☐ Author Biography p. 115	☐ ❶ Literature and Reading Center at **thinkcentral.com**
Teach	
☐ Narrative Nonfiction p. 115	
☐ Identify Author's Purpose p. 115	☐ Identify Author's Purpose CM—English p. 137, Spanish p. 138 **D**
☐ Vocabulary in Context p. 115	☐ Vocabulary Study CM p. 139 **D**

D = Resources for Differentiation

Student/Teacher's Edition Pages	Additional Resources CM = Copy Master T = Transparency
Practice and Apply: Guided Practice	
Selection and Teacher Notes	☐ *Audio Anthology CD* D
☐ *"from* Woodsong," pp. 116–121	☐ Summary CM—English and Spanish p. 133, Haitian Creole and Vietnamese p. 134 D
☐ "A Life in the Day of Gary Paulsen," p. 122	☐ Reading Fluency CM p. 145
	☐ i Audio Summaries at **thinkcentral.com**
	☐ **Best Practices Toolkit**
	☐ Comparison Matrix p. A24 [T] D
	☐ Evaluating a Story or Drama p. D18 [T] D
	☐ Jigsaw Reading p. A1 [T]
	☐ Words with Multiple Meanings p. E31 [T] D
Practice and Apply: After Reading	
☐ Selection Questions p. 123	☐ Reading Check CM p. 142
	☐ Narrative Nonfiction CM—English p. 135, Spanish p. 136 D
	☐ Question Support CM p. 143 D
	☐ Additional Selection Questions p. 129 D
	☐ Ideas for Extension pp. 130–131 D
☐ Vocabulary Practice p. 124	☐ Vocabulary Practice CM p. 140
☐ Academic Vocabulary in Writing p. 124	☐ Academic Vocabulary CM p. 3
☐ Vocabulary Strategy: Prefixes and the Latin Root *ject* p. 124	☐ Additional Academic Vocabulary CM p. 4
	☐ Vocabulary Strategy CM p. 141
	☐ i *WordSharp* Interactive Vocabulary Tutor CD-ROM and online at **thinkcentral.com**
	☐ i **Best Practices Toolkit**
	☐ Sensory Notes p. B30 [T] D
☐ Grammar in Context p. 125	☐ **Best Practices Toolkit**
☐ Writing Prompt p. 125	☐ Peer Response Guide p. C14 [T]
	☐ Maintain Pronoun-Antecedent Agreement CM p. 144
	☐ Grammar Handbook.—Student Edition p. R52
	☐ i GrammarNotes DVD-ROM at **thinkcentral.com**
	☐ i Interactive Revision Lessons on **WriteSmart CD-ROM** and online at **thinkcentral.com**

D = Resources for Differentiation

Student/Teacher's Edition Pages	Additional Resources CM = Copy Master T = Transparency
Assess and Reteach	
Assess	**Diagnostic and Selection Tests**
	☐ Selection Tests A, B/C pp. 44–45, 46–47 **D**
	☐ **ⓘ** ThinkCentral Online Assessment
	☐ ✎ ExamView Test Generator on the **Teacher One Stop DVD-ROM**
Reteach	
☐ Identify Author's Purpose	☐ **ⓘ** Level Up Online Tutorials on **thinkcentral.com**
☐ Prefixes and the Latin Word *ject*	☐ **ⓘ** Reteaching Worksheets on **think.central.com**
☐ Maintain Pronoun-Antecedent Agreement	☐ Reading Lesson 3: Determining Author's Purpose
	☐ Vocabulary Lesson 1: Word Parts
	☐ Grammar Lesson 8: Pronoun-Antecedent Agreement

D = Resources for Differentiation

from WOODSONG

Additional Selection Questions

Differentiation Use these questions to provide customized practice with comprehension and critical thinking skills.

Easy

1. **Does nature demand RESPECT?** In what way could Paulsen have shown more respect for nature in his encounter with the bear? (*Not throwing the stick and keeping his distance would have been two ways he could have shown more respect.*)

2. **Recall** What is the setting of Paulsen's memoir? (*The setting is a cabin near the wilderness in northern Minnesota.*)

3. **Recall** Why does Paulsen begin to relax around Scarhead? (*Scarhead comes around the kennels often. He doesn't harm the dogs even though he takes their food.*)

Average

4. **Examine Narrative Nonfiction** Which images have the most impact on the action the most? Explain. (*The conflict between Paulsen and Scarhead is brought about because Paulsen lives in the wilderness and raises dogs. The smell of the meat that is fed to the dogs attracts bears, including Scarhead. Paulsen's familiarity with the wilderness also causes him to relax his guard and become too casual in his interactions with Scarhead.*)

5. **Examine Author's Purpose** How would this selection differ if Paulsen's major purpose had been to inform? (*He might have included more facts about the appearance, habitat, and characteristics of black bears. He might not have revealed as many of his own thoughts. He might have chosen third-person point of view rather than first person.*)

Challenging

6. **Does nature demand RESPECT?** What are possible consequences of not respecting nature? (*Not respecting nature can put someone in danger. It can lead to destruction of the environment. It can lead to a lack of respect for people as well.*)

7. **Evaluate Author's Purpose** How does Paulsen's honest portrayal of himself in this memoir help him to accomplish his purpose? (*Paulsen describes his behavior and shares his thoughts before, during, and after his encounter with the bear. This helps readers connect with Paulsen and see him as a real person. It also highlights the significance of the lesson Paulsen learns and helps readers to see its impact upon his behavior.*)

8. **Analyze Narrative Nonfiction** The memoir and the newspaper article describe two of the places that Paulsen has lived. What does Paulsen's choice of these settings reveal about his values? (*He prefers nature to society. He enjoys solitude. He feels a kinship with animals. He likes the challenge of living primitively.*)

Resource Manager

Ideas for Extension

from WOODSONG

Differentiation These activities provide students with a variety of options for demonstrating understanding of lesson concepts.

EXPLORATIONS AND ACTIVITIES

COMPOSE ORIGINAL SONG: INTERPRET MAIN IDEAS

Ask students to name some songs that tell stories. Discuss how singers may use both the words and the music to establish setting, build character, direct the action, and convey emotion.

Have pairs or small groups of students write a song that tells the story of Paulsen's encounter with the bear. Their lyrics should include the most important details from the memoir. Encourage them to set their songs to familiar or original music and to rehearse. Then have students take turns performing their compositions. Discuss the strengths of each performance.

SAFETY GUIDE: EXAMINE AUTHOR'S PURPOSE

Direct students' attention to lines 56–118. Discuss how Paulsen's behavior in this part of the memoir illustrates what someone should and should not do during an encounter with a bear.

Ask pairs of students to create a guide to wilderness safety. They should focus specifically on dealing with bears, drawing from Paulsen's actions as well as the facts he shares in this section. Students may wish to have one "do" list and one "don't" list. Invite pairs to compare their safety guides with each other before sharing them with the class.

PUBLIC SERVICE CAMPAIGN: EXPLORE KEY CONCEPT

Discuss with students how important it is to respect nature, especially when in a national park. Point out that the premise of a national park is to make nature accessible to everyone and to preserve wildlife and vegetation for future generations.

Have students work in small groups of three to four to develop a public service campaign that will convey the importance of respecting national parks. The campaign should consist of two components: a formal public service announcement, either recorded or acted out in class, that includes a strong message persuading viewers to respect and preserve nature, and a billboard that identifies the campaign's message or slogan. Remind students that a slogan is a memorable phrase that expresses an idea or purpose. Examples of slogans include "Life is Calling" from the Peace Corps; "Nick is for Kids" from Nickelodeon; and "Think Different" from Apple Computer, Inc.

When groups have completed their work, have them present their public service announcements and their billboard designs to the rest of the class.

SMALL-GROUP DISCUSSION: EXPLORE THEME

Ask students if they have ever heard the saying "Familiarity breeds contempt." Have students volunteer their interpretations of its meaning.

Divide students into small groups and have them discuss how the saying is proved or disproved by events in the memoir. Encourage them to look closely at Paulsen's words and actions to support their view. Have students also consider how the saying is connected to the key idea and theme of the selection.

IDEAS FOR EXTENSION, CONTINUED

Have students create a graphic organizer in which they can record their insights. Invite small groups to share their organizers with each other before contributing to a whole-class discussion.

ROLE-PLAY: EXPLORE AUTHOR'S BACKGROUND

Have students work in pairs to find out more about Gary Paulsen's life and experiences. Students may use print or electronic resources. Encourage students to define a focus for their research. For example, they may want to find out more about his life on his boat or the years in which he raised dogs.

After students have gathered their facts, have them create interview questions that elicit the information they want to share. Have students record their questions and answers on separate index cards. Ask one student to play the role of the interviewer and the other to assume the character of Gary Paulsen.

Have students conduct mock interviews in front of the class. Afterwards, discuss what students learned from the interviews.

Pre-AP Challenge: After students have researched Paulsen, have them jointly or separately write an article in the style of the one on page 122. Encourage students to unify their articles by focusing on a single aspect of Paulsen's life. Remind them to develop one main idea per paragraph.

INQUIRY AND RESEARCH

BLACK BEARS

Divide the class into small groups. Have each group research a topic related to black bears in North America. For example, one group might investigate the different habitats in which the bears can thrive. Others may look into the population distribution, characteristics of the species, or threats to the black bear. Ask each group to present their information on an illustrated poster, which includes charts or graphs if appropriate.

Have each group present their poster to the class. Then display the posters around the room.

WRITING

EVALUATE STYLE: REVIEW

Ask students to write a review of this excerpt that might appear on a poster in a bookstore in which *Woodsong* is sold. Have students bring in specific details or quotations to support their opinion of the work.

EXAMINE GENRE: MEMOIR

Have students choose an incident from their own lives that taught them a lesson. Ask students to write about the event from first-person point of view and to incorporate elements of the memoir genre, such as an informal tone and personal insights. Encourage students to record details in a sequence chart or other graphic organizer before they begin to write.

Teacher Notes

Review and Evaluate Outcome

What did I want students to know or be able to do?

How successful was the lesson?

Evaluate Process

What worked?

- Strategies

- Resources

- Differentiation

What did not work? Why not?

Reflect

The next time I teach "Woodsong," what will I do differently? Why?

Plan Ahead

What must I do next?

Summary

FROM WOODSONG

Gary Paulsen

Setting: Northern Minnesota, present-day

Bears are always searching for food outside Gary Paulsen's Minnesota cabin. He is so used to seeing them that he gives them names and begins to think of them as pets. One day, Paulsen is burning trash and food scraps. A male bear he calls Scarhead is attracted by the smell. Scarhead begins to rip up the trash enclosure. Paulsen angrily throws a stick at the bear. The bear turns and comes toward Paulsen. Paulsen knows that Scarhead could kill him with one blow, but the bear suddenly turns away and goes back to searching through the trash. Paulsen then hurries to get his rifle.

DE LA CANCIÓN DEL BOSQUE

Gary Paulsen

Escenario: Norte de Minnesota, en la actualidad

Los osos siempre buscan comida afuera de la cabaña de Gary Paulsen en Minnesota. Está tan acostumbrado a verlos que les pone nombres y empieza a considerarlos mascotas. Un día, Paulsen está quemando basura y restos de comida. El olor atrae a un oso macho al que llama *Scarhead*. El oso empieza a destrozar el cerco de la basura. Enojado Paulsen le avienta una vara. El oso se voltea y va hacia Paulsen. Paulsen sabe que *Scarhead* podría matarlo de un golpe pero, de pronto, el oso se voltea y vuelve a buscar en la basura. Paulsen se apresura a ir por su rifle.

Summary

DEPI WOODSONG

Gary Paulsen

Espas ak tan: Nò Minesota, jodi a

Lous yo toujou ap chèche manje deyò kabin Gary Paulsen ki nan Minesota. Li tèlman abitye wè yo, sa fè li ba yo non epi li kòmanse panse pou fè yo vin tankou bèt nan kay. Yon jou, Paulsen ap boule fatra ak ti dechè manje. Odè a atire yon lous mal li rele Scarhead. Scarhead kòmanse rache kloti fatra a. Paulsen fache epi li tire yon baton sou lous la. Lous la vire epi li mache sou Paulsen. Paulsen konnen Scarhead kapab touye li avèk yon kou, men toudenkou lous la chanje direksyon epi li retoumen al chèche nan fatra a. Paulsen kouri al chèche fizi li.

theo WOODSONG

Gary Paulsen

Bối cảnh: Bắc Minnesota, thời hiện tại

Các chú gấu thường đến kiếm ăn bên ngoài căn buồng của Gary Paulsen ở Minnesota. Ông đã quen nhìn chúng đến nỗi ông đặt tên cho chúng và coi chúng như những con vật nuôi. Một hôm, Paulsen đang đốt rác và thức ăn thừa. Một con gấu đực tên Scarhead thấy mùi đó hấp dẫn. Scarhead bắt đầu bới đống rác. Paulsen tức giận ném một cây gậy vào con gấu. Con gấu quay lại và tiến về phía Paulsen. Paulsen biết rằng Scarhead có thể giết chết ông chỉ bằng một cái tát, nhưng con gấu bất ngờ quay đi và trở lại lục lợi trong đống rác. Khi đó Paulsen vội và đi lấy khẩu súng trường của ông.

from WOODSONG

Text Analysis

NARRATIVE NONFICTION

Narrative nonfiction tells true stories about events that really happened. Often these events surround a **conflict** between opposing forces. The author may create **suspense** that makes the reader unsure how the conflict will be resolved.

Directions: In the excerpt from *Woodsong*, each of the two forces that are in conflict has some advantages over the other. On the scale, record the different qualities that make the bear and the narrator strong. One example has been done for you. Then answer the question that follows.

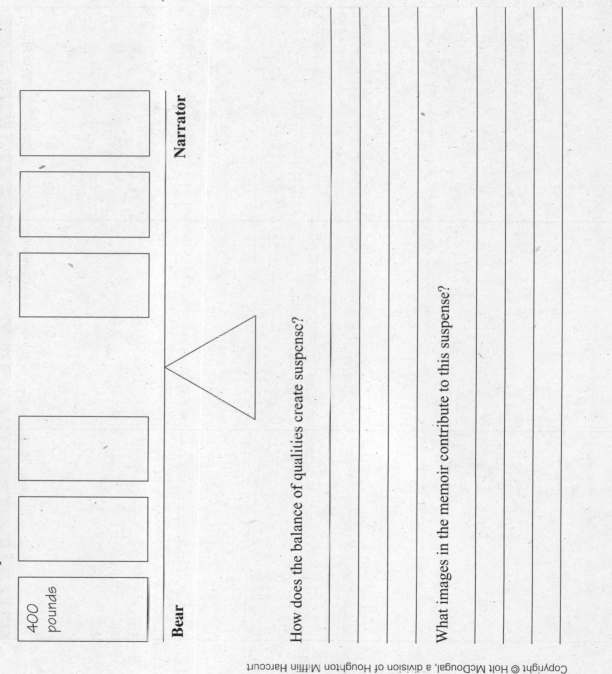

Narrator

Bear

400 pounds

How does the balance of qualities create suspense?

_____

_____

_____

What images in the memoir contribute to this suspense?

_____

_____

_____

from WOODSONG

Text Analysis

NARRATIVE NONFICTION

Una memoria, como *Woodsong* es una forma de narrativa de no ficción. La narrativa de no ficción hace uso de muchos de los elementos literarios que se encuentran en la ficción, incluyendo el conflicto, el suspenso y las imágenes.

Instrucciones: En la tabla registra algunos ejemplos del uso que Gary Paulsen hace en su memoria del conflicto, el suspenso y las imágenes.

Elementos de la narrativa de no ficción		
Conflicto	Suspenso	Imágenes

from WOODSONG

Reading Skill

IDENTIFY AUTHOR'S PURPOSE

Authors may write for a variety of purposes, but they often have one main reason for writing. This is called the **author's purpose.**

Directions: As you read the excerpt from *Woodsong,* record clues about the author's purpose for writing his memoir. Circle the main purpose.

Author's Purpose

Explain/Inform	Share Thoughts	Persuade	Entertain
Bears hibernate in winter and are very hungry in the spring (lines 15–16).			

DE CANCIÓN DEL BOSQUE

Reading Skill

IDENTIFY AUTHOR'S PURPOSE

Los autores pueden escribir con una variedad de propósitos, pero por lo general tienen una razón principal para escribir. Esta es el **propósito del autor.**

Instrucciones: Mientras lees el fragmento de *La canción del bosque,* anota pistas sobre el propósito del autor al escribir sus memorias. Encierra en un círculo el propósito principal.

Propósito del autor

Explicar/Informar	Compartir ideas	Persuadir	Entretener
Los osos hibernan durante el invierno y tienen mucha hambre en la primavera. (renglones 15-16)			

from WOODSONG

Vocabulary Study

CONTEXT CLUES

A. Directions: Cover up or fold under the right-hand column. As your teacher reads each sentence, listen for the boldfaced word. Discuss possible meanings for the word. Then check your answers by reading the definition in the right-hand column.

Word	How It Is Used	Definition
coherent	His thoughts during the event were jumbled. Later, he was able to give a more **coherent** account.	clear; logical
eject	He could not physically **eject** the huge bear from his trash area. Instead, he would have to scare the animal away.	to throw out from inside; to remove
hibernation	**Hibernation** helps bears and other animals survive winter, a time when food is scarce. In the spring, they stir and venture out again.	the state of being inactive through the winter
novelty	At first, the bears were a **novelty** to the campers. Then, they became a nuisance.	something new and unusual
scavenge	To avoid attracting animals that **scavenge,** campers should destroy their garbage completely.	to search for discarded scraps
truce	The bears and dogs established a **truce.** The bears would not hurt the dogs if they could eat all their food.	an agreement to end an argument or fight

B. Directions: On a separate sheet of paper, write a complete sentence for each word. If possible, make your sentences to tell a story.

Resource Manager

Vocabulary Practice

| coherent | eject | hibernation | novelty | scavenge | truce |

A. Directions: On each blank line, write the word from the box that fits the rhyme.

1. Although the car's a common sight, not odd to you or me

A hundred years ago it was indeed a _____.

2. One person's trash may be another person's treasure.

That is why so many people _____ for pleasure.

3. Because snoring on the sofa is his favorite thing to do;

A bear's long _____ would be bliss for Uncle Lou.

B. Directions: Write the word from the box that best completes each sentence.

4. Hoping to avoid a strike, the two sides agreed to a temporary

_____ to allow time for tempers to cool down.

5. The manager may _____ a rowdy customer from the store.

6. Elena made such a _____ argument for watching the show

that she was allowed to stay up for an hour past her usual bedtime.

C. Writing Option: Pretend you have spent a week visiting Gary Paulsen. Write a note to thank him for having you as a guest. Comment on your visit and use at least two of the vocabulary words.

_____

_____

_____

_____

_____

from WOODSONG

Vocabulary Strategy

PREFIXES AND THE LATIN WORD *JECT*

A **prefix** is a word part that appears at the beginning of a base word or root. It changes the meaning of the original base word. The Latin word *ject* means "throw." It is often combined with prefixes such as those below.

Prefix	Meaning
e-, ex-	from; out of
in-	in; into
pro-	forward; in front of
re-	back; again
sub-	under; down

A. Directions: Use the information on the chart and the meaning of the root *ject* to write a definition for each boldfaced word.

1. The boy's idea for a clubhouse was **rejected.**

_____

2. The actor needed to **project** his voice from the stage.

_____

3. The spy's car features an **ejection** seat.

_____

4. We were all **subjected** to the babysitter's harsh rules.

_____

5. He loved to **inject** humor into any situation.

_____

B. Directions: Write two sentences using boldfaced words from Exercise A.

6. _____

_____

7. _____

_____

from WOODSONG

from WOODSONG

Reading Check

Directions: Recall the characters and events in the selection. Then answer the questions in sentences or phrases.

1. Why do bears come to Paulsen's area?

_____

_____

2. Why does Paulsen say that naming a bear is a bad idea?

_____

_____

3. What provokes Paulsen to throw a stick at Scarhead?

_____

_____

4. How does Scarhead react when Paulsen throws the stick at him? Then what does Paulsen do?

_____

_____

5. Why does Paulsen decide not to shoot the bear? What causes him to change his mind?

_____

_____

from WOODSONG

Question Support

TEXT ANALYSIS

For questions 1–3, see page 123 of the Student Edition.

Directions: Answer the questions.

4. Make Inferences Reread lines 42–49. Then complete the following sentence.

The bears do not bother the yard animals because _____

_____

5. Analyze Author's Purpose Circle the word or phrase that names Paulsen's main purpose. Support your answer with an example from the memoir.

  a. Explain/Inform   **c.** Persuade

  b. Share Thoughts   **d.** Entertain

_____

_____

6. Examine Narrative Nonfiction Briefly describe one example of conflict from the memoir.

_____

_____

7. Synthesize Ideas Across Texts Reread lines 115–118. Then think about the article on page 122. Circle one word in parentheses and then complete the following sentence.

I (agree/disagree) with the idea that Paulsen loves nature because _____

_____

_____

_____

Resource Manager

from WOODSONG

Grammar in Context

MAINTAIN PRONOUN-ANTECEDENT AGREEMENT

A **pronoun** is a word that is used in place of a noun or another pronoun. The word that the pronoun refers to is its **antecedent**. Pronouns should always **agree in number** with their antecedents. *Anyone, nobody, no one,* and *somebody,* for example, are singular words that must be paired with singular pronouns.

Original: <u>Anyone</u> would have frozen in <u>their</u> tracks at the size of the bear.
Revised: <u>Anyone</u> would have frozen in <u>his</u> tracks at the size of the bear.

Directions: Rewrite each sentence to correct the pronoun-antecedent errors.

1. No one who sees a bear can keep their heart from pounding.

   _____

2. Anyone who thinks they don't need to respect bears is wrong.

   _____

3. Everyone should realize they are animals, too.

   _____

4. No one should think that they are better than any other creatures.

   _____

5. Everyone should watch their back when they are in the woods.

   _____

6. Nobody could ever convince me that they are right to disrespect animals.

   _____

from WOODSONG

Reading Fluency

LISTENING FOR PHRASING

When you read, you can increase your comprehension by grouping words into meaningful segments, or chunks. This technique is called **phrasing.** Look at how slash marks are used to indicate phrasing in this sentence:

A family of bears, / hungry after their winter sleep, / rummaged through our garbage, / eating whatever they could find.

Directions:

1. Listen to the first two paragraphs from *Woodsong* on the *Audio Anthology CD.* The words appear below. Then read along with the speaker as you listen again. Notice the speaker's phrasing.

2. Next, mark up the passage below to show how you would read these lines. Draw slash marks after punctuation marks and other places where you might pause to take a breath or to show emphasis.

3. Read the passage to a partner, paying attention to the marks you made.

4. Together, discuss ways to improve your phrasing.

We have bear trouble. Because we feed processed meat to the

dogs, there is always the smell of meat over the kennel. In the

summer it can be a bit high because the dogs like to "save" their

food sometimes for a day or two or four—burying it to dig up

later. We live on the edge of wilderness, and consequently the

meat smell brings any number of visitors from the woods.

Skunks abound, and foxes and coyotes and wolves and

weasels—all predators. We once had an eagle live over the kennel

for more than a week, scavenging from the dogs, and a group of

Excerpt from *Woodsong* by Gary Paulsen. Copyright © 1990 by Gary Paulsen. Reprinted by permission of Simon & Schuster Books for Young Readers, an imprint of Simon & Schuster's Children's Publishing Division.

Resource Manager

ravens has pretty much taken over the puppy pen. Ravens are

protected by the state and they seem to know it. When I walk

toward the puppy pen with the buckets of meat, it's a toss-up to

see who gets it—the pups or the birds. They have actually pecked

the puppies away from the food pans until they have gone through

and taken what they want. (175 words)

— Gary Paulsen, from *Woodsong*

Lesson at a Glance

THE HORSE SNAKE

Huynh Quang Nhuong

WHY THIS SELECTION?

This chapter from Huynh Quang Nhuong's memoir develops a suspenseful conflict and paints a vivid picture of life in a small Vietnamese village. His accessible style guarantees that students will enjoy learning about another culture.

ABOUT THIS SELECTION

Student/Teacher's Edition Pages: 126–137

Difficulty Level: Average

Readability Scores: Lexile: 1030; Fry: 8; Dale-Chall: 5.6

Summary "The Horse Snake," from Huynh Quang Nhuong's memoir, *The Land I Lost*, tells how Vietnamese villagers work together to capture a fearsome snake. After someone hears a snake in a field, the men of the village search for it. They discover a horse that the snake has squeezed to death. Finally, a farmer finds the snake cleverly emptying his fish pond so it can eat the fish. Men, women, and children cooperate to trap and kill the snake.

Engaging the Students This excerpt offers students an opportunity to explore the idea of teamwork. By working together the villagers have a chance to defeat the dangerous snake. Their success proves that teamwork can overcome many obstacles. As students read the memoir, they are able to see that teamwork goes beyond sports and can be used to solve real-life problems as well.

ⓘ Lesson resources are also available on the **Teacher One Stop DVD-ROM** and online at thinkcentral.com.

Lesson Plan and Resource Guide

The Horse Snake

Memoir by Huynh Quang Nhuong

Common Core Focus

RI 3 Analyze in detail how a key event is introduced, illustrated, and elaborated in a text. **RI 5** Analyze how a particular sentence, paragraph, or section fits into the structure and contributes to the development of ideas. **W 2** Write informative/explanatory texts to examine a topic. **L 1** Demonstrate command of the conventions of grammar. **L 4C** Consult dictionaries to find the pronunciation of a word or determine its precise meaning or part of speech. **L 5** Demonstrate understanding of nuances in word meanings.

Unless otherwise noted, resources can be found in the *Resource Manager.* **ⓘ** Lesson resources are also available on the **Teacher One Stop DVD-ROM** and online at **thinkcentral.com.** The Student Edition and selected copy masters are available electronically on the **Student One Stop DVD-ROM.**

Student/Teacher's Edition Pages	Additional Resources CM = Copy Master T = Transparency
Focus and Motivate	
☐ Big Question p. 126	
☐ Author Biography p. 127	☐ **ⓘ** Literature and Reading Center at **thinkcentral.com**
Teach	
☐ Setting in Nonfiction p. 127	
☐ Trace Chronological Order p. 127	☐ Trace Chronological Order CM—English p. 159, Spanish p. 160 **D**
☐ Vocabulary in Context p. 127	☐ Vocabulary Study CM p. 161 **D**

D = Resources for Differentiation

Student/Teacher's Edition Pages	Additional Resources CM = Copy Master T = Transparency
Practice and Apply: Guided Practice	
Selection and Teacher Notes	✎ **Audio Anthology CD** D
☐ "The Horse Snake," pp. 128–134	☐ Summary CM—English and Spanish p. 155, Haitian Creole and Vietnamese p. 156 D
	☐ Reading Fluency CM p. 167
	📦 **Best Practices Toolkit**
	☐ Setting Diagram p. D14 D
	☐ Setting Map p. B2 D
	☐ ⓘ Audio Summaries at **thinkcentral.com**
Practice and Apply: After Reading	
☐ Selection Questions p. 135	☐ Reading Check CM p. 165
	☐ Setting in Nonfiction CM—English p. 157 Spanish p. 158 D
	☐ Question Support CM p. 166 D
	☐ Additional Selection Questions p. 151 D
	☐ Ideas for Extension pp. 152–153 D
☐ Vocabulary Practice p. 136	☐ Vocabulary Practice CM p. 162
☐ Academic Vocabulary in Writing p. 136	☐ Academic Vocabulary CM p. 3
	☐ Additional Academic Vocabulary CM p. 4
☐ Vocabulary Strategy: Reading a Dictionary Entry p. 136	☐ Vocabulary Strategy CM p. 163
	☐ ⓘ *WordSharp* Interactive Vocabulary Tutor CD-ROM and online at **thinkcentral.com**
☐ Grammar in Context p. 137	📦 **Best Practices Toolkit**
☐ Writing Prompt p. 137	☐ Cluster Diagram p. B18
	☐ Create Compound Sentences CM p. 164
	☐ Grammar Handbook—Student Edition p. R52
	☐ ⓘ GrammarNotes DVD-ROM at **thinkcentral.com**
	☐ ⓘ Interactive Revision Lessons on **WriteSmart CD-ROM** and online at **thinkcentral.com**

D = Resources for Differentiation

Student/Teacher's Edition Pages	Additional Resources CM = Copy Master T = Transparency
Assess and Reteach	
Assess	☐ **Diagnostic and Selection Tests**
	☐ Selection Tests A, B/C pp. 47–48, 49–50 **D**
	☐ **ⓘ** ThinkCentral Online Assessment
	☐ ✎ ExamView Test Generator on the **Teacher One Stop** **DVD-ROM D**
Reteach	☐ **ⓘ** Level Up Online Tutorials on **thinkcentral.com**
☐ Trace Chronological Order	☐ **ⓘ** Reteaching Worksheets on **thinkcentral.com**
☐ Reading a Dictionary Entry	☐ Reading Lesson 6: Recognizing Sequence and Chronological Order
	☐ Vocabulary Lesson 25: Etymologies

D = Resources for Differentiation

Copyright © Holt McDougal, a division of Houghton Mifflin Harcourt

THE HORSE SNAKE

Additional Selection Questions

Differentiation Use these questions to provide customized practice with comprehension and critical thinking skills.

Easy

1. ***When is there strength in NUMBERS?***
How does teamwork enable the villagers to catch the snake? (*All of the villagers, including women and children, work together to trap and then kill the snake.*)

Average

2. ***When is there strength in NUMBERS?***
Do you think the villagers are used to working as a team? Explain. (*Yes. They are described as rushing to help Minh in line 121. Then the village chief quickly organizes an attack in line 122, suggesting that he has had to coordinate similar efforts before. The villagers work together, following directions efficiently and without question in lines 122–143.*)

3. **Analyze Setting in Nonfiction** In lines 150–152, the author writes, "We rejoiced that the danger was over. But we knew it would only be a matter of time until we would once again have to face our most dangerous natural enemy—the horse snake." What does Huynh's comment reveal about the setting and his life in the village? (*The villagers' lives were not easy. They often had obstacles to overcome. They lived with a daily threat of dangerous and deadly snakes.*)

4. **Trace Chronological Order** Imagine that the selection had begun with the villagers catching and defeating the snake. How would the effect be different? (*Much of the suspense was built up by not knowing the outcome until the end of the selection. Therefore, the suspense would have decreased. Also, the importance of the cooperation among villagers might have been minimized.*)

Challenging

5. ***When is there strength in NUMBERS?***
What lesson does the author's experience teach about teamwork? (*People working together can solve problems that individuals might not be able to. There can be power in numbers.*)

6. **Evaluate Setting in Nonfiction** Does your knowledge that the events, setting, and participants are real affect your reaction to the tale? Explain. (*Yes. The reality of the events makes them more fascinating and suspenseful to read about. Also, real people performed great acts of courage, which shows what people are capable of doing. The fact that these people often face danger increases feelings of admiration for them and understanding of the culture in which the author lived.*)

7. **Trace Chronological Order** Lines 1–9 are not a part of the chronology of events. Why does the author choose to include these details before the major conflict is introduced? (*In order to appreciate the seriousness of the events, readers must understand the qualities of the horse snake.*)

Resource Manager

Ideas for Extension

Differentiation These activities provide students with a variety of options for demonstrating understanding of lesson concepts.

EXPLORATIONS AND ACTIVITIES

BOOK POSTER: ANALYZE NARRATIVE NONFICTION

Have students skim "The Horse Snake," jotting down several (four to eight) significant quotations. These quotations might help to tell the story, reveal important themes, or develop understanding of the setting or the people involved.

Then have students divide a large poster into several sections. In each section, ask them to write one of the quotations and then illustrate it with original art, pictures from magazines or newspapers, or computer graphics.

Have students present their posters to the class, explaining their choice of quotations and illustrations.

COLLAGE: EXPLORE KEY CONCEPT

Discuss examples of teamwork that are present in aspects of daily life.

Then have students work in pairs to create a collage of real-life examples. Students should gather their materials from magazines, newspapers, ads, or other print sources. Students may also choose to include original text. Encourage students to design their collages to reinforce a message about the importance of teamwork in life.

Have pairs present their collages to the class. Talk about the similarities and differences among the examples and the lessons that they communicate.

STORYTELLING: EXPLORE GENRE

Point out to students that Huynh's memoir reveals some important insights about his culture and his village in addition to narrating an experience from his own life. Discuss how readers can learn a great deal about other cultures from memoirs.

Ask students to brainstorm incidents from their own lives that might form the basis of a good story while also revealing something about the community or environment in which they live. For example, students might tell about a family tradition, a cultural or community celebration, or an interesting place in their community.

Have each student create a storyboard for his or her memoir. Encourage students to share their storyboards with the rest of the class.

Pre-AP Challenge: Have students use their storyboards to write a draft of their own memoir or personal narrative. Invite students to share their stories with the rest of the class. Then ask students to reflect on the process of writing a memoir and sharing it with others in the form of a journal entry.

IDEAS FOR EXTENSION, CONTINUED

INQUIRY AND RESEARCH

SNAKES

Divide the class into small groups. Assign each group a different type of snake to research: cobras, pit vipers, garter snakes, racer snakes, king snakes, boas, or pythons.

Ask students to write informational articles that explain important facts about their snakes. Encourage students to organize their articles with headings and to include illustrations with captions. Have groups present their articles to the class. Then combine the articles into one volume to be displayed in the classroom.

WRITING

ANALYZE KEY IDEA: ORIGINAL POEM

Ask students to write an acrostic poem for the word *teamwork*. Remind students that this type of poem uses the letters in the key word to start each line. In this case, the first line will start with *T*, the second with *E*, and so on.

Have students use a cluster chart or other organizer to collect their thoughts and ideas about the concept before they begin to write. Encourage them to incorporate insights that they have gained from their reading.

EXPLORE VIEWPOINT: SPEECH

Draw students' attention to lines 121–122. Ask them to imagine what the village chief might have said as he organized the villagers to fight the snake. Have students write his speech. Have them base their ideas upon the content of the passage and include an inspirational and motivating introduction. Suggest that students outline what they wish to say in their speech before they begin to write.

EXAMINE GENRE: LETTER

Have students reflect on their reactions to Huynh's memoir. Ask them to write a personal letter to the author expressing these feelings, asking questions, or discussing what they found most interesting.

Resource Manager

THE HORSE SNAKE

Teacher Notes

Review and Evaluate Outcome

What did I want students to know or be able to do?

How successful was the lesson?

Evaluate Process

- Resources

- Strategies

What worked?

- Differentiation

What did not work? Why not?

Reflect

The next time I teach "The Horse Snake," what will I do differently? Why?

Plan Ahead

What must I do next?

THE HORSE SNAKE

Summary

THE HORSE SNAKE

Huynh Quang Nhuong
Setting: a jungle village in Vietnam, mid-twentieth century

One night, a friend of the narrator's family frantically bangs on the door. He explains that while on his way home from a wedding he heard the hiss of a horse snake. The horse snake is the most dangerous animal in the jungle. The family sends a warning to the villagers. The next day, the men of the village go hunting for the snake. That night, the women stay up to listen for the snake. The narrator's grandmother tells a story about a father and son who conquer a snake. The children are relieved to hear that a snake can be defeated. The next day, a farmer named Minh calls for help because a horse snake is attacking his fishpond. Everyone in the village rushes to fight the dangerous beast.

LA SERPIENTE CABALLO

Huynh Quang Nhuong
Escenario: una aldea en la selva de Vietnam a mediados del siglo XX

Una noche, un amigo de la familia del narrador golpea la puerta con desesperación. Explica que cuando regresaba a su casa después de una boda, escuchó el siseo de una serpiente caballo. La serpiente caballo es el animal más peligroso de la selva. La familia envía una advertencia a los demás aldeanos. Al día siguiente, los hombres de la aldea salen a cazar la serpiente. Esa noche, las mujeres permanecen despiertas por si escuchan a la serpiente. La abuela del narrador relata un cuento sobre un hombre y su hijo quienes vencen a una serpiente. Los niños sienten alivio al escuchar que se puede derrotar a una serpiente. Al día siguiente, un granjero llamado Minh pide ayuda porque una serpiente caballo está atacando su estanque de peces. Todos en la aldea se apresuran a combatir la peligrosa bestia.

Summary

KOULÈV CHEVAL

Huynh Quang Nhuong

Espas ak tan: yon vilaj jeng, nan mwatye ventyèm syèk la

Yon lannwit, yon zanmi fanmi naratè a frape nan pòt la avèk dezespwa. Li eksplike pandan li sou wout li pou li sòti nan yon maryaj pou li ale lakay li, li tande yon koulèv fè-a-cheval k ap sifle. Koulèv fè-a-cheval se bèt ki pi danjere nan jeng lan. Fanmi an voye yon avètisman pou tout moun ki nan vilaj la. Nan jòu apre a, gason vilaj yo ale lachas pou kenbe koulèv la. Jou swa sa a, tout fi yo al kouche ta pou yo te ka tande koulèv la. Grann naratè a rakonte yon istwa sou yon papa ak pitit gason l ki kenbe yon koulèv. Timoun yo soulaje lè yo tande yo ka touye yon koulèv. Nan lòt jou apre a, yon kiltivatè ki rele Minh mande sekou paske yon koulèv fè-a-cheval atake letan pwason li. Tout moun nan vilaj la kouri al goumen ak bèt danjere a.

CON RẮN NGỰA

Huynh Quang Nhượng

Bối cảnh: một ngôi làng trong rừng ở Việt Nam, giữa thế kỷ 20

Một đêm, một người bạn của gia đình người kể chuyện điên cuồng đập mạnh vào cửa. Ông ta giải thích rằng trên đường đi đám cưới về nhà ông nghe tiếng rít của một con rắn ngựa. Rắn ngựa là con vật nguy hiểm nhất trong rừng. Gia đình người kể chuyện cảnh báo bà con dân làng. Hôm sau, những người đàn ông trong làng đi săn lùng con rắn. Đêm đó, đàn bà thức cạnh nghe ngóng về con rắn. Bà của người kể chuyện kể về hai cha con nọ bắt được một con rắn. Trẻ con trong làng cảm thấy nhẹ nhõm khi biết rằng người ta có thể đánh được con rắn. Hôm sau, một bác nông dân tên Minh kêu cứu vì bị một con rắn ngựa tấn công ao cá của bác. Mọi người trong làng đổ xô đến bắt con ác thú nguy hiểm đó.

Name _____

Date _____

THE HORSE SNAKE

Text Analysis

SETTING IN NONFICTION

A **memoir** is about real events in the author's life. The **setting** in a memoir is like the setting in fiction. It includes details of time and place that help a reader picture the scene.

Directions: In the chart, record details from the memoir that describe the locations, times during the day, and surroundings. Then circle the details that seem most vivid to you.

Details About Setting

Location	Times	Surroundings

LA SERPIENTE CABALLO

Text Analysis

SETTING IN NONFICTION

Las **memorias** se ocupan de sucesos reales de la vida del autor. El **escenario** en unas memorias es como el escenario en la ficción. Incluye detalles del tiempo y el lugar que ayudan al lector a visualizar la escena.

Instrucciones: Anota en la tabla detalles de las memorias que describan los lugares, las horas del día y los alrededores. Luego, encierra en un círculo los detalles que te parezcan más vívidos.

Detalles del escenario

Lugar	Horas del día	Alrededores

Name _____ Date _____

THE HORSE SNAKE

Reading Skill

TRACE CHRONOLOGICAL ORDER

Writers of narrative nonfiction often present events in the same order in which they happened in real life. This is called **chronological order** or time order. To recognize time order, look for clue words that tell when events took place, such as *a few seconds, later* or *the next day.*

Directions: As you read "The Horse Snake," use this timeline to keep track of the order in which the events happened. The first event has been provided for you.

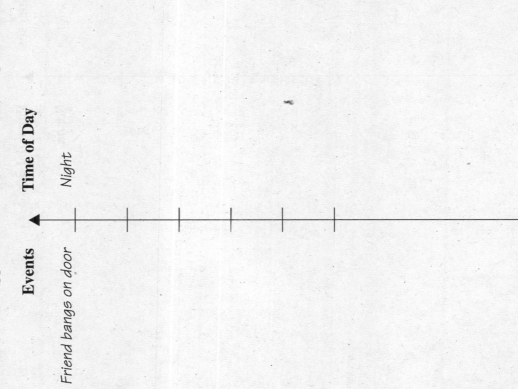

Time of Day

Night

Events

Friend bangs on door

Resource Manager

Reading Skill

TRACE CHRONOLOGICAL ORDER

Los escritores de narrativa informativa a menudo presentan sucesos en el mismo orden en el que ocurrieron en la vida real. Esto se llama **orden cronológico**. Para identificar el orden cronológico, busca palabras clave que indiquen cuándo tuvieron lugar los sucesos, como *algunos segundos después* o *al día siguiente*.

Instrucciones: Mientras lees "La serpiente caballo" usa esta línea cronológica para seguir el orden en el que ocurrieron los sucesos. Te damos el primer suceso.

Sucesos	Parte del día
Un amigo golpea la puerta	Noche

Vocabulary Study

SELF-ASSESSMENT OF WORD MEANING

A. Directions: As your teacher reads each set of sentences, listen for the boldfaced word and clues to its possible meaning.

1. The men prepared to **assume** defensive positions around the snake. They held their knives ready.

2. After he heard the snake in the field, the man walked with a fast **gait** to the nearest house.

3. The jungle was never silent, even at night. The movements and cries of **nocturnal** creatures provided a constant background of noise.

4. The sight of the snake swinging from the tree was frightening enough to **petrify** the group of villagers. For a long minute, they felt frozen with fear.

5. To avoid alarming the snake, the men moved **stealthily** on tiptoe through the long grass.

6. The venom of the snake was powerful. The man knew he would **succumb** in minutes if he were bitten.

B. Directions: To determine how well you understand each vocabulary word, fill in the chart. As you read the selection, revise your definitions as needed.

Vocabulary Word	New	Seen Before	Can Use in a Sentence	Possible Meanings
1. assume				
2. gait				
3. nocturnal				
4. petrify				
5. stealthily				
6. succumb				

Vocabulary Practice

| assume | gait | nocturnal | petrify | stealthily | succumb |

A. Directions: Fill in each blank with the correct word from the box.

1. Never _____ that an unfamiliar snake is harmless.

2. At the same time, snakes should never _____ you unnecessarily.

3. If you _____ to fear, you will never learn to respect these animals.

4. While a horse has a steady _____, a snake slithers because it has no feet.

5. Making no noise at all, they can creep up on you _____

6. Some snakes, like bats, are _____

B. Directions: Write the word from the box that means the same or nearly the same thing as each of the following words.

7. frighten _____

8. surrender _____

9. nighttime _____

10. sneakily _____

11. pace _____

12. suppose _____

Name _____ Date _____

Vocabulary Strategy

READING A DICTIONARY ENTRY

One important part of a word entry in a dictionary is the **etymology**, or information about a word's origin. Etymologies can help you understand the meaning of unfamiliar words. The etymology is found at the end of an entry and is enclosed in brackets.

A. Directions: Use a dictionary to find the etymology of each word in the chart. Record the word's original language and original meaning.

Word	Original Language	Original Meaning
1. corset		
2. idiom		
3. jungle		
4. sloop		
5. zebra		

B. Directions: Use each word listed in the chart in a sentence.

6. _____

7. _____

8. _____

9. _____

10. _____

Resource Manager

Grammar in Context

CREATE COMPOUND SENTENCES

A run-on sentence is two or more sentences written as one. You can change a run-on sentence to a **compound sentence** by using a comma and a coordinating conjunction (such as and, but, or, for, or so) to separate the two sentences.

Original: The snake had not struck again, the farmers returned to their fields.

Revised: The snake had not struck again, so the farmers returned to their fields.

Directions: Rewrite the following sentences. Use a comma and a coordinating conjunction to create a compound sentence.

1. One night a frightened villager banged on our door, he asked us to let him in.

   _____

2. I stayed up that night, I listened to all the sounds outside.

   _____

3. The snake usually eats chickens and monkeys, sometimes it attacks people and cattle.

   _____

4. The animal might have been killed by a horse snake, it could have been a king python.

   _____

5. The villagers caught and killed the snake, we could rest easy.

   _____

Name _____ Date _____

COPY MASTER

THE HORSE SNAKE

Reading Check

Directions: Recall the events in Huynh Quang Nhuong's memoir. Then answer the questions in phrases or sentences.

1. How does the horse snake get its name?

_____

_____

2. Why does the narrator's cousin blow the buffalo horn?

_____

_____

3. Why does the grandmother's story make the narrator more cheerful?

_____

_____

4. How does the horse snake try to steal from Minh?

_____

_____

5. How does the whole village take part in killing the snake?

_____

_____

Resource Manager

Question Support

TEXT ANALYSIS

For questions 1–3, see page 135 of the Student Edition.

Directions: Answer the questions.

4. **Understand Chronological Order** Match each event to the time at which it happened.

_____ first night

_____ early morning of second day

_____ second night

_____ morning of third day

_____ afternoon of third day

   a. men divide up and search for snake

   b. Minh calls for help

   c. a friend bangs on door

   d. Grandmother tells a story

   e. farmers return to their fields

5. **Make Inferences** Reread lines 121–149. Then complete the following sentence.

During the battle with the horse snake, I think Huynh was probably _____

6. **Analyze Imagery** Complete the following graphic organizer with images from "The Horse Snake."

Image	Sense

7. **Examine Setting** Complete the following sentence.

The story of the snake in Huynh's memoir could not have taken place in a cold climate because _____

8. **Draw Conclusions** Complete the following sentence.

Teamwork was important to the community because _____

Name _____ Date _____

THE HORSE SNAKE

Reading Fluency

ORAL RECITATION

When you read a story aloud, speak loudly, clearly, and with expression. Use these symbols to plan how to read a story aloud:

L = louder	↑ = raise pitch	/ = pause or stop
S = softer	↓ = lower pitch	underscore = add stress

Directions: Listen as your teacher reads this article about snakes. Use the marks above to plan how you would read the passage. Then read it to your partner.

There are over 100 species of snakes in Vietnam. While some species are harmless, others can be dangerous and even deadly. Several of the 30 or more venomous species can be classified as pit vipers or cobras.

Pit vipers get their name from two deep, heat sensing "pits" located between the snake's eyes and nostrils. These pits help the snake locate its warm-blooded prey. When a pit viper bites, venom flows from glands above its jaw into two fangs at the back of its mouth. These fangs swing down to inject the venom into the victim. Enzymes in the venom start to destroy the victim's body tissue and blood vessels. They can also cause the blood to thicken. This change in blood pressure can lead to death.

Cobras belong to an ancient family of snakes called *Elapids.* The cobra's most outstanding feature is its hood, the flap of skin that surrounds its head. A cobra flares its hood as a warning when it feels threatened. To find and capture its prey, the cobra relies on its forked tongue, excellent vision, and sensitivity to motion. A cobra has two short, hollow fangs at the front of its mouth. Venom flows through these fangs to attack the victim's motor nervous system. As poison spreads to the organs, muscles and glands, the victim experiences breathing problems or even a heart attack. (228 words)

Lesson at a Glance

Reading for Information | Le Mat Village Holds On to Snake Catching Tradition

WHY THIS SELECTION?

This radio transcript exposes students to facts about a Vietnamese village that prides itself on its tradition of catching snakes. The transcript develops their understanding of the characteristics of this type of writing.

ABOUT THIS SELECTION

Student/Teacher's Edition Pages: 138–141
Difficulty Level: Average
Readability Scores: Lexile: 1030; Fry: 8; Dale-Chall: 5.6

Summary This radio transcript describes the village of Le Mat in modern Vietnam, which is famous for its tradition of catching snakes. In Le Mat, villagers actually learn how to catch snakes. According to an 11th century legend, a giant snake had killed the king's daughter. A Le Mat villager found and killed the snake, and then brought it and the princess's body to the king. In return, the king granted the villagers a swampy area that they turned into a prosperous land. The rest of the villagers learned how to catch snakes and passed along the tradition.

COMMON CORE STANDARDS FOCUS

- Author's Purpose
- Compare Authors' Purposes

LESSON RESOURCES

Plan and Teach

Student Copy Masters

ⓘ Lesson resources are also available on the **Teacher One Stop DVD-ROM** and online at <ins>thinkcentral.com</ins>.

Resource Manager

Lesson Plan and Resource Guide

Le Mat Village Holds On to Snake Catching Tradition

Radio Transcript

Common Core Focus

RI 3 Analyze in detail how a key idea is introduced, illustrated, and elaborated in a text. **RI 6** Determine an author's purpose and explain how it is conveyed in the text. **W 2** Write informative/explanatory texts to examine a topic.

Unless otherwise noted, resources can be found in the *Resource Manager:* ❶ Lesson resources are also available on the **Teacher One Stop DVD-ROM** and online at **thinkcentral.com.** The Student Edition and selected copymasters are available electronically on the 💿 **Student One Stop DVD-ROM.**

Student/Teacher's Edition Pages	Additional Resources CM = Copy Master T = Transparency
Focus and Motivate	
☐ What's the Connection? p. 138	☐ 🧰 **Best Practices Toolkit** ☐ Connecting p. A8 [T]
Teach	
☐ Author's Purpose p. 138	☐ Author's Purpose CM—p. 177, Spanish p. 179 ❶
Practice and Apply: Guided Practice	
Selection and Teacher Notes	
☐ "Le Mat Village Holds On to Snake Catching Tradition," pp. 139–140	☐ 💿 **Audio Anthology CD** ❶ ☐ Summary CM—English and Spanish p. 175, Haitian Creole and Vietnamese p. 176 ❶ ☐ ❶ Audio Summaries at **thinkcentral.com**

❶ = Resources for Differentiation

Student/Teacher's Edition Pages	Additional Resources CM = Copy Master T = Transparency
Practice and Apply: After Reading	
☐ Selection Questions p. 141	☐ Reading Check CM p. 181
	☐ Question Support CM p. 182 Ⓓ
	☐ Additional Selection Questions p. 172 Ⓓ
	☐ Author's Purpose CM—p. 177, Spanish p. 179 Ⓓ
☐ Read for Information: Compare Authors' Purposes p. 141	☐ Compare Authors' Purposes CM—p. 178, Spanish p. 180 Ⓓ
Assess and Reteach	
Assess	☐ **Diagnostic and Selection Tests**
	☐ Selection Tests A, B/C pp. 51–52, 53–54 Ⓓ
	☐ ⓘ ThinkCentral Online Assessment
	☐ ✏ ExamView Test Generator on the **Teacher One Stop**
	DVD-ROM
Reteach	☐ **Level Up Online Tutorials on thinkcentral.com**
☐ Author's Purpose	**Reteaching Worksheets on thinkcentral.com**
☐ Compare Authors' Purposes	☐ Reading Lesson 3: Determining Author's Purpose
	☐ Reading Lesson 12: Comparing and Contrasting

Ⓓ = Resources for Differentiation

Resource Manager

Additional Selection Questions

Differentiation Use these questions to provide customized practice with comprehension and critical thinking skills.

Use to supplement the questions on SE page 141.

Easy

1. **Recall** What is the village of Le Mat famous for? (*Le Mat is famous for its tradition of snake catching.*)

2. **Recall** Where does the tradition come from? (*According to legend, the tradition dates back to the 11th century, when a villager killed a snake that had killed the king's daughter.*)

Average

3. **Analyze Radio Transcript** What does a radio transcript allow the reader to do that the listener might have difficulty doing? (*It allows the reader to reread passages to increase understanding.*)

4. **Analyze Author's Purpose** Describe the main idea expressed in the radio transcript. (*Le Mat villagers love their snake catching tradition and continue to practice it.*)

5. **Draw Conclusions** Based on this transcript, what conclusion can you draw about the villagers' familiarity with nature? (*The residents of Le Mat know the various snake species and their characteristics, so they are probably fairly knowledgeable about nature in general.*)

Challenging

6. **Compare Authors' Purposes** What is the purpose of this radio transcript? In what way is the purpose different from that of an article that describes the dangers of encountering snakes in the wild? (*The purpose of the transcript is to inform the reader about a Vietnamese village's proud tradition of catching snakes and how it represents the village's history of dealing with threats. It doesn't include many details about which snakes are dangerous and which ones aren't, and it doesn't explain how to avoid dangerous snake encounters in the wild, which the article probably would include.*)

7. **Evaluate Radio Transcript** Sound effects can help engage a listener with a radio broadcast by making subject seem more real to the listener. How might a radio transcript attempt to achieve a similar effect? (*Photographs or other images used to illustrate the subject of the transcript can help make it seem more real for the reader.*)

LE MAT VILLAGE HOLDS ON TO SNAKE CATCHING TRADITION

Teacher Notes

Review and Evaluate Outcome

What did I want students to know or be able to do?

How successful was the lesson?

Evaluate Process

What worked?
- Strategies

- Resources

- Differentiation

What did not work? Why not?

Reflect

The next time I teach "Le Mat Village Holds On to Snake Catching Tradition," what will I do differently? Why?

Plan Ahead

What must I do next?

LE MAT VILLAGE HOLDS ON TO SNAKE CATCHING TRADITION

Summary

LE MAT VILLAGE HOLDS ON TO SNAKE CATCHING TRADITION
Radio Transcript

This radio transcript describes a modern Vietnamese village that prides itself on its tradition of catching snakes. The transcript tells of the village of Le Mat, near Hanoi, the Vietnamese capital, where the activity of catching snakes dates back to the 11th century. A legend says that a giant snake had carried the king's daughter away. The king offered a reward to whomever found his daughter's body. A villager, Trung, found the body but refused the reward in exchange for the villagers' right to settle in a new area. But first the villagers had to clear the new area of poisonous snakes. The transcript states that modern-day villagers remain very knowledgeable about snakes and continue to practice the skill of snake catching.

LE MAT VILLAGE HOLDS ON TO SNAKE CATCHING TRADITION
Transcripción radial

Esta transcripción radial describe una aldea moderna de Vietnam que se enorgullece por su tradición de cazar serpientes. La transcripción narra acerca de la aldea de Le Mat, cerca de Hanoi, la capital de Vietnam, donde la actividad de cazar serpientes se remonta al siglo XI. Una leyenda cuenta que una serpiente gigante se había llevado a la hija del rey. El rey ofreció un premio para el que encontrara el cuerpo de su hija. Un aldeano, Trung, encontró el cuerpo pero se rehusó a recibir el premio a cambio del derecho de los aldeanos de asentarse en una nueva área. Pero primero los aldeanos tuvieron que limpiar el área de serpientes venenosas. La transcripción dice que los aldeanos actuales son aún muy conocedores de las serpientes y continúan practicando la habilidad de cazar serpientes.

Summary

VILAJ LE MAT TOUJOU GENYEN TRADISYON POU KENBE KOULÈV

Transkripsyon Radyo

Transkripsyon radyo sa a dekri yon vilaj vyetnamyen jodi a ki fyè pou tradisyon yo genyen pou kenbe koulèv. Transkripsyon an bay temwayaj sou vilaj Le Mat, yon vilaj ki toupre Hanoi, kapital peyi Vyetnam, kote y ap mennen aktivite kenbe koulèv depi 11 yèm syèk. Dapre yon lejann, te genyen yon gwo koulèv ki te ale avèk pitit fi wa a. Wa a te ofri yon rekonpans pou nenpòt moun ki te jwenn kò pitit fi li a. Yon moun nan vilaj la, ki rele Trung, te jwenn kò a men alaplas rekonpans lan li te mande pou moun nan vilaj la te jwenn dwa pou yo al abite nan yon lòt zòn. Men, toudabò fòk moun nan vilaj la te elimine koulèv venime (ki gen pwazon) ki nan nouvo zòn lan. Transkripsyon an endike moun k ap viv nan vilaj la nan tan modèn yo toujou genyen ampil konesans sou koulèv epitou yo kontinye ap pratike ladrès pou kenbe koulèv.

LÀNG LỆ MẬT GIỮ VỮNG TRUYỀN THỐNG BẮT RẮN

Ghi Chép từ Radio

Bài viết từ radio này miêu tả một làng Việt Nam đương đại tự hào với truyền thống bắt rắn. Bài kể về làng Lệ Mật, gần Hà Nội, thủ đô của Việt Nam, nơi mà hoạt động bắt rắn có từ thế kỷ thứ 11. Một truyền thuyết kể rằng một con rắn khổng lồ đã bắt cóc chúa đi. Vua treo giải thưởng cho bất cứ ai tìm được xác công chúa. Một người dân làng tên Trung tìm được xác nhưng từ chối giải thưởng để đổi lấy việc dân làng được quyền định cư ở một vùng mới. Nhưng trước tiên dân làng phải diệt sạch các loại rắn độc khỏi vùng mới. Bài viết nói rằng người dân làng thời nay vẫn rất hiểu biết về rắn và tiếp tục thực tập các kỹ năng bắt rắn.

Skill Focus

ANALYZING AN AUTHOR'S PURPOSE

Most authors will not come right out and state their purpose for writing. They will suggest their purpose through the information they present. To determine an author's purpose, ask yourself three things:

- For what reason is the author telling me *this?*
- Why is the author telling me this *in this way?*
- What *point* do the author's ideas make?

Directions: Use the chart below to discover the author's purpose in the radio transcript. As you read, list the important details the author shares about snake hunting. Then, state the main idea of the text. (Hint: the main idea may be in the title or in the final paragraph.) Finally, decide the author's purpose.

"Le Mat Village Holds On to Snake Catching Tradition"
Detail 1:
Detail 2:
Detail 3:
Main Idea:
Author's Purpose:

Read for Information

COMPARE AUTHORS' PURPOSES

Directions: Complete the chart below with details from each selection. Try to choose examples that show both similarities and differences between the texts. Then, identify the main ideas and determine the writer's purpose for each. You may use the chart you created earlier for "Le Mat Village . . ." to help you complete this one.

Selection	Details	Main Idea	Author's Purpose
"Le Mat Village Holds On to Snake Catching Tradition"			
"The Horse Snake"			

In a sentence or two, describe the differences between the two authors' purposes:

_____

_____

_____

LE MAT VILLAGE HOLDS ON TO SNAKE CATCHING TRADITION

COPY MASTER

Skill Focus

ANALYZING AN AUTHOR'S PURPOSE

La mayoría de los autores no establecen expresamente su propósito para escribir. Sugieren su propósito por medio de la información que presentan. Para determinar el propósito de un autor, pregúntate tres cosas:

- ¿Cuál es el motivo de que el autor me diga esto?
- ¿Por qué me dice el autor esto de esta manera?
- ¿Cuál es el punto que establece el autor con sus ideas?

Instrucciones: Usa la siguiente tabla para descubrir el propósito del autor en la transcripción de radio. Mientras lees, lista los detalles importantes que el autor comparte acerca de la caza de serpientes. (Pista: la idea principal puede estar en el título o en el último párrafo). Finalmente, decide cuál es el propósito del autor.

"Le Mat Village Holds On to Snake Catching Tradition"		
Detalle 1:	Detalle 2:	Detalle 3:
Idea principal:		
Propósito del autor:		

Resource Manager

Read for Information

COMPARE AUTHORS' PURPOSES

Instrucciones: Completa la tabla siguiente con los detalles de cada selección. Intenta elegir ejemplos que muestren tanto las similitudes como las diferencias que hay entre los textos. Luego, identifica las ideas principales y determina el propósito que tiene el autor con el uso de cada uno de ellos. Puedes usar la tabla que hiciste antes para "Le Mat Village . . ." para ayudarte a completar ésta.

Selección	Detalles	Idea principal	Propósito del autor
"The Horse Snake"			
"Le Mat Village Holds On to Snake Catching Tradition"			

En una o dos oraciones describe las diferencias que hay entre los propósitos de los dos autores:

_____

_____

_____

LE MAT VILLAGE HOLDS ON TO SNAKE CATCHING TRADITION

COPY MASTER

Reading Check

Directions: Recall the information in the radio transcript. Then answer the questions in phrases or sentences.

1. Where is Le Mat located?

_____

_____

2. Do all the villagers make their livings catching snakes?

_____

_____

3. When did the tradition of snake catching in Le Mat begin?

_____

_____

4. According to legend, what did Trung's people gain from his success against the snake?

_____

_____

5. What title did Trung receive because of his skill?

_____

_____

Resource Manager

LE MAT VILLAGE HOLDS ON TO SNAKE CATCHING TRADITION

Question Support

TEXT ANALYSIS

For questions 1–2, see page 141 of the Student Edition.

Directions: Answer the questions.

3. Draw Conclusions What do the modern Le Mat villagers have in common with Trung?

_____

_____

_____

_____

4. Analyze Author's Purpose If the author's purpose is to explain the importance of snake catching in Le Mat, give one detail from the transcript to support this idea.

_____

_____

_____

_____

_____

_____

Lesson at a Glance

The Walrus and the Carpenter
Lewis Carroll

WHY THIS SELECTION?

This poem, from Lewis Carroll's *Through the Looking Glass*, is a classic narrative poem that will be enjoyed by students and teachers alike.

ABOUT THIS SELECTION

Student/Teacher's Edition Pages: 142–149

Difficulty Level: Challenging

Summary In this narrative poem, the Walrus and the Carpenter invite the Oysters to go for a walk along the beach. The oldest and wisest Oyster turns down the offer, but many younger ones eagerly comply. About a mile away from the oyster bed, the Walrus and the Carpenter tell the Oysters it is time to chat. Instead, they take this opportunity to ready their bread and butter in preparation for their feast. Then they eat every last oyster.

Engaging the Students This poem offers students an opportunity to explore the key idea of a trick. The Walrus and the Carpenter trick the Oysters in order to satisfy their own hunger. As students read the poem, they should think about the motives behind tricks and the possible consequences.

COMMON CORE STANDARDS FOCUS

- Narrative Poetry
- Visualize

LESSON RESOURCES

Plan and Teach

Student Copy Masters

ℹ Lesson resources are also available on the **Teacher One Stop DVD-ROM** and online at **thinkcentral.com**.

Lesson Plan and Resource Guide

The Walrus and the Carpenter

Narrative Poem by Lewis Carroll

Common Core Focus

RL 5 Analyze how a particular stanza fits into the structure of a text and contributes to the development of the setting or plot. **SL 1c** Pose and respond to specific questions with elaboration and detail.

Unless otherwise noted, resources can be found in the *Resource Manager.* ❶ Lesson resources are also available on the **Teacher One Stop DVD-ROM** and online at **thinkcentral.com**. The Student Edition and selected copy masters are available electronically on the ✎ **Student One Stop DVD-ROM**.

Student/Teacher's Edition Pages	Additional Resources CM = Copy Master T = Transparency
Focus and Motivate	
☐ Big Question p. 142	
☐ Author Biography p. 143	☐ ❶ Literature and Reading Center at **thinkcentral.com**
Teach	
☐ Narrative Poetry p. 143	☐ Narrative Poetry CM—English p. 191, Spanish p. 192 ᴅ
☐ Visualize p. 143	

ᴅ = Resources for Differentiation

Student/Teacher's Edition Pages	Additional Resources CM = Copy Master T = Transparency
Practice and Apply: Guided Practice	
Selection and Teacher Notes	☐ ✎ **Audio Anthology CD** Ⓓ
☐ "The Walrus and the Carpenter," pp. 144–148	☐ Reading Fluency CM p. 196
	☐ **Best Practices Toolkit**
	☐ Two-Column Chart p. A25 [T] Ⓓ
	☐ Making Inferences p. A13 [T] Ⓓ
	☐ Jigsaw Reading p. A1 Ⓓ
Practice and Apply: After Reading	
☐ Selection Questions p. 149	☐ Visualize CM—English p. 193, Spanish p. 194 Ⓓ
	☐ Question Support CM p. 195 Ⓓ
	☐ Additional Selection Questions p. 200 Ⓓ
	☐ Ideas for Extension pp. 201–202 Ⓓ
Assess and Reteach	
Assess	☐ **Diagnostic and Selection Tests**
	☐ Selection Tests A, B/C pp. 55–56, 57–58 Ⓓ
	☐ ❶ ThinkCentral Online Assessment
	☐ ✎ ExamView Test Generator on the **Teacher One Stop**
	DVD-ROM
Reteach	☐ ❶ Level Up Online Tutorials on **thinkcentral.com**
☐ Narrative Poetry	☐ ❶ Reteaching Worksheets on **thinkcentral.com**
	☐ Literature Lesson 16: Narrative vs. Lyric Poetry

Ⓓ = Resources for Differentiation

Resource Manager

Additional Selection Questions

Differentiation Use these questions to provide customized practice with comprehension and critical thinking skills.

Easy

1. **Have you ever been FOOLED?** Are the Walrus and the Carpenter good at playing tricks? Explain. (*Yes. They are able to deceive the young Oysters quite easily.*)

2. **Define Narrative Poetry** What is the purpose of a narrative poem? (*to tell a story*)

3. **Recall** How many Oysters did the Walrus originally invite on the walk? Why? (*He originally invited four. He could hold the hands of two and so could the Carpenter.*)

Average

4. **Analyze Narrative Poetry** How does the setting influence the plot of the poem? (*The setting is a beach, a natural location for the characters of the poem, namely the Oysters and the Walrus, who perform the action.*)

5. **Visualize** Reread lines 49–54. What words in this stanza help you to build a mental image? What picture do you see? (*Students may say that "thick and fast" in line 51, "hopping through the frothy waves" in line 53, and "scrambling" in line 54 create a vivid image of the large number of oysters hurrying to go for a walk with the Walrus and the Carpenter.*)

Challenging

6. **Have you ever been FOOLED?** Why doesn't the eldest Oyster warn the young ones about the trick? (*Perhaps he thinks that the young Oysters deserve their fate if they are foolish enough to be taken in by the Walrus and the Carpenter. Or, perhaps he thinks that they would not heed his warning anyway.*)

7. **Make Inferences** Do you think the Walrus or the Carpenter is the leader? Explain. (*Students may say that since the Walrus is the one who convinces the Oysters and does most of the talking throughout the poem, he is the leader of the two. The Carpenter mainly comments on the distribution of the food.*)

8. **Evaluate Narrative Poetry** How does the rhyme contribute to the mood of the poem? (*The rhyme makes the mood lighthearted and fun.*)

9. **Visualize** Does the illustration on page 145 match your mental image of the Walrus and the Carpenter? Why or why not? (*There are no physical characteristics of the characters provided in the poem. But students may say that they think both characters would look like those in the illustration based on their personality traits.*)

THE WALRUS AND THE CARPENTER

Ideas for Extension

Differentiation These activities provide students with a variety of options for demonstrating understanding of lesson concepts.

EXPLORATIONS AND ACTIVITIES

DIALOGUE: ANALYZE CHARACTER

Have students review the conversations that the Walrus and the Carpenter have with each other and with other characters. Encourage students to note the manner in which they speak and the kinds of words they use.

Then have pairs of students outline a short dialogue describing what the Walrus and the Carpenter might have said after their oyster feast.

Have students rehearse their dialogues and perform them for the class. Then have audience members vote on which dialogue most closely reflects the personalities of the two characters.

CREATE ILLUSTRATIONS: INTERPRET POEM

Have students work in pairs to create a series of illustrations for two or three additional parts of the poem. Students may wish to depict original interpretations of the characters or retain elements of John Tenniel's illustration.

Have students present their illustrations to the class, identifying which part of the poem is being depicted.

STORYBOARD: ADAPT PLOT

Discuss with students how this poem might be made into a book for young children. Then divide students into small groups and have them produce storyboards for their version of "The Walrus and the Carpenter." Encourage students to browse through a variety of children's books to help them understand how writers and illustrators tell stories.

Ask groups to present their storyboards. Have students discuss how each version is the same or different from Carroll's poem.

Pre-AP Challenge: Have students create a children's book based on their storyboards. Encourage students to choose an interesting format, such as a big board book, a pop-up book, or even a coloring book version. Have students read and show their books to the class. Display the books in the classroom.

POETRY FESTIVAL: EXPLORE GENRE

Ask students to find other examples of narrative poems that are nonsensical or humorous. Students might choose selections from poets such as Shel Silverstein or Dr. Seuss.

Have students practice reading their poems aloud with appropriate expression. Ask them to prepare a short introduction explaining why they chose the poem and what they enjoyed about it.

Hold a poetry festival in the classroom. Invite students from other classes to be part of the audience.

Resource Manager

INQUIRY AND RESEARCH

OYSTERS

Have students put together an oyster cookbook. Ask students to investigate the oyster specialties of different cultures and countries. Encourage students to find a recipe that appeals to them. Then have students design a "recipe card" using their recipe. Encourage students to experiment with format, fonts, color, and illustrations.

Have students present their recipe to the class with a brief introduction about where the recipe comes from and why they chose it. After the presentations, hold a class discussion to compare and contrast the ways in which oysters are enjoyed by people around the world. Finally, compile a class cookbook for display.

WRITING

EXPRESS POINT OF VIEW: INTERNAL MONOLOGUE

What do you think the eldest Oyster was thinking? Ask students to reread lines 37–42. Have them write the Oyster's thoughts as he refuses the Walrus's invitation and then quietly observes as the young Oysters are led into a trap. Remind students to use first-person point of view throughout. They may wish to outline possible ideas before they begin to write.

IDENTIFY ELEMENTS OF POETRY: STANZA

Read one or two stanzas aloud. Discuss rhyme, rhythm, and other sound devices found throughout the poem. Then ask students to work together or alone to create an additional stanza for the poem. The stanza may be inserted anywhere. Encourage students to organize their ideas in a cluster chart before they begin to write.

EVALUATE POEM: REVIEW

Ask students whether or not they would recommend this poem to a friend. Then ask them to write a brief review in which they state their opinion of the poem and offer support, based on the text, for their view.

Students may find it helpful to discuss their ideas in small groups before they write their reviews. Remind students to craft a strong topic sentence and to use examples from the poem to support their opinion.

THE WALRUS AND THE CARPENTER

Teacher Notes

Review and Evaluate Outcome

What did I want students to know or be able to do?

How successful was the lesson?

Evaluate Process

What worked?
- Strategies

- Resources

- Differentiation

What did not work? Why not?

Reflect

The next time I teach "The Walrus and the Carpenter," what will I do differently? Why?

Plan Ahead

What must I do next?

Name _____

Date _____

COPY MASTER

THE WALRUS AND THE CARPENTER

Text Analysis

NARRATIVE POETRY

Narrative poetry is poetry that tells a story. It contains the same narrative elements as a work of fiction, such as setting, characters, and plot.

Directions: As you read "The Walrus and the Carpenter," record details about the setting, characters, and plot events in this story map.

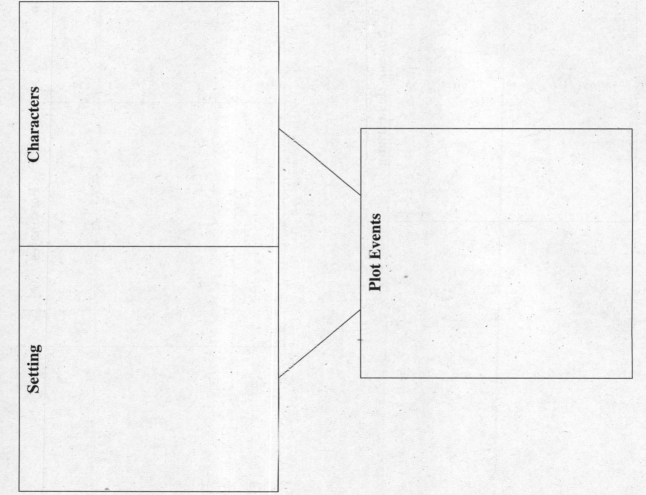

Name _____ Date _____

LA MORSA Y EL CARPINTERO

Text Analysis

NARRATIVE POETRY

La **poesía narrativa** es poesía que relata un cuento. Contiene los mismos elementos narrativos que una obra de ficción, como escenario, personajes y trama.

Instrucciones: Mientras lees "La Morsa y el Carpintero", anota detalles sobre el escenario, los personajes y la trama en este mapa del cuento.

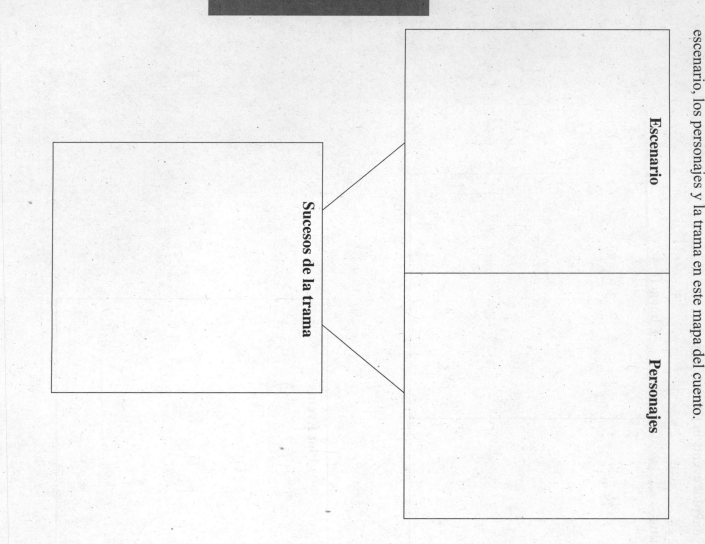

Escenario

Personajes

Sucesos de la trama

Name _____ Date _____

THE WALRUS AND THE CARPENTER

Reading Strategy

VISUALIZE

When you read a narrative poem, it helps to picture the setting and characters in your mind. If you can **visualize** what is being described, you will probably enjoy the poem more and understand it better.

Directions: Chooose a stanza from page 146 in your textbook and think about the mental picture you formed when you read it. Record notes in the following diagram to show what helped you viusalize.

Details from My Imagination

Words and Phrases from the Poem

Description of the Picture in My Mind

LA MORSA Y EL CARPINTERO

Reading Strategy

COPY MASTER

VISUALIZE

Cuando lees un poema narrativo, es bueno que formes en tu mente imágenes del escenario y los personajes. Si puedes **visualizar** lo que se describe, es probable que disfrutes más el poema y que lo entiendas mejor.

Instrucciones: Elige una estrofa de la página 146 de tu libro de texto y piensa en la imagen mental que formaste cuando la leíste. Haz anotaciones en el diagrama siguiente para mostrar qué fue lo que te ayudó a visualizar.

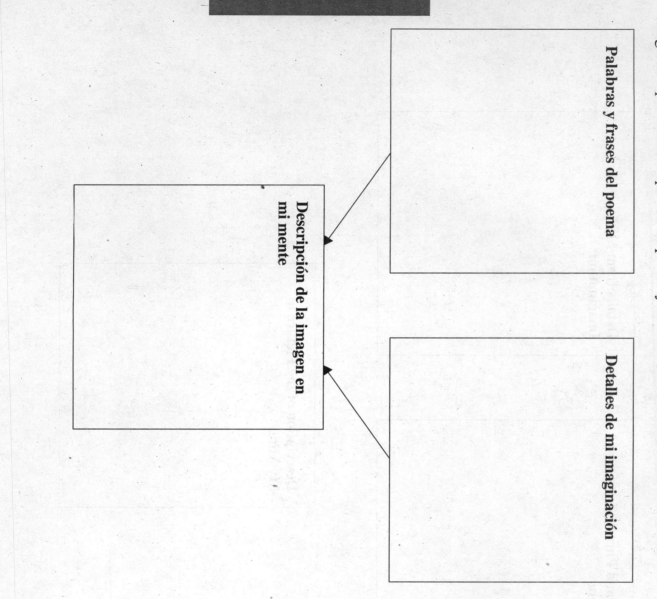

Palabras y frases del poema

Detalles de mi imaginación

Descripción de la imagen en mi mente

Name _____ Date _____

THE WALRUS AND THE CARPENTER

Question Support

TEXT ANALYSIS

For questions 1–2, see page 149 of the Student Edition.

Directions: Answer the questions.

3. Make Inferences Reread lines 37–42. The eldest Oyster lived longer than most

oysters because _____

_____

4. Visualize Reread lines 31–36. Describe what you see in your mind as you
read the lines.

_____

_____

5. Identify Rhyme

Which three words rhyme in lines 7–12? _____

Which three words rhyme in lines 13–18? _____

6. Evaluate Narrative Poetry Look at your story map. Circle the word that tells
how you feel about the poem. Then explain your feelings on the lines.
a. amused   **b.** disturbed

_____

_____

7. Draw Conclusions

How were the oysters tricked? _____

_____

What might the author tell you to do to avoid being tricked? _____

_____

Resource Manager

Unit 1 **195**
Grade 6

Name _____

Date _____

COPY MASTER

Reading Fluency

READING WITH EXPRESSION

To make a story or poem come alive for your listeners, you must read with expression. To read with expression means to read with feeling and emotion. Here are some tips for making your reading more expressive.

- Read at a natural pace, or speed. Speed up or slow down as necessary. Avoid reading word-by-word.
- Change the volume of your voice to signal that a word or idea is important.
- Vary your pitch, the rise and fall of your voice, to avoid sounding dull. A sudden change in pitch can add meaning to your words.
- Group words into meaningful phrases. Pause or stop to signal the end of a thought or idea.

L = louder
S = softer

↑ = raise pitch
↓ = lower pitch

/ = pause or stop
underscore = add stress

Directions: Follow along as your teacher reads an excerpt from "The Walrus and the Carpenter." Listen for changes in the volume and pitch of your teacher's voice. Notice where your teacher pauses. Then use these marks to prepare your own reading of the passage:

"The time has come," the Walrus said,
"To talk of many things:
Of shoes—and ships—and sealing-wax—
Of cabbages—and kings—
5   And why the sea is boiling hot—
And whether pigs have wings."

"But wait a bit," the Oysters cried,
"Before we have our chat;
For some of us are out of breath,
10   And all of us are fat!"
"No hurry!" said the Carpenter.
They thanked him much for that.

—Lewis Carroll, from "The Walrus and the Carpenter"

Essential Course of Study ECOS **Lesson at a Glance**

THE

PAUPER
AND THE

MARK TWAIN
Dramatized by Joellen Bland

WHY THIS SELECTION?

This dramatization of the novel by Mark Twain is a classic and enduring story that will entertain students and present some thought-provoking themes.

ABOUT THIS SELECTION

Student/Teacher's Edition Pages: 150–165

Difficulty Level: Average

Summary In this dramatic adaptation of Mark Twain's novel *The Prince and the Pauper*, Tom Canty, a poor boy, makes the acquaintance of the Prince of Wales, a boy his own age who is heir to the throne of England. A series of events leads them to be mistaken for each other. Under the guise of Tom Canty, the prince is thrust into the rough world of thieves and poverty. Meanwhile, Tom must adapt to palace life. Finally, after many adventures, the prince is able to regain his true identity and his throne.

Engaging the Students This play offers students an opportunity to explore the key idea of trading places. The Prince of Wales envies Tom's freedom, and Tom, who is poor, can only imagine a life of luxury. After exchanging identities, however, they find out that everyone's life has trials and tribulations. As students read the play, they are motivated to think about the lessons they might learn from walking in someone else's shoes and what they should appreciate about their own lives.

COMMON CORE STANDARDS FOCUS

- Conflict in Drama
- Reading a Play

LESSON RESOURCES
Plan and Teach

ⓘ Lesson resources are also available on the **Teacher One Stop DVD-ROM** and online at **thinkcentral.com**.

Resource Manager

Lesson Plan and Resource Guide

The Prince and the Pauper

Novel by Mark Twain
Dramatized by Joellen Bland

Common Core Focus

RL 3 Describe how a particular drama's plot unfolds as well as how the characters respond or change as the plot moves toward a resolution. **W 7** Conduct short research projects to answer a question, drawing on several sources.

Unless otherwise noted, resources can be found in the *Resource Manager.* ❶ Lesson resources are also available on the **Teacher One Stop DVD-ROM** and online at **thinkcentral.com**. The Student Edition and selected copy masters are available electronically on the ⊙ **Student One Stop DVD-ROM.**

Student/Teacher's Edition Pages	Additional Resources CM = Copy Master T = Transparency
Focus and Motivate	
☐ Big Question p. 150	☐ ❶ PowerNotes DVD-ROM and <u>thinkcentral.com</u>
☐ Author Biography and Background Information p. 151	☐ ❶ Literature and Reading Center at <u>thinkcentral.com</u>
Teach	
☐ Conflict in Drama p. 151	☐ ❶ PowerNotes DVD-ROM and <u>thinkcentral.com</u>
☐ Reading a Play p. 151	☐ Reading a Play CM—English p. 209, Spanish p. 210 ⅅ
	☐ ❶ PowerNotes DVD-ROM and <u>thinkcentral.com</u>
☐ Vocabulary in Context p. 151	☐ Vocabulary Study CM p. 211 ⅅ
	☐ ❶ PowerNotes DVD-ROM and <u>thinkcentral.com</u>

ⅅ = Resources for Differentiation

Student/Teacher's Edition Pages	Additional Resources CM = Copy Master T = Transparency

Practice and Apply: Guided Practice

Selection and Teacher Notes

☐ *The Price and the Pauper,* pp. 152–164

☐ 🔊 **Audio Anthology CD** D

☐ Summary CM—English and Spanish p. 205, Haitian Creole and Vietnamese p. 206 D

☐ Reading Fluency CM p. 214

☐ 📦 **Best Practices Toolkit**

☐ New Word Analysis p. E8 [T] D
☐ Reciprocal Teaching p. A35 [T] D
☐ Venn Diagram p. A26 [T] D
☐ Plot Diagram p. D12 [T] D
☐ Sequence Chain p. B21 [T] D
☐ Read Aloud/Think Aloud p. A34 [T] D
☐ Cluster Diagram p. B18 [T] D
☐ ℹ️ ThinkAloud Models and Audio Summaries at **thinkcentral.com**

Practice and Apply: After Reading

☐ Selection Questions p. 165

☐ Reading Check CM p. 212
☐ Conflict in Drama CM—English p. 207, Spanish p. 208 D
☐ Question Support CM p. 213
☐ Additional Selection Questions p. 200 D
☐ Ideas for Extension pp. 201–202 D

Assess and Reteach

Assess

☐ **Diagnostic and Selection Tests**
☐ Selection Tests A, B/C pp. 59–60, 61–62 D
☐ ℹ️ ThinkCentral Online Assessment
☐ 🔊 ExamView Test Generator on the **Teacher One Stop**
DVD-ROM

Reteach

☐ Conflict in Drama

☐ ℹ️ Level Up Online Tutorials on **thinkcentral.com**
☐ ℹ️ Reteaching Worksheets on **thinkcentral.com**
☐ Literature Lesson 6: Conflict

D = Resources for Differentiation

If you are following the *Essential Course of Study*, this selection may also be found in
- **Interactive Reader**
- **Adapted Interactive Reader**
- 🔊 **Adapted Interactive Reader: Audio Tutor**
- **English Language Learner Adapted Interactive Reader**

Additional Selection Questions

Use to supplement the
questions on SE page 165.

Differentiation Use these questions to provide customized practice with comprehension
and critical thinking skills.

Easy

1. ***Who would you BE if you could?***
What are some reasons that people might want to trade places with each other? *(They
might think the other person has more possessions, more talent or skills, an easier life,
or is just generally happier.)*

2. **Identify Conflict in Drama** What is the major conflict in the play? *(The prince
must find a way to regain the throne and convince people that he is really the royal heir.)*

Average

3. **Analyze Conflict in Drama** What events intensify the major conflict? How do
they add suspense to the plot? *(Significant events include the prince's escape from John
Canty, the death of King Henry VIII, the kidnapping of the prince by Canty and Hugo,
the prince's trial for robbery, and the imprisonment of Miles and the prince. These
events add suspense because they make the outcome or resolution of the conflict more
uncertain.)*

4. **Reading a Play** What information may be provided by stage directions? *(Stage
directions describe the setting, props, and scenery. They indicate the passage of
time. They describe the music, sound effects, and lighting. They identify characters'
movements, behavior, and manner of speaking.)*

5. **Analyze Theme** Based on the play, how should future leaders prepare themselves
for their role? *(All leaders should live as ordinary citizens first in order to understand
the problems and needs of their population. This point is reinforced by the prince's
declaration in lines 673–676.)*

Challenging

6. ***Who would you BE if you could?***
How might trading places improve society? *(By trading places, people would achieve
a greater understanding of each other and might develop greater tolerance for each
other's differences.)*

7. **Analyze Conflict in Drama** Why doesn't the prince remember where he put the
Great Seal? If he hadn't recalled its location, what might have happened? *(The prince
doesn't remember the location of the Great Seal because he has been through so much
since that day. If he hadn't remembered, Lord Hertford might have imprisoned him. But,
more likely, Tom would have insisted that they ask something else as a test.)*

8. **Reading a Play** Why is the play divided into scenes? *(Scenes organize the action.
Each scene takes place in a different location and develops the plot further.)*

THE PRINCE AND THE PAUPER

Ideas for Extension

Differentiation These activities provide students with a variety of options for demonstrating understanding of lesson concepts.

EXPLORATIONS AND ACTIVITIES

BRAINSTORM: EXTEND CONFLICT

Draw students' attention to lines 513–521. In this speech, the prince summarizes some of the adventures he has had. Have students work in small groups to develop one of these incidents, or others that the prince might have had, into an additional scene in the play.

Have students brainstorm details such as setting and character. Remind them to stay consistent with the other scenes. Then have them sketch out possible dialogue for their scene.

Pre-AP Challenge: Have students create a script for their scene. Ask groups to perform their scenes for the class.

COMIC STRIP: SUMMARIZE PLOT

Invite students to create a series of frames for a comic strip version of the play.

Have students identify the incidents that they want to include and decide how they want to portray the characters. Remind them to develop the plot through the dialogue as well as the illustrations.

Have students present their comic strips to the class. Discuss the strengths of each set.

BUILD A STAGE SET: EXPLORE SETTING

Tell students that building a miniature stage set often helps designers to determine how they want to portray a particular setting.

Have small groups of students choose one of the scenes from the play. Ask them to create their own stage set for that scene in a shoebox. They should paint backdrops and arrange their furniture or props on their stage. Students might even position the actors. Remind them to pay close attention to the stage directions in the scene they choose.

Have students present their models to the class and give a brief explanation of the design decisions they made. Display the stage sets around the room.

HERALDIC DESIGN: ANALYZE CHARACTER

Explain to students that a coat of arms is an arrangement of symbols, appearing on a shield or pennant, identifying a person and his background. As a baronet, Miles would have a coat of arms. Tom may also have been entitled to one after he becomes the King's Ward.

Have students design a coat of arms for either Tom or Miles. Ask students to base their choice of symbols on the traits that the character reveals throughout the play. Students should also include a motto, or short saying, expressing the character's philosophy of life. If necessary, help students locate web sites on the Internet to find examples of coats of arms.

Have students present their designs and explain their choices of symbols and saying.

IDEAS FOR EXTENSION, CONTINUED

VENN DIAGRAM: COMPARE AND CONTRAST GENRES

Have students read a chapter of Mark Twain's novel *The Prince and the Pauper* corresponding to one of the scenes in the play. Ask them to note similarities and differences in character portrayal, setting, and plot.

Have them present their insights in a Venn diagram. Discuss the advantages of each genre.

INQUIRY AND RESEARCH

THE HOUSE OF TUDOR

Have students find out more about Edward's lineage. Assign small groups to research one of the historical figures associated with the Tudor family. For example, students might investigate Henry VII, Henry VIII, one of his six wives, one of Edward's half sisters, either Mary or Elizabeth, or Edward himself. Have students organize their information on small posters. They should include the dates of birth and death of their subject as well as the time in which he or she ruled, if applicable. They should also include significant and interesting facts about the person and a portrait, if possible.

Have students present their information to the class. Then have students place their posters on a wall of the classroom in the arrangement of a family tree.

WRITING

EXPLORE KEY IDEA: ROYAL MEMO

Discuss ways in which the prince's view on life in the palace may have changed after his experiences. Then ask students to imagine how he might alter palace practices as a result of his new insights.

Have students write a memo, using the royal "we," that the prince might send to palace personnel, outlining new policies or procedures. Encourage students to organize their ideas before beginning to write.

EXPLORE VIEWPOINT: JOURNAL ENTRY

Point out that the prince has some horrifying moments in the course of his adventures. There must have been times when he wondered if he would live to tell the tale.

Ask students to skim the play and to choose one of these moments, such as his first encounter with John Canty or his trial. Have them write what the prince might have been thinking and feeling in a journal entry. Remind students to use first person and to base their ideas on their knowledge of his character and the plot.

THE PRINCE AND THE PAUPER

Teacher Notes

Review and Evaluate Outcome

What did I want students to know or be able to do?

How successful was the lesson?

Evaluate Process

What worked?
- Strategies

- Resources

- Differentiation

What did not work? Why not?

Reflect

The next time I teach "The Prince and the Pauper," what will I do differently? Why?

Plan Ahead

What must I do next?

THE PRINCE AND THE PAUPER

Summary

THE PRINCE AND THE PAUPER

Mark Twain

Setting: Westminster Palace, England, 1547

Tom, a young beggar, tries to see the Prince of Wales. When he looks through the gates of the palace, a guard throws him into the street. The Prince sees what happens and makes the guards open the gates. The two boys talk. The Prince envies Tom's freedom to play. Tom envies the Prince's fine clothes. They decide to exchange clothes. No one recognizes them in their new clothing, so they are forced to exchange lives as well. The Prince is sent into the street and ends up in jail. Tom is sent to live in the palace. When the King dies, Tom will be crowned king. How will the real Prince claim his rightful throne?

EL PRINCIPE Y EL MENDIGO

Mark Twain

Escenario: Palacio de Westminster, Inglaterra, 1547

Tom, un joven mendigo, intenta ver al príncipe de Gales. Cuando mira a través de la reja del palacio, un guardia lo empuja hacia la calle. El príncipe ve lo que ocurre y hace que los guardias abran la reja. Los dos muchachos conversan. El príncipe envidia la libertad que tiene Tom para jugar. Tom envidia la fina ropa del príncipe. Deciden intercambiar la ropa. Nadie los reconoce con su nueva ropa, por lo que se ven forzado a intercambiar también sus vidas. Al príncipe lo mandan a la calle y termina en la cárcel. A Tom lo mandan a vivir en el palacio. Cuando muere el rey, Tom será coronado rey. ¿Cómo podrá el verdadero príncipe reclamar su derecho al trono?

THE PRINCE AND THE PAUPER

Summary

PRENS LAN AK PÒV LA

Mark Twain

Espas ak tan: Palè Westminster, Angletè, 1547

Tom, yon jenn pòv k ap mande, eseye wè prens Wales la. Lè li gade atravè baryè palè a, yon gad pouse li toumen nan lari a. Prens lan wè sa ki pase a epi li fè gad yo louvri baryè a. De mesye yo pale. Prens lan anvi jwenn libète Tom lan pou li ka jwe. Tom anvi jwenn bèl abiman Prens lan. Yo deside boukante rad. Pèsòn pa rekonèt yo nan nouvo abiman yo, kidonk yo fòse boukante lavi tou. Yo voye Tom pou li al viv nan palè a epi li ale nan prizon. Yo voye Prens lan nan lari a epi kouwone wa. Kouman vrè Prens lan ap reklame twòn lejitim li a?

HOÀNG TỬ VÀ CẬU BÉ ĂN MÀY

Mark Twain

Bối cảnh: Cung điện Westminster, Anh, 1547

Tom là một cậu bé ăn mày cố tìm cách gặp Hoàng tử xứ Wales. Khi cậu nhìn qua hàng rào cung điện, một người lính canh ném cậu ra đường. Hoàng tử nhìn thấy cảnh đó và yêu cầu người lính canh mở cổng. Hai cậu bé nói chuyện với nhau. Hoàng tử ghen tị với Tom vì cậu được tự do chơi. Tom ghen tị với hoàng tử vì quần áo đẹp của cậu. Cả hai quyết định đổi quần áo cho nhau. Trong trang phục mới của mình không ai nhận ra họ, vì vậy họ cũng buộc phải tráo đổi cả cuộc sống của họ với nhau. Hoàng tử bị tống ra đường và cuối cùng vào tù. Tom được đưa vào sống trong cung điện. Khi đức vua qua đời, Tom lên làm vua. Làm sao vị hoàng tử đích thực có thể giành lại quyền kế vị ngôi vua chính đáng của mình?

Name _____ Date _____

COPY MASTER

THE PRINCE AND THE PAUPER

Text Analysis

CONFLICT IN DRAMA

In drama, as in short stories, the plot revolves around a central **conflict.** The conflict in a drama unfolds through action and dialogue. A play is divided into acts and scenes. The conflict becomes more complicated with each act and scene.

Directions: To see how the conflict develops during the play, use this chart to summarize the main events of each scene. Circle the scene in which the conflict is resolved.

Scene 1	The guards mistake the Prince for Tom, and the King thinks that Tom is the Prince.
Scene 2	
Scene 3	
Scene 4	
Scene 5	
Scene 6	
Scene 7	

SPANISH

COPY MASTER

Text Analysis

CONFLICT IN DRAMA

En un drama, como en los cuentos cortos, la trama gira en torno a un **conflicto** central. El conflicto en un drama se desarrolla a través de la acción y el diálogo. Una obra de teatro se divide en actos y escenas. El conflicto se vuelve más complicado con cada acto y escena.

Instrucciones: Para ver cómo se desarrolla el conflicto durante la obra, usa esta tabla para resumir los sucesos principales de cada escena. Encierra en un círculo la escena en la que se resolvió el conflicto.

Escena 1	Los guardias confunden al príncipe con Tom y el rey piensa que Tom es el príncipe.
Escena 2	
Escena 3	
Escena 4	
Escena 5	
Escena 6	
Escena 7	

Resource Manager

THE PRINCE AND THE PAUPER

Reading Strategy

READING A PLAY

In a play, stage directions provide key information that readers would normally see or hear in an actual performance such as the following:

- the setting, scenery, and props
- the music, sound effects, and lighting
- the characters' movements, behavior, or ways of speaking.

Directions: As you read "The Prince and the Pauper," record examples of stage directions and tell what they help you understand. An example has been done for you.

Stage Direction	Type of Directions	What It Tells Me
Fanfare of trumpets is heard (Scene 3, line 282)	Sound effects	Someone is entering.

EL PRÍNCIPE Y EL MENDIGO

Reading Strategy

READING A PLAY

En una obra de teatro, las direcciones escénicas proporcionan información clave que los lectores por lo regular verían o escucharían en una representación real como:

- el escenario, la decoración y los accesorios.
- la música, los efectos de sonido y la iluminación.
- los movimientos, el comportamiento o la forma de hablar de los personajes.

Instrucciones: Mientras lees "El príncipe y el mendigo", anota ejemplos de direcciones escénicas y di qué te ayudaron a entender. Te damos un ejemplo.

Dirección escénica	Tipo de dirección	Qué me dice
Se escucha una fanfarria de trompetas (escena 3, renglón 282).	efectos de sonido	Alguien está entrando.

Name _____

Date _____

THE PRINCE AND THE PAUPER

Vocabulary Study

STORY PREDICTIONS

A. Directions: Listen as your teacher reads each sentence about *The Prince and the Pauper*. Together discuss what you know about the word or how it might be used. Write your ideas on the lines.

1. To explain his odd behavior, the palace said that the prince was suffering from an **affliction.**

   _____

2. Sir Hugh accused Miles, the rightful baronet, of being an **impostor.** As a result, Miles was thrown into prison.

   _____

3. A **pauper** could hope to earn a few pennies by begging near the palace grounds.

   _____

4. His **recollection** of the event was fuzzy. Too much had happened since he left the palace.

   _____

5. He knew he was perfectly **sane**, even if the rest of the world thought he was crazy.

   _____

6. The Prince of Wales was the **successor** to the throne. Therefore, he would be next in line for the crown.

   _____

plot	character	theme	conflict

B. Directions: How might each boldfaced word in Part A relate to the words in the box? Write your predictions on the line below.

_____

_____

_____

Reading Check

Directions: Recall the events in the Joellen Bland play based on Mark Twain's novel.
Then answer the questions in phrases or sentences.

1. Why does Prince Edward want to exchange places with Tom?

2. What starts the rumor that the Prince is mad?

3. Why does the Constable arrest Edward?

4. Why is Miles Hendon put in prison?

5. How does Edward prove that he is the king of England?

Name _____ Date _____

THE PRINCE AND THE PAUPER

Question Support

TEXT ANALYSIS

For questions 1–3, see page 165 of the Student Edition.

Directions: Answer the questions.

4. Make Inferences

How does Miles treat the prince? Why? _____
_____

How do the members of the royal court treat Tom? Why? _____
_____

5. Evaluate Stage Directions

Write two stage directions that helped you understand the setting. _____
_____

Write two stage directions that helped you understand the characters. _____
_____

6. Analyze Conflict in Drama Skim the play. Circle the scene in which the conflict is resolved.

a. Scene Three   b. Scene Five   c. Scene Seven

7. Analyze Character

Why do people at court think the "prince" is mad? _____
_____

Why does Tom behave so strangely? _____
_____

8. Evaluate Resolution Complete the following sentence. Trading places helped

the boys learn _____

Reading Fluency

READERS THEATER

Readers Theater is a way of performing a play in which the actors read their parts from a script. Using only their voices, the actors make the characters come alive for the audience. You can perform most plays as Readers Theater. Here are some tips for giving a successful performance:

- Read at a natural pace, or speed, as you do when you talk. Adjust your pace to bring out the personality of your character.
- Experiment with phrasing. How you group words can sometime affect their meaning.
- Vary your pitch, the rise and fall of your voice, to express emotion and to keep listeners interested.
- Speak louder or softer to call attention to important words or ideas.

A. Directions: With two or more classmates, choose a scene from *The Prince and the Pauper* (pages 152–164 in the anthology) to perform as Readers Theater. Fill in the chart below to explain how to read your character's lines.

Character:	
Description:	
Manner of Speaking:	

B. Directions: Now read the scene as a group. Evaluate your performance on the lines below.

_____

_____

Essential Course of Study ECOS **Lesson at a Glance**

Reading for Information | Twain's Tale Transplanted to Today

WHY THIS SELECTION?

This film review introduces students to a modern version of Twain's classic and develops their understanding of an increasingly common form of informational text.

ABOUT THIS SELECTION

Student/Teacher's Edition Pages: 166–169

Difficulty Level: Average

Readability Scores: Lexile: 1310; Fry: 9; Dale-Chall: 9.10

Summary This film review compares and contrasts a recent movie version of Mark Twain's *The Prince and the Pauper* to its original version. The review explains how Twain's story has been updated but still retains the essential elements of the original story. For example, the basic plot and characters are similar, although the setting is modern-day Florida rather than sixteenth-century England. The review reminds us of the timelessness of Twain's tale.

COMMON CORE STANDARDS FOCUS

• Compare and Contrast Versions of a Story

LESSON RESOURCES

Plan and Teach

Student Copy Masters

ⓘ Lesson resources are also available on the **Teacher One Stop DVD-ROM** and online at <u>thinkcentral.com</u>.

Resource Manager

Lesson Plan and Resource Guide
Twain's Tale Transplanted to Today
Film Review

Common Core Focus

RL 1 Cite textual evidence to support analysis of what the text says explicitly. **RL 7** Compare and contrast a drama to a video version of the text. **W 2** Write informative/explanatory texts to examine a topic.

Unless otherwise noted, resources can be found in the *Resource Manager*. ❶ Lesson resources are also available on the **Teacher One Stop DVD-ROM** and online at **thinkcentral.com**. The Student Edition and selected copymasters are available electronically on the ✏ **Student One Stop DVD-ROM.**

Student/Teacher's Edition Pages	Additional Resources CM = Copy Master T = Transparency
Focus and Motivate	
☐ What's the Connection? p. 166	☐ ✏ **Best Practices Toolkit** ☐ Connecting p. A8[T] ☐ ❶ **PowerNotes DVD-ROM** and thinkcentral.com
Teach	
☐ Compare and Contrast Versions of a Story p. 166	☐ Compare and Contrast Versions of a Story CM—p. 223, Spanish p. 225 **D** ☐ ❶ **PowerNotes DVD-ROM** and **thinkcentral.com**
Practice and Apply: Guided Practice	
Selection and Teacher Notes	☐ ✏ **Audio Anthology CD D**
☐ Twain's Tale Transplanted to Today pp. 223–226	☐ Summary CM—English and Spanish p. 221, Haitian Creole and Vietnamese p. 222 **D** ☐ ❶ ThinkAloud Models at **thinkcentral.com** ☐ ❶ Audio Summaries at **thinkcentral.com**

D = Resources for Differentiation

Practice and Apply: After Reading

- [ ] Selection Questions p. 169
- [ ] Read for Information: Compare and Contrast Versions of a Story p. 169

- [ ] Reading Check CM p. 227
- [ ] Compare and Contrast CM—English p. 223, Spanish p. 225
- [ ] Question Support CM p. 228 **D**
- [ ] Additional Selection Questions p. 218 **D**
- [ ] Compare and Contrast Versions of a Story CM—p. 224, Spanish p. 226

Assess and Reteach

Assess

- [ ] Diagnostic and Selection Tests
  - [ ] Selection Test CM pp. 63–64
  - [ ] Selection Test B/C CM pp. 65–66
  - [ ] **i** Interactive Selection Test on **thinkcentral.com**

Reteach

- [ ] Compare and Contrast

- [ ] **i** Level Up Online Tutorials on **thinkcentral.com**
- [ ] **i** Reteaching Worksheets on **thinkcentral.com**
- [ ] Reading Lesson 12: Comparing and Contrasting

D = Resources for Differentiation

If you are following the *Essential Course of Study*, this selection may also be found in

- **Interactive Reader**
- **Adapted Interactive Reader**
- **Adapted Interactive Reader: Audio Tutor CD**
- **English Language Learner Adapted Interactive Reader**

Additional Selection Questions

Use to supplement the questions on SE page 169.

Differentiation Use these questions to provide customized practice with comprehension and critical thinking skills.

Easy

1. **Recall** What is the name of the rich "prince" in the modern version of the story? *(He is named Eddie Tudor.)*

2. **Recall** What do the boys do together at the end of the film? *(The boys act together in a traditional film version of Twain's story.)*

3. **Summarize** How is the modern version updated over the traditional version of the story? *(The modern version is set in Miami Beach and Palm Beach instead of England; the story revolves around the world of movies and acting instead of a royal court; and the boys not only look alike, they also have many of the same feelings in common.)*

Average

4. **Note Similarities and Differences** What are the similarities between the lessons learned by the pairs of boys in each version? *(In each version, each pair of boys learns something important about life, but the lessons themselves are different.)*

5. **Analyze Setting and Characters** Could the story be told with two female characters in the lead roles? What might the modern setting be? *(Yes, two females could trade places. The story could be set in the world of music or dance.)*

6. **Compare and Contrast Versions of a Story** What is one important difference between the modern Tom's situation and the original Tom's situation when both pairs of boys trade places? *(Students may say that the modern Tom could really have a career as an actor, but the original Tom couldn't become a real prince.)*

Challenging

7. **Compare and Contrast Versions of a Story** Think about the "princes" in each version of the story. Explain one major difference in the two characters' personalities. *(The prince in the original version thinks about life's important questions, while the "prince" in the updated version isn't very thoughtful and seems not to care for the feelings of others.)*

8. **Evaluate Film Reviews** What might be some of the challenges facing a writer of film reviews? Keep in mind the characteristics of the genre. *(One challenge might be to include enough information about the film to interest the reader without giving so much information that the review spoils the story. Another challenge would be to provide a fair review in a short amount of space.)*

TWAIN'S TALE TRANSPLANTED TO TODAY

Teacher Notes

Review and Evaluate Outcome

What did I want students to know or be able to do?

How successful was the lesson?

Evaluate Process

What worked?
- Strategies

- Resources

- Differentiation

What did not work? Why not?

Reflect

The next time I teach "Twain's Tale Transplanted to Today," what will I do differently? Why?

Plan Ahead

What must I do next?

Summary

TWAIN'S TALE TRANSPLANTED TO TODAY
Film Review

This film review describes a recent movie version of *The Prince and the Pauper* that sets the story in modern times. In the new version, the "prince" is a wealthy teen actor with millions of fans. The "pauper" is a boy from a difficult background who works as a landscaper. The boys look alike, but both are also lonely and feel that adults don't understand them. Eddie, the actor, and Tom, the landscaper, switch places. As in Twain's version, the boys each learn lessons about life. Tom learns that his dream of a better life isn't just a fantasy but a real possibility. Eddie has a much harder time learning to be considerate and respectful of others, but he eventually changes his ways. The film ends with Tom becoming an actor like Eddie. The two boys make a traditional film version of *The Prince and the Pauper* together.

EL CUENTO DE TWAIN TRANSPLANTADO AL DÍA DE HOY
Crítica cinematográfica

Esta crítica cinematográfica describe una versión reciente de la película *El príncipe y el mendigo* ambientada en tiempos modernos. En la nueva versión, el "príncipe" es un rico actor adolescente que tiene millones de fans. El "mendigo" es un joven de antecedentes difíciles que trabaja como jardinero. Los jóvenes se parecen, pero ambos se sienten también solos y consideran que los adultos no los comprenden. Eddie, el actor, y Tom, el jardinero, intercambian lugares. Como en la versión de Twain, cada joven aprende lecciones acerca de la vida. Tom aprende que su sueño de una mejor vida no es sólo una fantasía sino una posibilidad real. La experiencia de Eddie es mucho más difícil al aprender a ser considerado y respetuoso para con los otros, pero con el tiempo cambia su forma de ser. La película termina al Tom convertirse en actor como Eddie. Juntos, los dos jóvenes hacen una versión tradicional de la película *El príncipe y el mendigo*.

Summary

ISTWA TWAIN YO RAKONTE JODI A
Kritik Film

Kritik film sa a dekri yon denye vèsyon film *The Prince and the Pauper* (Prens lan ak Malere a) kote istwa a ap dewoule nan tan modèn yo. Nan nouvèl vèsyon an, "prens" lan se yon jenn aktè rich ki genyen anpil milyon fanatik. "Malere" a se yon ti gason ki sòti nan yon milye defavorize epi k ap travay kòm yon jadinye. Ti gason yo sanble, men toulède se moun ki poukont yo, epi yo santi adilt yo pa konprann yo. Eddie, aktè a, ak Tom, jadinye a, chanje plas. Menm jan ak vèsyon Twain lan, chak ti gason aprann leson sou lavi a. Tom aprann rèv li pou yon lavi miyò pa senpleman yon imajinasyon men yon vrè posiblite. Eddie limenm gen plis difikilte pou aprann genyen konsiderasyon ak respè pou lòt moun, men li vin chanje fason li yo. Film lan fini avèk Tom ki vin yon aktè tankou Eddie. Toulède ti gason yo fè yon vèsyon tradisyonèl film *The Prince and the Pauper* ansanm.

TRUYỆN CỦA TWAIN ĐƯỢC CHUYỂN ĐẾN HÔM NAY
Bình Phẩm Phim

Bài bình phẩm này miêu tả một phiên bản phim mới đây của Hoàng Tử và kẻ Khốn Cùng lấy bối cảnh thời nay. Trong phiên bản mới, "hoàng tử" là một diễn viên thiếu niên giàu có với hàng triệu người hâm mộ. "Kẻ khốn cùng" là một cậu bé xuất thân trong nghèo khó làm công việc tạo cảnh quan. Hai cậu bé nhìn giống nhau, nhưng cả hai đều cô đơn và cảm thấy người lớn không hiểu các em. Eddie, diễn viên, và Tom, người tạo cảnh quan, đối vị trí. Như trong phiên bản của Twain, hai cậu bé đều học được các bài học về cuộc sống. Tom học được rằng giấc mơ của cậu về một cuộc sống tốt hơn không chỉ là viễn vông mà là khả năng thực sự. Eddie phải vất vả hơn nhiều để học cách ý tứ và tôn trọng người khác, nhưng cuối cùng cậu thay đổi cách sống. Bộ phim kết thúc với Tom trở thành diễn viên như Eddie. Hai cậu bé cũng nhau tạo nên phiên bản phim truyền thống của *The Prince and the Pauper*.

TWAIN'S TALE TRANSPLANTED TO TODAY

COPY MASTER

Skill Focus

COMPARE AND CONTRAST VERSIONS OF A STORY

Some stories are so popular that different versions of them are told through different forms of literature or media. For example, a novel might become a Broadway play, which is then made into a movie. Although different versions of a story might have different characters or settings, the basic plot, or story line, usually remains similar.

Directions: In the center column of the chart below, record what you know about the play. Then, as you read, record in the right-hand column what you learn about the setting, characters, and plot of the film. You will use the chart to compare the play and the film.

The Prince and the Pauper	Play	Film
Setting		
Characters		
Plot		

Read for Information

COMPARE AND CONTRAST VERSIONS OF A STORY

To **compare and contrast** means to examine the similarities and the differences between two things. Two versions of a story will almost certainly have both similarities and differences.

Directions: Now that you have read both the play and the film review, think about the similarities and differences between the two versions of the story. List them in the chart below. The completed chart will help you write a well-organized comparison/contrast essay on the two versions of *The Prince and the Pauper.*

Setting:	
similarities	
differences	
Characters:	
similarities	
differences	
Plot:	
similarities	
differences	

TWAIN'S TALE TRANSPLANTED TO TODAY IN SPANISH

COPY MASTER

Skill Focus

COMPARE AND CONTRAST VERSIONS OF A STORY

Algunas historias son tan populares que se han contado diversas versiones de ellas por medio de los distintas formas de literatura o los medios. Por ejemplo, una novela puede volverse una obra de Broadway, la que luego se hace en película. A pesar de que las distintas versiones de una histori podrían tener personajes o escenarios diferentes, la trama básica, o línea de la historia, usualmente permanece similar.

Instrucciones: En la columna central de la siguiente tabla, registra lo que sabes de la obra. Luego, mientras lees, registra en la columna de la derecha lo que has aprendido sobre el escenario, los personajes y la trama de la película. Usa la tabla para comparar la obra con la película.

The Prince and the Pauper	Obra	Película
Escenario		
Personajes		
Trama		

Resource Manager

TWAIN'S TALE TRANSPLANTED TO TODAY

Read for Information

COMPARE AND CONTRAST VERSIONS OF A STORY

Comparar y contrastar los medios de examinar las similitudes y las diferencias entre ambas cosas. Las dos versiones de una historia casi con certeza tienen tanto similitudes como diferencias.

Instrucciones: Ahora que has leído las críticas de la obra y de la película, piensa sobre las similitudes y diferencias que hay entre las dos versiones de a historia. Listalas en la siguiente tabla. La tabla completa te ayudará a escribir un ensayo bien organizado de comparación y contraste de las dos versiones *The Prince and the Pauper*.

Escenario	similitudes	
	diferencias	
Personajes:	similitudes	
	diferencias	
Trama:	similitudes	
	diferencias	

TWAIN'S TALE TRANSPLANTED TO TODAY

Reading Check

Directions: Recall the information in the film review. Then answer the questions in phrases or sentences.

1. Which well-known television stars portray the modern "prince" and "pauper" in the film?

_____

_____

_____

2. Before he becomes an actor, what kind of work does Tom do?

_____

_____

3. How successful an actor is Tom?

_____

_____

4. What does Eddie tell his mother when he returns to the movie set?

_____

_____

5. What does Miles help Eddie realize in the end?

_____

_____

Resource Manager

Question Support

TEXT ANALYSIS

Directions: Answer the questions.

For questions 1–3, see page 169 of the Student Edition.

4. **Analyze Setting and Characters** Name one alternative setting for a modern version that might appeal to audiences today.

_____

_____

5. **Compare and Contrast Versions of a Story** How is the personality of Tom in the play similar to the personality of Tom in the film version?

_____

_____

6. **Compare and Contrast Versions of a Story** Name at least one plot feature that is the same in both the play and the film.

_____

_____

_____

Essential Course of Study **EOS** Lesson at a Glance

Writing | Workshop | Argument

WHAT'S THE CONNECTION?

By writing an argument, students will be able to utilize many of the techniques they have studied throughout the unit, including these:

• Make Inferences

• Analyze

• Connect

• Monitor

In addition, students will have opportunities to incorporate what they have learned in the unit by developing a claim and supporting it with reasons and evidence, organizing ideas in a logical order, restating ideas in a conclusion, using transitions to show relationships among ideas, and using intensive pronouns correctly. Finally, using the Common Core Traits to develop their own arguments will help students acquire a stronger understanding of claims, reasons, and evidence.

ABOUT THE WRITING WORKSHOP

Student/Teacher's Edition Pages: 170–181

The Writing Workshop reinforces the unit focus of story elements by asking students to cite effective story elements as evidence to persuade readers to agree with a claim. The workshop provides step-by-step instructions, suggestions, and models for the writing process.

LESSON RESOURCES

Plan and Teach

ℹ Lesson resources are also available on the **Teacher One Stop DVD-ROM** and online at <u>thinkcentral.com.</u>

Resource Manager

Lesson Plan and Resource Guide

Writing Workshop
Writing Workshop: Argument

Common Core Focus

W 1a–e Write arguments to support claims with clear reasons and relevant evidence; use words, phrases, and clauses to clarify the relationships among claim(s), and reasons; maintain a formal style. **W 4** Produce clear and coherent writing appropriate to task, purpose, and audience. **W 5** Strengthen writing as needed by planning, revising, editing, rewriting, and trying a new approach. **W 6** Demonstrate sufficient command of keyboarding skills. **W 9a (RL 5)** Draw evidence from literary texts; analyze how a scene contributes to development. **W 10** Write routinely over shorter time frames. **L 1b** Use intensive pronouns. **L 2** Demonstrate command of the conventions of standard English capitalization, punctuation, and spelling. **L 3b** Maintain consistency in style and tone.

Unless otherwise noted, resources can be found in the *Resource Manager*. ❶ Lesson resources are also available on the **Teacher One Stop DVD-ROM** and online at **thinkcentral.com**. The Student Edition and selected copymasters are available electronically on the ✏ **Student One Stop DVD-ROM**.

Student/Teacher's Edition Pages	Additional Resources CM = Copy Master T = Transparency
Focus and Motivate	
☐ Write with a Purpose p. 170	☐ ✏ **WriteSmart CD-ROM**
	☐ ❶ Writing Center at **Writing Center at thinkcentral.com**
Teach	
☐ Planning/Prewriting pp. 171–172	☐ ❶ Planning/Prewriting CM p. 233
	☐ ❶ Interactive Graphic Organizers on **WriteSmart CD-ROM** and online at **thinkcentral.com**
Practice and Apply: Guided Practice	
☐ Drafting p. 173	☐ Drafting CM p. 234
	☐ Writing Support CM p. 240 **D**
	☐ 📦 **Best Practices Toolkit**
	☐ Spider Diagram p. B22 [T]
	☐ Writing Template: Responding to Literature p. C41 (T)
	☐ ❶ Writing Templates on **WriteSmart CD-ROM** and online at **thinkcentral.com**

D = Resources for Differentiation

Student/Teacher's Edition Pages	Additional Resources CM = Copy Master T = Transparency
Practice and Apply: Guided Practice	
☐ Revising pp. 174–176	☐ Revising and Editing 1 CM p. 235
	☐ Ask a Peer Reader CM p. 237
	☐ For interactive revision tools, see
	☐ **Write*Smart* CD-ROM**
	☐ **Writing Center** on <u>thinkcentral.com</u>
	☐ **GrammarNotes DVD-ROM**
	☐ Interactive Revision Lessons on **Write*Smart* CD-ROM** and online at <u>thinkcentral.com</u>
	☐ **GrammarNotes DVD-ROM** and online at <u>thinkcentral.com</u>
Editing and Publishing	
☐ Editing and Publishing p. 177	☐ Revising and Editing 2 CM p. 236
	☐ **GrammarNotes DVD-ROM** and online at <u>thinkcentral.com</u>
Assess and Reteach	
☐ Scoring Rubric p. 178	☐ Scoring Rubric CM p. 238
	☐ Rubric Generator on **Write*Smart* CD-ROM** and online at <u>thinkcentral.com</u>
	☐ Level Up Online Tutorials on <u>thinkcentral.com</u>
	☐ Reteaching Worksheets on <u>thinkcentral.com</u>
Listening and Speaking	
☐ Participating in a Discussion p. 566	☐ Speaking and Listening CM p. 239

D = Resources for Differentiation

WRITING WORKSHOP
Teacher Notes

Review and Evaluate Outcome

What did I want students to learn about writing an argument

How successful was the lesson?

Evaluate Process

• Resources

• Strategies

What worked?

• Writing Prompts

• Listening and Speaking Workshop (Participating in a Discussion)

What did not work? Why not?

Reflect

The next time I teach this Writing Workshop, what will I do differently? Why?

Plan Ahead

What must I do next?

Name _____ Date _____

COPY MASTER

WRITING WORKSHOP

Argument

PLANNING/PREWRITING

Use a graphic organizer to help you choose a story element that is particularly powerful and that makes the story memorable.

Directions: In center of the diagram, record the title of the story or novel you have chosen. Then jot down reasons why each story element is effective and powerful. Circle the element for which you have listed the most reasons. It is the element you can focus on in your argument.

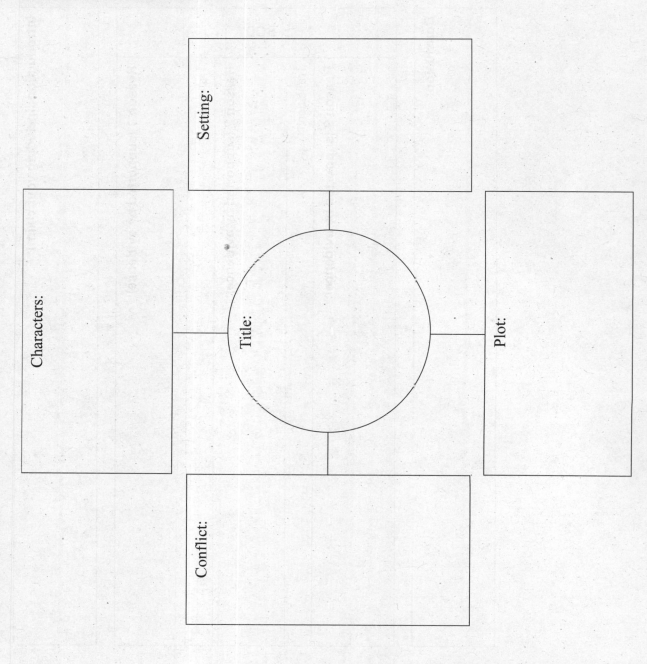

Characters:

Setting:

Title:

Conflict:

Plot:

Resource Manager

Argument

DRAFTING

For your argument to be persuasive, you must present it in a clear and logical order. Use the chart to order your ideas into a coherent, or easy to follow, argument.

Directions: In the chart, draft your ideas for your argument's introduction, body, and conclusion. In the body, list your reasons in order of importance (from most important to least, or least to most). Then add transitions between each reason.

Introduction (including your claim):

BODY	
Reason 1 (supported by evidence):	
Transition:	
Reason 2 (supported by evidence):	
Transition:	
Reason 3 (supported by evidence):	

Conclusion:

Name _____

Date _____

COPY MASTER

WRITING WORKSHOP
Argument

REVISING AND EDITING 1

The following model is an excerpt from a draft one student wrote arguing that the unique setting of the story "All Summer in a Day," by Ray Bradbury, makes it truly memorable.

Directions: Ask yourself the following questions as you revise and edit the excerpt. Mark your changes on this page. Then copy your corrected draft on a separate sheet of paper.

- Does the introduction grab the audience's attention?
- Does it include all the background readers need?
- Does it include a strong claim and reasons to support it?
- Are intensive pronouns used properly?

A World without Sun

Think of how you feel when it's been raining for two days in a row. Now imagine if it rained for seven years straight! In the story "All Summer in a Day," by Ray Bradbury, humans live on the planet Venus where the sun only shines for one hour every seven years. The story's strange setting makes it very memorable.

The setting affects the characters in the story in different ways. The children who were born on Venus don't remember the sun. They were only two years old the last time the sun appeared. All they know is rain and they don't seem to mind it. Margot was born on Earth, though, and she remembers the sun. She misses it a lot, and she seems to hate the rain. She wouldn't take a shower once, "screaming that the water mustn't touch her head." She is pale, thin, and quiet. Margot's parents themselves seem to be worried about her, and they may take her back to Earth.

Argument

WRITING WORKSHOP

REVISING AND EDITING 2

To measure your ability to express ideas clearly and correctly, some tests may ask you to identify errors in grammar and usage and to improve sentences and paragraphs.

Directions: Read each question and select the correct answer.

1. What change, if any, should be made in this sentence?

   I was surprised by the childrens cruelty.

   A. Change *childrens* to *children's*

   B. Change the period to an exclamation point.

   C. Add quotation marks around the word *surprised.*

   D. Make no change.

2. What change, if any, should be made to this sentence?

   The teacher herself should have stopped the bullying.

   A. Insert commas after *teacher* and *herself.*

   B. Capitalize *teacher.*

   C. Change *herself* to *herselves.*

   D. Make no change.

Directions: Read the paragraph and select the correct answer to the question that follows:

   The setting also contributes to the main conflict in the story. They hate her because she is different from them. She is the only one who can remember the sun. She never plays with the other children and she spends her time alone and sad. The way Margot responds to the rain makes the other children hate her.

3. What is the best way to improve the organization of this paragraph?

   A. Delete sentence 3.

   B. Move sentence 5 before sentence 2.

   C. Move sentence 1 to the end of the paragraph.

   D. Move sentence 4 to the beginning of the paragraph.

WRITING WORKSHOP

Argument

ASK A PEER READER

To see whether your argument is coherent, ask a peer reviewer to read it.

Directions: Give your peer reader this sheet and have him or her record answers to the following questions and then give you suggestions for revision.

1. Does the introduction grab the audience's attention?

_____

_____

_____

2. Do I provide the background information that my audience needs?

_____

_____

3. Does the introduction have a strong claim?

_____

_____

4. Are there at least two clear reasons that support the claim? Does at least one piece of relevant evidence support each reason?

_____

_____

5. Does my argument include transitions that show the relationships among my claim and reasons?

_____

_____

6. Does the concluding section follow logically from the argument and restate my claim and reasons?

_____

Argument

SCORING RUBRIC

Use the rubric below to evaluate your argument from the Writing Workshop.

ARGUMENT

SCORE	COMMON CORE TRAITS
6	• **Development** Effectively presents a strong claim; supports the claim with clear reasons and relevant evidence; has a powerful concluding section • **Organization** Capably arranges reasons and evidence; effectively uses transitions to show relationships among ideas • **Language** Consistently maintains a formal style and tone; shows a strong command of conventions
5	• **Development** Presents a strong claim; supports the claim with clear reasons and relevant evidence; has a strong concluding section • **Organization** Clearly arranges reasons and evidence; uses transitions to show relationships among ideas • **Language** Maintains a formal style and tone; has a few errors in conventions
4	• **Development** States a sufficient claim; supports the claim with reasons and evidence; has an adequate concluding section • **Organization** Arranges the reasons and evidence clearly with some exceptions; uses transitions adequately, but could use more • **Language** Mostly maintains a formal style and tone; includes a few distracting errors in conventions
3	• **Development** States a claim; provides some reasons and evidence, but needs more; has a somewhat weak concluding section • **Organization** Arranges the reasons and evidence in a somewhat confusing way; needs more transitions • **Language** Often lapses into an informal style and tone; has several errors in conventions
2	• **Development** Has a weak claim; offers some unclear reasons and needs more evidence; has a weak concluding section • **Organization** Arranges reasons and evidence in a confusing way; uses few transitions • **Language** Uses an informal style and tone; has many errors in conventions
1	• **Development** Lacks a clear claim; offers unclear reasons and not enough evidence; has no concluding section • **Organization** Has no overall organization; lacks transitions • **Language** Lacks a formal style and tone; has major problems with conventions

Name _____ Date _____

COPY MASTER

WRITING WORKSHOP

Speaking and Listening Workshop

PARTICIPATING IN A DISCUSSION

When you participate in a group discussion, you must contribute ideas both as a speaker and as a listener.

Directions: Use the organizers below to plan your argument and to evaluate the argument of another member of your group.

Plan Your Argument:

My goal is to _____

Claim: _____

Reasons	Evidence

Evaluate an Argument:

My goal is to _____

Checklist

☐ Did the speaker state a strong claim?

☐ Did the speaker provide reasons and evidence to support the claim?

☐ Did I ask questions, paraphrase key points, and offer opinions?

	Notes

Resource Manager

Writing Support

WRITE SENTENCES WITH TRANSITIONS

Use these words and phrases to connect your ideas in an argument.

Transitions: Argument		
Order of Importance	Cause and Effect	Summary
first	as a result	finally
first of all	so then	in conclusion
most important	consequently	to sum up
second	for this reason	after all
least important	therefore	
also		
in addition		

A. Write transition words to finish these sentences. Choose one of the words or phrases in parentheses.

1. The setting in "All Summer in a Day" makes the story memorable for three reasons. _____, it affects the characters in the story in different ways. (*First of all, Consequently*)

2. It rains very hard every day on Venus. _____ people must live under ground. (*Finally, As a result*)

3. _____, the setting contributes to the conflict in the story. (*In addition, After all*)

4. Margot remembers the sun and the other children do not. _____, the other children hate her. (*Most important, For this reason*)

5. _____, the setting makes readers think about basic things most people take for granted, such as sunshine. (*Finally, Consequently*)

WRITE AN ARGUMENT

B. Write an argument that persuades readers that a certain story element makes a story unforgettable. Use these sentence frames to state your claim and to give three reasons that support your claim.

The element _____ makes the story _____ unforgettable for several reasons.

First, _____.

Secondly, _____.

Finally, _____.

Introductory Unit
Answer Key

Note Taking
p. I-2

Students' notes will vary. Sample answers are given.

Key Terms

- nonfiction
- dramas
- poetry
- media

plot: a series of events that traces a problem

stage directions: the writer's notes to the actors in a play

dialogue: what characters in a drama say

biography: the true story of a person's life, told by someone else

autobiography: the true story of a person's life, told by that person

essay: a short piece of writing about one subject

news article: reports on recent events

consumer document: printed material with a product or service

Web sites: pages on the World Wide Web

Note Taking
p. I-3

Students' notes will vary. Sample responses are shown.

Key Terms

Preview: Look at title, pictures, 1st paragraph

Connect: Does this relate to people & experiences in your own life?

Set a Purpose: Know why you're reading.

Use Prior Knowledge: Use what I know to make sense of what I don't know.

Predict: Guess what will happen next.

Visualize: Picture what the writer describes.

Monitor: Check your understanding as you read.

Make Inferences: Make logical guesses about characters and events.

Reading Strategies

Know Your Purpose

Take Notes

Create a Personal Word List

Note Taking
p. I-4

Students' wording may vary.

Definition: Academic vocabulary refers to the language one uses to talk about school subjects, such as language arts, math, science, and social studies.

Benefits of learning: Knowing the meaning of academic vocabulary words will help students become more successful in school and on tests.

Three examples: influence, affect, impact

Three Strategies:

1. Use the chart to preview words.
2. Look for activities in the book labeled Academic Vocabulary i Writing or in Speaking.
3. Use the activities as opportunities to use the words in writing and in discussions.

Note Taking
p. I-5

Students' outlines will vary. Sample responses are provided.

I.A.2. to inform or explain, to persuade, to describe, to express thoughts and feelings

I.B. Audience

I.B.2. classmates, teacher, friends, myself, Web users

1.C Format

I.C.1. Which format will best suit my purpose/audience?

I.C.2 essay, speech, letter, review, research paper

II.A.2. freewriting

II.B. Drafting

II.B.2. draft from an outline; draft to discover

II.C. Revising and Editing

II.C.1. rubric

II.C.2. peer reader

II.C.3. Proofread

II.D.1 readers

II.D.2 purpose, audience and format

Unit 1 Answer Key

Unit Opener Copy Masters

Academic Vocabulary
p. 2

B.
1. analyze
2. impact
3. affect
4. provide
5. evidence

Additional Academic Vocabulary
p. 3

B.
1. participate
2. define
3. approach
4. constitute/economy

Note Taking
p. 9

Students' outlines should demonstrate their understanding of the information in the Reader's Workshop.

Note Taking
p. 10

Bullet 1: plot; Bullet 2: exposition;
Bullet 3: climax; Bullet 4: resolution;
Bullet 5: rising action; Bullet 6: falling action;
Bullet 7: rising action; Bullet 8: exposition

The School Play

Text Analysis
p. 21

Exposition—Robert is in a school play and will need to remember only two lines.
Rising Action—Robert has trouble remembering his lines during rehearsal and Belinda, the class bully, threatens to bury his face in the ground if he messes up during the actual play.
Climax—Robert decides to say the parts of his lines that he can remember even if they aren't perfect
Falling Action—The play goes on and Robert gets into it completely.

Reading Strategy
p. 23

Students' questions and answers will vary.

Vocabulary Study
p. 25

A.
1. *narrative*—Clues: "very interesting," "told us," "amazing adventures"; Possible meaning: tale
2. *prop*—Clues: "sunglasses," "in the play," "to use"; Possible meaning: something used by an actor
3. *relentless*—Clues: "two days," "no end insight"; Possible meaning: persistent
4. *smirk*—Clues: "effortlessly," "struggle"; Possible meaning: smile in a superior way

B. Sentences will vary. Accept responses that accurately use the words in part A.

Vocabulary Practice
p. 26

A.
1. prop
2. smirk
3. narrative
4. relentless
5. mystery word: roses

B.
6. prop
7. smirked
8. relentless

C. Advice will vary. Accept responses that accurately use at least two of the vocabulary words.

Vocabulary Strategy
p. 27

A.
1. brassy
2. arrogant
3. skinny
4. fawning
5. indifferent

B. Sentences will vary.

Resolution—Belinda only pinches Robert and Robert is satisfied with his performance.

The Good Deed

Reading Check
p. 28

1. He plays a pioneer. He has two lines to say to a pioneer woman. He tells her that nothing is wrong and that he can see.
2. Belinda is a bully. She chews gum all the time, and she beats up boys.
3. Belinda has threatened to beat him up if he forgets his lines. He prepares by repeating the lines constantly.
4. He wants to be someone who recalls facts. He thinks the job involves having a "supergreat" memory, sitting around at home, and getting phone calls from important people.
5. He is happy that he didn't completely forget his lines. Belinda is annoyed, but is glad that he didn't do even worse.

Question Support
p. 29

Text Analysis

4. Questions will vary.
5. Robert: **a.** relieved, **c.** nervous, **d.** timid, **f.** satisfied
   Belinda: **d.** timid, **e.** angry
6. The audience seems to follow it (line 158) and claps afterward (line 190), so they appear to like it.
7. e, a, d, c, b
8. Answers will vary. Accept answers that reasonably explain how Robert makes use of a personal quality other than fear.

Grammar in Context
p. 30

A.

Our school put on a play called The Last Stand. It was performed by the students in Mrs. Bunnin's class. It was about a group of people from Illinois and nearby states who were headed for California. Alonso played the narrator, and he told about the historic background of the Donner party. Some of the other students in the class played trees and snowflakes. Belinda Lopez played a pioneer woman, and Robert Suarez played a pioneer man. They got their roles by scoring high on their spelling tests!

Text Analysis
p. 43

Responses will vary. Possible answers are provided.

External Conflicts

1. Risa seems to be horning in on Heather's good deed.
2. Heather loses Miss Benson's book.

Internal Conflicts

1. Heather wants to earn another badge, but she is scared to visit Miss Benson.
2. Heather feels guilty for putting the book in the wastebasket.

Explanations will vary. Accept responses that accurately describe resolutions following the climax.

Reading Strategy
p. 45

Students' connections will vary.

Vocabulary Study
p. 47

A.

1. *accusation*—Predicted Meaning: "statement of blame"; Meaning in Story: "the act of charging someone with wrong doing"
2. *generic*—Predicted Meaning: "ordinary, plain"; Meaning in Story: "having no particularly distinctive or noteworthy quality"
3. *impaired*—Predicted Meaning: "limited, damaged"; Meaning in Story: "being in a less than perfect condition"
4. *incredibly*—Predicted Meaning: "difficult to believe"; Meaning in Story: "unbelievably"
5. *pert*—Predicted Meaning: "rude, unpleasant"; Meaning in Story: "offensively bold; saucy"
6. *trite*—Predicted Meaning: "commonplace"; Meaning in Story: "boring because overused; not fresh or original"

Vocabulary Practice
p. 48

A.

1. impaired
2. pert

3. trite
4. incredibly
5. mystery word: deed

B.
6. general, universal, wide
7. bright, lively, spirited
8. blame, charge, claim

C. Letters will vary. Accept responses that accurately use at least two of the vocabulary words.

Vocabulary Strategy
p. 49

A.
1. generate(e); a thing that generates
2. discuss; the act of discussing
3. occur; the act of occurring
4. open; a thing that opens
5. resemble(e); the condition of resembling

B.
6. introduction
7. actor
8. writer
9. assistance
10. concentration
11. absence

Reading Check
p. 50

1. Heather needs to do a good deed to earn a Girl Scout badge, and she has been assigned to help Miss Benson.
2. Heather is glad that she does not have to face a sight-impaired person on her own. However, she does not want her good deed to be outdone by Risa.
3. Heather notices that Risa moves her lips while reading silently. Heather decides that Risa must be a poor reader because Heather has not done this since the first grade.
4. Risa's mother works and is not allowed to receive phone calls at work. Risa must take care of her three younger brothers.
5. Heather reads to Miss Benson, helps watch Risa's brothers, and offers to take turns reading to Risa's brothers.

Question Support
p. 51

Text Analysis
4. Answers will vary.
5. Possible conflict with outside force: Heather has a conflict with Risa, Possible conflict in her own mind: Heather is guilty about the book.
6. Most students will say that Heather realizes how frightened Risa is about the baby and about having to take risks to care for it. This realization is a climax because from this point forward, Heather no longer feels anger or resentment toward Risa.
7. Most students will say that she does do a good deed, not only by reading to Miss Benson, but by finally making friends with Risa. Others will say that Heather does not do a good deed because she accuses Risa of taking the book.
8. The speaker is more like Miss Benson, who is friendly and open.

Grammar in Context
p. 52

1. I knew Risa stole the book from Miss Benson, but I didn't know how to prove it.
2. I went over to Risa's apartment. She was reading one of the stories to her brothers.
3. Risa hid the book behind her back. She didn't answer when I asked why she took it.
4. I went back over to Miss Benson's apartment, and I told her who had the book.
5. I thought Miss Benson would yell at Risa, but she let Risa keep the book.

All Summer in a Day

Text Analysis
p. 65

Responses will vary. Possible answers are provided.
Plot Event/Venus: The children are amazed when the rain stops and the sun comes out.
Plot Event/Earth: The children might be happy that the rain had stopped, but they wouldn't be surprised.
Plot Event/Venus: The teacher warns the children that they only have an hour to enjoy themselves. **Plot Event/Earth:** The teacher might have made the same warning.

Plot Event/Venus: The children felt guilty about locking Margot in the closet, spoiling her enjoyment. **Plot Event/Earth:** This event would not have been different.

Reading Skill
p. 67

Row 2

The children have never seen the sun.

+ Seeing something unusual can make you excited.

= The children are excited.

Row 3

Margot looks pale and washed out.

+ The sun can add color to your face.

= Margot misses the sun.

Row 4

The children insist that Margot is a liar.

+ I know that Margot is telling the truth.

= The children don't want to believe that Margot knows anything.

Row 5

The children cannot meet each other's glances when they remember where Margot is.

+ Guilt can make you unable to look someone in the eye.

= The children feel terribly guilty.

Vocabulary Study
p. 69

A.

1. Word in context: exercise, <u>apparatus</u>
2. Part of word I recognize: *appar–*
3. I think it means . . . : a kind of tool
4. It is . . . : a noun
5. It is not . . . : a person
6. Examples of: a sewing machine, a DVD player
7. Related words: *apparel*

B. Accept all reasonable responses. Examples relating to first boldfaced word: Students might describe futuristic machines they would find at home and at school. Each **apparatus** would have a different function, such as providing entertainment or making things.

Vocabulary Practice
p. 70

A.

1. apparatus
2. resilient
3. savor
4. tumultuously
5. slacken
6. immense

B.

7. apparatus
8. savor

C. Descriptions will vary. Accept responses that accurately use at least two of the vocabulary words.

Vocabulary Strategy
p. 71

A.

1. suspicions
2. remark
3. rivals
4. hike
5. immense
6. peaceful

B.

7. a
8. c

Reading Check
p. 72

1. It has jungle–like vegetation, in shades of black and white. It rains constantly.
2. They came with their parents who went to Venus to set up a new civilization.
3. She is unhappy because she can't stand the lack of sun and the unending rain. She remembers the sun from Ohio.
4. The other children resent Margot because she grew upon Earth and remembers the sun. They don't want her to enjoy the hour of sunlight they're about to experience on Venus.
5. They might try to be very nice and be sure she got out in the sun. They understand now what she's been missing, and they might want to make up for their cruelty.

Question Support
p. 73

Text Analysis

4. Answers will vary.
5. Margot was unhappy because she missed life on Earth. The children on Venus were mean to her.

6. A sunny day on Earth lasts longer. A sunny day on Earth is not rare.

7. Most students will say that the children are an internal conflict as they walk to the closet because they are struggling with feelings about what they did to Margot. Other students may say that they are an external conflict because they stopped Margot from seeing the sun.

8. Student answers will vary, but could include the ideas that the emotions and behavior of the children are realistic, or that life on Venus in the future is more of a fantasy.

Grammar in Context
p. 74

A.

1. "It's been raining for years," the girl said.
2. "Let's go outside," the teacher said.
3. The boy asked, "What are you waiting for?"
4. "The sun looks like a penny," Margot said.

B. —Juan said, "I don't like science fiction."

—"Why not?" asked Teresa.

—"I don't think it is realistic enough," he responded. "Who could believe people walking around on Saturn?"

—"But if the story tells you something about the way people really think and feel," Teresa suggested, "isn't that realistic enough?"

Settling in Space
Skill Focus
p. 85

"Weather That's Out of This World"

Column 2: Ideas

- Temperature on Venus versus other planets
- Venus and Mercury
- Rain on Venus versus rain on Earth

Column 3: Supporting Details

- Venus is hotter than the other planets.
- Venus has an atmosphere, but Mercury doesn't.
- Earth rain is water; rain on Venus is made of sulfuric acid.

"Space Settlements"

Column 2: Ideas

Life on Earth versus life on a space station.

Column 3: Supporting Details

On the space station:

- housing will be similar to that on Earth: houses, apartments, etc.
- people will still go to movies, visit with friends, etc., as they do on Earth
- people will live inside an enclosed spacecraft, which will rotate to produce gravity, as opposed to living on the outside surface of spinning Earth, which is much larger
- air and water will be limited and must be constantly monitored, as opposed to on Earth, where air and water are much more plentiful and a part of a natural ecosystem
- space and materials will be very limited; there will be no room for waste, as there is on Earth, so everything will have be recycled
- agriculture will exist in very small, carefully controlled rooms, as opposed to outdoors in natural conditions
- building materials will come from the Moon, asteroids, or comets
- all energy will come from the sun, unlike Earth, where we use only some solar-generated electricity
- telecommunication will be similar to the technology we use on Earth

Read for Information
p. 86

Students may record any of the following details, or others.

Fictional Venus:

rainy
warm
cloudy/sunless
overgrown with jungle
inhabited by human beings
children go to school

Real Venus:

very hot
no protective atmosphere; only greenhouse gases
sulfuric rain

Space Colony:

people live in communities similar to Earth
air and water are limited and carefully monitored
agriculture is grown under highly controlled conditions
all life is technically indoors
space is limited

waste is recycled

all energy comes from the sun

Students' main ideas will vary, but should include support from the details in their chart.

Reading Check
p. 89

1. The rain on Venus is dangerous because it is made of sulfuric acid, which is corrosive and burns everything it touches.

2. Venus, the second planet from the sun, has an atmosphere of carbon dioxide gas that traps heat coming from the sun. The heat builds up like a blanket over the planet because it has nowhere to go.

3. People will do the same things in space that they do on Earth: go shopping and to work, school, concerts, sporting events, and parties.

4. Earth is thousands of kilometers across.

5. It would be too expensive (between $2,000 and $14,000 per pound) to transport materials from Earth.

Question Support
p. 90

Text Analysis

3. "What Will Life Be Like?" It will be like living on Earth with several important differences. "How Will We Build One?" It will require materials, energy, transportation, communications, life support, and radiation protection. "How Big Will the Colonies Be?" They may hold tens of thousands of people.

4. Possible answers include: It is nonfiction; It tells about a scientific subject; Its purpose is to explain or inform.

5. Sample: They are alike because people go about their normal lives there. They are different because they are enclosed

Lob's Girl
Text Analysis
p. 101

Hint 2: "Don came home very late and grim-faced." (line 258)

Hint 3: ". . . that dog has walked the length of England—twice—to be with that girl"? (lines 309–310)

What Happened: Lob was killed and sunk at sea with a lump of concrete tied to his collar, but his ghost came back to find Sandy.

Reading Skill
p. 103

Responses will vary. Possible responses are provided.

Clue Word or Phrase: "after supper"
Event: Lob bounces through the kitchen window.

Clue Word or Phrase: "A week passed"
Event: Lob returned after walking 400 miles.

Clue Word or Phrase: "In ten days' time"
Event: Lob returns for good.

Clue Word or Phrase: "Nine years went by"
Event: Lob changes less than Sandy.

Clue Word or Phrase: "One evening in October"
Event: Sandy and Lob are hit by a truck.

Clue Word or Phrase: "At tea-time"
Event: Granny Pearce finds Lob and brings him to Sandy.

Vocabulary Study
p. 105

A.

1. *agitated*—"upset"
2. *atone*—"make up for"
3. *decisively*—"confidently"
4. *erupt*—"burst out"
5. *melancholy*—"gloomy"
6. *reluctant*—"unwilling"

B.

1. decisively
2. melancholy
3. agitated
4. erupt
5. atone
6. reluctant

Vocabulary Practice
p. 106

A.

1. melancholy
2. agitated
3. atone
4. decisively
5. reluctant
6. erupt
7. canine

B.
8. c
9. b
10. a

Vocabulary Strategy
p. 107

A.
1. to wash, give a bath to, to wash or pour over
2. animal feed, something to talk about
3. bed covering used for warmth or a kind of covering, a layer that covers
4. to come open or fly apart suddenly or violently, an abrupt, intense increase

B.
5. George hitched the mule to its harness.
6. George was a mule when it came to taking a bath.

Reading Check
p. 108

Sample responses follow.
1. Lob became the family pet and was loved by all. He attached himself mostly to Sandy. He was very important in their lives.
2. Lob found Sandy on the beach, and she immediately felt a connection to him. They understood and loved each other.
3. Sandy and I were walking along the road in the dark. It was raining, but we were laughing as we hurried along. Suddenly there was a horrible noise, so loud, and then I felt something hit me.
4. Lob's spirit came back to help Sandy live. Lob may have realized that Sandy was very sick and that only seeing him would give her the strength to awaken and go on.
5. Sandy missed Lob a great deal, and she thought of him often. She never forgot him and would go into the garden and sit to remember the good times they had together.

Question Support
p. 109

Text Analysis
4. She feels cross and miserable.
5. Don found Lob after Sandy was taken to the hospital.

6. **Part 1:** Lob is dead, **Part 2:** Lob will find Sandy again.
7. **Part 1:** It is a sunny August day in the fishing village of Cornwall, England, **Part 2:** It is a windy, damp October day in Cornwall and the approach to this village is by a narrow, steep hill. The wet conditions and the hill are the two causes of Sandy's accident, **Part 3:** The settings are important to the plot because Cornwall and Liverpool (where Lob comes from) are 400 miles apart. This creates a conflict since Sandy cannot go there on a regular basis to visit Lob. In the second part, the rain and the hill cause Sandy's accident.
8. Student answers will vary, but might include any of the following ideas:
   • Lob's relationship with the family, especially with Sandy, is realistic.
   • Lob's visit to the hospital is unusual, but not unheard of; dogs are known for their loyalty and sometimes traveling great distances to get home or to the people they are loyal to.
   • When you realize that Lob had died in the accident, his visits to Sandy seem like fantasy.

Grammar in Context
p. 110

1. Lob's collar seemed heavy and damp.
2. The two nurses' chatter could be heard upstairs.
3. No one could repair Sandy's injuries.
4. Originally, Lob was Mr. Dodsworth's dog.
5. The twins' shrieks made Lob lick their faces harder.
6. Sandy could see the fishermen's boats far out at sea.

from Bud, not Buddy
Text Analysis
p. 113

Row 1
Many people out of work without money for food or clothes

Row 3
Mother and father who say "Clarence" is part of their family and let him into the line for food. Sharing breakfast with his pretend family.

Media Study

Viewing Guide
p. 121

Example: A long shot of Olaf's car stuck in the middle of the train tracks

Example: A medium shot of Violet and Klaus as they scramble to find an escape,

Example: A close-up shot of the clock inside the car as it changes from 11:14 A.M. to 11:15 A.M. Each of these shots creates suspense: the viewer is able to piece together Olaf's plan from the different visual clues. The viewer is also drawn into the action as the children realize the danger of their situation.

Example: Music plays in the background as Violet talks on the car phone to Mr. Poe.

Example: The warning bell that signals a train is approaching.

Example: Violet yells into the phone, slightly panicked, but Mr. Poe can't hear her because of the train. These sound techniques all stress that the children need to help themselves because no one else will help them. The warning bell and Violet's conversation with Mr. Poe signal that the train is very close and there's no time to waste.

Close Viewing
p.122

Count Olaf's car: The locks are remote-controlled, so the Baudelaires have no way to escape the car. A book about inheritance laws and a train schedule in the backseat make Violet and Klaus aware of the danger they're in.

The train tracks: The children are trapped in the car, which Olaf left parked on the tracks, and the train is bearing down on them. Klaus figures out that the only way to reroute the train is to pull the track-switching lever located outside the car.

Mr. Poerquos car: Mr. Poe is driving alongside the train, which the audience knows is heading for Count Olaf's car. The noise from the train keeps Mr. Poe from being able to hear what Violet is saying to him on the phone. Answers will vary. One possible answer: Violet uses a metal coil, the head of toy, and a piece of fabric from the inside of the car to invent a device to pull the track switch.

from Woodsong

Text Analysis
p. 135

Bear: 400 pounds; powerful; unafraid
Narrator: gun; intelligence; house for protection
Both the bear and the narrator have important but different strengths. The suspense comes from not knowing which strengths will prove more important in the confrontation between the bear and the narrator.

Images contributing to suspense:
Possible answers include: living on the edge of a wilderness; narrator's wife chased by a bear; dogs killed by rough bear swats; bear unafraid of the fire; bear standing over the narrator

Reading Skill
p. 137

Answers will vary. Most students will say that by sharing the story about the bear, Paulsen wants to persuade readers that a bear's place in nature is equal to humans. Some possible answers are given.

Row 1

Share thoughts on: Paulsen grows accustomed to Scarhead and treats him like a yard animal (lines 31–37).

Persuade: Don't make the mistake of treating bears as pets (line 30).

Entertain: The truce between the bears and the yard animals (lines 42–49).

Row 2

Explain/Inform: Bears are strong enough to kill a dog with a swat (lines 21–24).

Share thoughts on: Paulsen is frightened when Scarhead turns on him (lines 84–93).

Persuade: A bear's place in nature is equal to a human's (lines 115–118)

Entertain: The image of Scarhead walking through the tomato garden (lines 73–74).

Row 3

Explain/Inform: Nothing draws bears like burning food (line 56).

Share thoughts: Paulsen is angry enough to think about killing the bear (lines 104–107).

Row 4

Explain/Inform: Bears know that the sound of gunshot means there will be food (lines 58–62).

Vocabulary Study
p. 139

A.

1. *coherent*—Clue: "jumbled"; Possible meaning: organized
2. *eject*—Clues: "physically," "Instead," "scare the animal away"; Possible meaning: get rid of
3. *hibernation*—Clues: "survive winter," "stir and venture out"; Possible meaning: sleep
4. *novelty*—Clues: "at first," "became a nuisance"; Possible meaning: something to be enjoyed
5. *scavenge*—Clue: "destroy their garbage completely"; Possible meaning: eat garbage
6. *truce*—Clue: "bears would not hurt the dogs"; Possible meaning: understanding

B. Sentences will vary. Accept responses that accurately use the vocabulary words.

C. Thank-you notes will vary. Accept responses that use at least two of the vocabulary words.

Vocabulary Practice
p. 140

A.

1. novelty
2. scavenge
3. hibernation

B.

4. truce
5. eject
6. coherent

Vocabulary Strategy
p. 141

A.

1. thrown back or again
2. throw forward or in front of
3. thrown out of
4. thrown under ordown
5. throw into

B. Sentences will vary.

Reading Check
p. 142

1. They are in search of food and are attracted by Paulsen's trash.
2. Because naming bears makes them seem like pets and this makes people feel too relaxed around them. It gives people a false sense of security.
3. Paulsen is having a bad day and isannoyed when he finds Scarhead tearing up things in the yard. He's trying to chase the bear away.
4. Scarhead threatens Paulsen by looming over him. Paulsen freezes in place until the bear relaxes and moves away. Then Paulsen backs away and gets his gun.
5. Paulsen realizes that the bear could easily have killed him, but instead spared his life. He feels that he should do the same for the bear.

Question Support
p. 143

Text Analysis

4. Possible answers: they prefer the dogs' food, or they have some kind of truce with the goats and chickens
5. Some students will circle "Share Thoughts." Paulsen shares his experience with Scarhead to show readers that bears and humans are equals in nature. Although Scarhead could have killed Paulsen, he backed off and let Paulsen go. When Paulsen, he backed off and the chance to kill Scarhead, he, too, backs off and puts his gun away. Other students will circle "Persuade," making the point that the whole reason Paulsen shares his experiences about Scarhead is to persuade readers that a bear's place in nature is equal to a human's.
6. Student answers may vary. Most students will cite the confrontation between Scarhead and the narrator as an example.
7. Most students will agree with the idea that Paulsen loves nature, citing his understanding of the beauty and the danger and his willingness to live close to a wilderness.

Grammar in Context
p. 144

1. No one who sees a bear can keep his/her/his or her heart from pounding.
2. Anyone who thinks he/she/he or she doesn't need to respect bears is wrong.
3. Everyone should realize that he/she/he or she is an animal, too.
4. No one should think that he/she/he or she is better than any other creature.
5. Everyone should watch his/her/his or her back when he/she/he or she is in the woods.
6. Nobody could ever convince me that he/she/he or she is right to disrespect animals.

The Horse Snake

Text Analysis
p. 157

Row 1

Location: farm on the edge of the Vietnamese jungle

Times: night

Surroundings: rice fields, house, farm animals

Row 2

Location: rice field

Times: early morning

Surroundings: dead horse

Row 3

Location: sitting room in the house

Times: late at night

Surroundings: mother sewing;

Reading Skill
p. 159

Events:

Men look for snake.

The men give up.

Grandmother tells a story.

Farmers return to fields.

Minh calls for help.

Time of Day:

Early morning

Nightfall

Second night

Next morning

Late afternoon

Vocabulary Study
p. 161

A.

1. *assume*—Clues: "defensive positions," "held their knives ready"
2. *gait*—Clues: "walked," "fast," "nearest house"
3. *nocturnal*—Clue: "night"
4. *petrify*—Clues: "frightening," "frozen with fear"
5. *stealthily*—Clues: "avoid alarming," "tiptoe"
6. *succumb*—Clues: "venom . . . was powerful," "in minutes," "bitten"

B.

7. *assume*: "take"
8. *gait*: "step"
9. *nocturnal*: "nighttime"
10. *petrify*: "keep still out of fear"

11. *stealthily*: "quietly"
12. *succumb*: "die"

Vocabulary Practice
p. 162

A.

1. assume
2. petrify
3. succumb
4. gait
5. stealthily
6. nocturnal

B.

7. petrify
8. succumb
9. nocturnal
10. stealthily
11. gait
12. assume

Vocabulary Strategy
p. 163

A.

1. Latin; "body"
2. Greek; "own, personal, private"
3. Sanskrit; "wasteland"
4. Old Dutch; "to glide"
5. Old Portuguese; "wild ass"

B. Sentences will vary but should show modern-day meanings.

Grammar in Context
p. 164

Sentences may vary. Sample sentences:

1. One night a frightened villager banged on our door, and he asked us to let him in.
2. I stayed up that night, and I listened to all the sounds outside.
3. The snake usually eats chickens and monkeys, but sometimes it attacks people and cattle.
4. The animal might have been killed by a horse snake, or it could have been a king python.
5. The villagers caught and killed the snake, so we could rest easy.

Reading Check
p. 165

1. The villagers call the creature the horse snake because it can move as fast as a thoroughbred.

2. He wants to alert the villagers to the presence of a dangerous animal in the area.
3. The story gives him new confidence that people can defeat the horse snake.
4. The snake wants to eat the fish, so it hooks itself between two trees and then swings itself back and forth like a hammock to splash the water out of the pond.
5. The men surround the snake and strike at it with their knives. The women and children keep the snake from going into the jungle while half the men keep it from the river. Then the hunting party surrounds the snake and kills it.

Question Support
p. 166

Text Analysis

4. c. a friend bangs on door
a. men divide up and search for snake
d. Grandmother tells a story
e. farmers return to their fields
b. Minh calls for help
5. yelling loudly to scare the snake
6. **Column 1:** Image friend banged on the door he heard the hiss of a horse snake cousin blew three times on the buffalo horn narrator stayed up listening to sounds outside neighing of a horse calls of nocturnal birds and rearing of tigers
Column 2: Sense all images appeal to sense of hearing
7. snakes are reptiles and must live in a warm environment.
8. by working together, they were stronger and smarter than the horse snake
Main Idea of the Article: Types of spiders and the webs they make

Le Mat Village Holds On to Snake Catching Tradition

Skill Focus
p. 177

Answers will vary. Sample answers:

Detail 1: Everyone in Le Mat learns how to catch snakes.

Detail 2: The tradition of snake catching dates back to 11th century.

Detail 3: Despite changes in their village, the villagers still love their tradition of snake catching.

Main Idea: The tradition of snake catching is very important to the people of Le Mat.

Author's Purpose: To show why snake catching is such an important tradition to the people of Le Mat.

Read for Information
p. 178

Answers will vary. Most students will use their responses for the previous page to complete Row 2.

Sample answers:

Row 1, "The Horse Snake":

Detail: A deadly horse snake threatens the villagers and their animals.

Detail: The people of the village work together to hunt down the snake.

Detail: The people find and kill the snake.

Main Idea: The snake is so dangerous that people have to work together to get rid of it.

Author's Purpose: To show how teamwork and cooperation can overcome even the most serious obstacles

Reading Check
p. 181

Answers will vary. Sample answers:

1. Le Mat is a village near Hanoi, in Vietnam.
2. Not all villagers make their living by catching snakes, but everyone in the village learns how to catch snakes.
3. The tradition of snake catching dates back to the 11th century.
4. Trung's people were granted new land to clear and make into new farms and a village.
5. Trung was called the Genie of Le Mat.

Question Support
p. 182

Answers will vary. Sample answers:

3. Modern villagers share a knowledge of snakes, a pride in their village, and courage with Trung.
4. The modern village is in an area with lots of poisonous snakes, so it is important to be familiar with them and to know how to handle them.

The Walrus and the Carpenter

Text Analysis
p. 191

Setting

sun shining
middle of night
quantities of sand
wet sea
no clouds

Characters

sneaky Walrus
sympathetic Carpenter
sulky Moon
eager Oysters
wise eldest Oyster

Plot Events

1. Walrus and Carpenter walk on beach and weep over quantities of sand.

2. They invite the Oysters to walk with them.

3. The young Oysters walk, despite the eldest Oyster's refusal.

4. Walrus and Carpenter have a friendly conversation with the Oysters and then eat them.

Reading Strategy
p. 193

Students' responses will vary.

Question Support
p. 195

Text Analysis

3. He was wise; he did not leave his oyster bed.
4. Students' descriptions will vary.
5. Lines 7–12: sun, done, fun, Lines 13–18: dry, sky, fly
6. Students' responses will vary.
7. **Part 1:** They were lured away and eaten by the Walrus and the Carpenter, **Part 2:** Do not go off with strangers.

The Prince and the Pauper

Text Analysis
p. 207

Scene 2: The Prince runs into Tom's father and barely escapes from him.

Scene 3: Tom attends a royal banquet. Heralds announce the king's death. The Prince hears the news from outside the palace gates.

Scene 4: The Prince eats with Miles, who has rescued him from the crowd. He humors the Prince, thinking him simply mad. Tom's father sneaks in and kidnaps the sleeping Prince.

Scene 5: Tom's father tries to get the Prince to steal. Villagers attack the Prince, but Miles comes to help him. Both are brought before the Justice.

Scene 6: Miles and the Prince are in chains. They have been to Miles's father's home, where they found Miles's brother had stolen his bride and estate. They hear news of the good deeds of the new King. The Prince realizes that it must be Tom.

Scene 7: Miles loses the Prince in the crowd on Coronation Day. The Prince claims the crown, and Tom agrees that it is his. Tom and the Prince prove it by recalling where the Prince hid the Great Seal. The Prince rewards Miles and Tom for their loyalty and kindness and pledges to be a merciful king. Scene 7 should be circled.

Reading Strategy
p. 209

Row 1

Guards open gates and Tom slowly passes through, as if in a dream. (Scene 1, lines 30–31)

Characters' movements and behavior

Tom is amazed by his experience.

Row 2

eagerly (Scene 2, line 250)

Character's way of speaking

The prince is interested and excited.

Row 3

Miles' room at the inn (Scene 4, line 329)

Setting

The action has moved from the palace to an inn.

Row 4

springing to Miles' side (Scene 5, line 428)

Character's movements

The prince is moving rapidly.

Row 5

sitting, with head in hands (scene 6, line 542)

Character's movements and behavior

Miles is upset.

Vocabulary Study
p. 211

A.

1. "Suffering" hints at the meaning of affliction.
2. "Rightful baronet," "as a result," and "thrown into prison" suggest the meaning of impostor.
3. "Begging" and "hope to earn" indicates the meaning of pauper.
4. "Fuzzy" and "too much had happened" hint at the meaning of recollection.
5. "Crazy" suggests the meaning of sane.
6. "To the throne," "next in line," and "Therefore" hint at the meaning of successor.

B. Accept all thoughtful answers that show an understanding of the vocabulary words and the discussion of the key concept. For example: Based on the title of the play, I think the conflict might involve the successor to the throne trading places with a pauper. The adventures of both impostors probably form the basis of the plot. The characters know that they are sane, but their story appears too farfetched for others to believe. Instead they are thought to be suffering from an affliction. Their recollections of their experiences help them learn some valuable lessons, providing the play's theme.

Reading Check
p. 212

1. Edward would like to watch Punch and Judy shows, fight in the street, run races, swim in the river, and wallow in the mud. He would like some of Tom's freedom.
2. Everyone believes Tom is the Prince, so when Tom denies this and insists that he is only a pauper, people question his state of mind.
3. Edward, dressed as Tom, is accused of stealing a pig.
4. Miles's brother, Hugh, accuses Miles of being an imposter. Hugh claims that his brother, the real Miles Hendon, is dead.
5. With Tom's help, he recalls where he hid the Great Seal of England.

Question Support
p. 213

Text Analysis

4. **Part 1:** Miles acts as friend and protector to the prince. He is a good-hearted man who feels sorry for the poor confused boy. **Part 2:** Members of the court think Tom is mad, but they treat him with respect because they are required to do so.

5. Choices will vary but should include two descriptions of setting and two stage directions that describe characters' feelings.

6. c

7. **Part 1:** He insists that he is not the Prince, **Part 2:** He does not know how to behave in court.

8. how other people live. Tom learns that he doesn't want to be a prince; he misses the freedom he had in his old life. Edward learns how his poor subjects actually live; he sees the need for more merciful laws and better treatment for his subjects.

Twain's Tale Transplanted to Today

Skill Focus
p. 223

Responses will vary. Sample responses:

Column 2 - Setting: England in the 16th century; **Characters:** Edward, the Prince of Wales, Tom Canty, a poor boy, members of the royal court; **Plot:** The prince and Tom, who look like they could be twins, switch places. Tom takes the prince's place in court, and the prince tries to move about London as a common boy. Each boy has some exciting and even dangerous adventures, and each boy learns important lessons about life.

Column 3 - Setting: Modern-day Palm Beach and Miami Beach; **Characters:** Eddie Tudor, a famous young actor, and Tom Canty, a less fortunate boy who works in his grandfather's landscaping company; **Plot:** the boys meet decide to switch places to see what the other's life is like. Tom demonstrates talent for acting, but Eddie has trouble. The boys must overcome obstacles to return to their places, but each learns lessons. In the end, both boys act in a traditional film version of Twain's story.

Read for Information
p. 224

Responses will vary. Sample responses:

Column 2 - Setting/Similarities: a rich world and a poor world, adults trying to tell the boys how to think and behave; **Differences:** England in the 1500s instead of modern-day Florida. **Characters/Similarities:** rich boy and a boy without money; the boys look like twins; each boy is curious about the like of the other; Differences: prince instead of actor; street boy instead of landscape worker; the prince is thoughtful and kind, but Eddie is not. **Plot/Similarities:** the boys switch places; each boy has difficulties in the other boy's world; the boys return to their original places eventually; **Differences:** original Tom is almost crowned king, while modern Tom becomes an actor; original boys help each other, but modern boys fight before the conflict is resolved; prince makes original Tom his ward, but modern boys both become actors.

Reading Check
p. 227

Responses will vary. Sample responses:

1. Dylan and Cole Sprouse
2. Tom works in his grandfather's landscaping business.
3. Tom is a good actor—even better than Eddie.
4. He says he understands that she is hard on him because she cares about him.
5. He helps Eddie realize that it is important to be kind and respectful.

Question Support
p. 228

Responses will vary. Sample responses:

4. The film could have a sports setting. One boy could be a star on a well-known club and the other might just play the sport on the playground.
5. In both versions, Tom is honest and kind, and he feels uncomfortable in the other boy's place.
6. The boys switch places.

Writing Workshop
Revising and Editing 1
p. 235

Think of how you feel when it's been raining for two days in a row. Now imagine if it rained for seven years straight! In the story "All Summer in a Day,"

by Ray Bradbury, humans live on the planet Venus where the sun only shines

~~makes it very~~

for one hour every seven years. The story's strange setting makes it very
~~memorable.~~

The rest of the time it rains. As a result, the people must live underground. ^

The story's strange setting ^
affects the characters, contributes to the conflict, and makes readers think about think

about basic things most people take for granted, such as sunshine.

First of all, the

The setting affects the characters in the story in different ways. The
^
children who were born on Venus don't remember the sun. They were only two years old the last time the sun appeared. All they know is rain and they don't seem to mind it. Margot was born on Earth, though, and she remembers the sun. She misses it a lot, and she seems to hate the rain. She wouldn't take a shower once, "screaming that the water mustn't touch her head." She is pale, thin, and quiet. Margot's parents ~~themselves~~ seem to be worried about her, and they may take her back to Earth.

Revising and Editing 2
p. 236

1. A
2. D
3. B

Writing Support
p. 240

A.
1. First of all
2. As a result
3. In addition
4. For this reason
5. Finally

B. Answers will vary depending on students' arguments, but the claims should be stated clearly and the reasons should support the claim.